Service Integration in Schools

Research and Policy Discourses, Practices
and Future Prospects

Edited by

Joan Forbes
University of Aberdeen, Scotland, UK

and

Cate Watson
University of Aberdeen, Scotland, UK

SENSE PUBLISHERS
ROTTERDAM / TAIPEI

A C.I.P. record for this book is available from the Library of Congress.

ISBN 978-90-8790-586-6 (paperback)
ISBN 978-90-8790-587-3 (hardback)
ISBN 978-90-8790-588-0 (e-book)

Published by: Sense Publishers,
P.O. Box 21858, 3001 AW Rotterdam, The Netherlands
http://www.sensepublishers.com

Cover picture:
Joan Eardley – *Brother and Sister*, Aberdeen Art Gallery and Museums Collections
© The Eardley Estate

Printed on acid-free paper

TABLE OF CONTENTS

PREFACE

In the context of globalisation and globalised policy talk about the emergence of a knowledge economy, nations around the world have recognised the overwhelming significance of the quality and quantity of human capital to economic development and regeneration, to social cohesion, as well as to the international competitiveness of the (putative) national economy. In this context, education policy has become a central component of economic policy. Different nations have pursued this human capital development goal in different ways. The Anglo-American nations have tended to take a neo-liberal approach through a restructuring of the state, public/private partnerships, market reforms and choice, while other models, for example, those in the Scandinavian countries as well as those in East Asia, have taken a different policy direction with more state-centric policies, but for the same policy purposes. This improving educational achievement agenda has both qualitative and quantitative aspects, that is, there is a policy concern within the nations of the Global North for improving the quality and amount of education provided for all young people.

The evidence is overwhelming that those who do poorly at school and who do not complete a full secondary education are from socio-economically disadvantaged families. Thus improvements in educational achievement and enhancing the amount of education received by all come up against this issue of the social class/educational achievement nexus. Central to the policy agenda then has been a recognition that there is need to break the nexus between social class of origin and educational opportunities, achievements and retention at school. The achievement of equal opportunities in education, more equal outcomes and greater retention to the end of secondary schooling, however, remain intractable policy goals. In the UK, for example, a policy focus attempts to ameliorate disadvantage for those young people not in education, employment or training. The Rudd Labor government in Australia, elected in late 2007, sees socio-economic based inequalities in educational opportunities and outcomes as unacceptable on social justice grounds, but also in terms of the economic well being of the nation and the related need for better prepared human capital. In England, the Department for Education and Skills in 2004 in its Five Year Strategy document stated:

> We fail our most disadvantaged children and young people - those in public care, those with complex family lives are those most at risk…Internationally our rate of child poverty is still high, as are the rates of worklessness in one-parent families, the rate of teenage pregnancies and the level of poor diet among children. The links between poor health, disadvantage and low educational outcomes are stark. (Department for Education & Skills, 2004, para. 24)

There is then a wide-spread recognition of this policy problem; the question is what can and should be done about it in relation to the broader policy purposes? The research evidence would suggest that the socio-economic experiences of families (parental educational levels, cultural practices, income, types of jobs, aspirations) and the quality of pedagogies and relationships in classrooms are the two most salient factors in school achievement.

Given our social science based knowledge of the epidemiology of educational disadvantage then and its seeming intractability through traditional policies in education, an interesting policy response in the UK to this social, educational and ultimately economic problem has been the concept of 'joined-up government' and 'inter-professional agency work', grouped in and around schools. This has been a discursive policy response, arguing the necessity of a new way of working for the policy bureaucracies and for partnerships and collaboration between a range of professionals and their practices. (In the US and in some parts of Australia, the idea of the full-service school is a related policy development.) Accompanying this discursive reframing in the UK has been a legislative one. In England, The Green Paper, *Every Child Matters* (HM Treasury, 2003) and the ensuing legislation, Children Act, 2004, Education and Inspections Act, 2006, reconstituted education as a children's service, demanding the integration of education, health and social services in an attempt to improve and expand educational outcomes for all and in a move away from a one size fits all approach.

This new policy configuration sees learning and support for it in homes and communities, as well as schools, as central to the policy goals of improved educational outcomes for all, including those disadvantaged by socio-economic circumstances. In my view, in some ways this is an historical moment in the evolution of educational provision, part of the concept of lifelong learning, and as significant in its potential impact as the 1944 Education Act which ensured some secondary education for all (Lingard, Nixon & Ranson, 2008).

While a joined-up approach might result in positive synergy in addressing educational and social disadvantage, the broader policy frame of neo-liberalism adopted to varying degrees among the countries that make up the UK has resulted in more economic inequality. This joined-up policy response is a wonderful exemplification then of the ways in which policies construct the problem to which they are the proposed solution: here, education to overcome socio-economic disadvantage. The social class/education success nexus is not so entrenched in the Scandinavian countries. We need to recognise that these countries have less social inequality than is the case in the UK as demonstrated in their comparative Gini coefficients (a measure of the inequality of income/wealth distribution). Finland's success on the Organisation for Economic Co-operation and Development's (OECD) Programme for International Student Assessment (PISA), where it achieves high quality and socially just outcomes, probably reflects this comparative equality and a comprehensive government school system, where one might be able to argue that all young people in local areas go to the same school. This situation can be starkly contrasted with that in England, where one policy response to improving outcomes and overcoming educational disadvantage is to widen the

PREFACE

types of schools available within the government sector and to strengthen parental choice. While Scotland still has a comprehensive schooling system, there is a socio-economic based achievement gap beginning in upper primary schools and reflected as well in differential retention in the senior years of schooling (OECD, 2007).

It is this range of discursive, policy and organisational developments associated with a reconstruction of children's services, that Joan Forbes and Cate Watson's edited collection, *Service Integration in Schools*, seeks to address. In addressing these policy developments the collection has multiple readerships in mind and seeks to be both academic and policy relevant. That is, the collected papers seek to speak to policy makers in ways that the critiques offered might provoke some potential paths forward; the papers also speak to academics in the fields of both professional practice and policy in education and social work. The papers demonstrate that joined-up policy and professional practices will not magically appear through simple discursive exhortation. Rather, these are matters which need to be debated and discussed amongst and between relevant professionals, policy makers, academic theorists and researchers, set against recognition that a more equal society is necessary to the achievement of the policy goals of higher quality education and more educational equality for all. These goals have become almost universal ones across the globe in an age of educational multilateralism and thus the collection ought to be read by relevant professionals around the world and should have particular purchase across the UK, in Europe, in North America and in Australia and New Zealand, where the topics traversed have particular policy and practice salience.

REFERENCES

Department for Education & Skills (2004). *Five Year Strategy for Children and Learners*. London: DfES.

HM Treasury (2003). *Every child matters*. London: HMSO

Lingard, B., Nixon, J., & Ranson, S. (2008). Remaking Education for a Globalized World: policy and pedagogic possibilities. In B. Lingard, J. Nixon, & S. Ranson (Eds.), *Transforming Learning in Schools and Communities* (pp. 3-33). London: Continuum.

Organisation for Economic Co-operation and Development (2007). *Quality and Equity of Schooling in Scotland*. Paris: OECD.

Bob Lingard
School of Education
The University of Queensland
Australia

ix

JOAN FORBES

INTRODUCTION

The question of changing children's services is one which countries in the United Kingdom and elsewhere are attempting to address and the issues and challenges raised by such transformations are many. The integration of services in schools, how education should now work differently – and better – with health, social care and other services to children, is a topical issue. The current children's services integration agenda emerged fairly recently and moves to integrate services are proving to be neither easy nor straightforward. As new policy enjoinders drive changing governance, management, leadership and practices in interprofessional and interagency working a number of practical and cultural problems are being encountered by practitioners and professional groups where policy fails to work in practice. This edited collection of papers presents to the reader some such challenging instances of policy-practice disjuncture through informative critical analyses of key ideas in the children's services research and policy discourses and by introducing to the reader a series of alternative perspectives, questions and suggestions that explore what is at stake and what is worthwhile retaining and changing in public services to children. A feature of the book is the necessary and apposite cross-disciplinary approach which it takes to the many issues and challenges in an agenda which cuts across research disciplines as much as professions and agencies.

THE RESEARCH SEMINARS AT THE UNIVERSITIES OF ABERDEEN, ULSTER AND BIRMINGHAM

This book has emerged from an Economic and Social Research Council (ESRC) research seminar series held at the universities of Aberdeen, Ulster and Birmingham between May 2006 and April 2007. The aim of the series of meetings was to bring together practitioners, researchers and policy makers from the different disciplines that inform policy and practice in education, health and social care, together with representatives of voluntary agencies working with/for children, professional associations, and the users of children's public services to explore a number of important questions for practitioners and professional groups arising from the children's services transformations agenda that is currently unfolding in the UK countries and in other places. The first seminar in the series at the

University of Aberdeen, Scotland, in May 2006: *The research and policy discourses of service integration, interprofessional and interagency working* mapped the research and policy discourses that are currently constructing the reformation of children's services and how professional groups work together in schools and communities in Scotland, Northern Ireland and England. The seminar aimed to examine the professional values to which different groups subscribe and to uncover the purposes that underlie service integration. We analysed current issues concerning demarcations of practice and professional boundaries in multi-agency working and examined the effects of specific models of co-practice on professionals' practices and identities.

In October 2006 the second of our seminars: *How service integration is operating in practice in the Scotland, Northern Ireland and England and Wales policy contexts* was held at the University of Ulster, Northern Ireland. This meeting explored the variety of emergent models of partnership within children's services, drawing on examples from across the United Kingdom countries. Focusing on the relationships between children's services, families and communities, the seminar provided a forum for researchers and practitioners to share and learn about current models of practice across the UK policy contexts, to map evolving models of implementation and to identify the implications for governance and administration arrangements.

The third seminar in the series: *Leading and managing collaborative practice: The research* was held at the University of Birmingham, England, in January 2007. The Birmingham seminar both built on and challenged some of the understandings from the first two seminars. It explored notions of leadership and management as constructed and conceptualised within disciplines which collaborate in multidisciplinary work. The seminar specifically examined discourses of power as these play out in professional status, gender and ethnicity within and across disciplines and how, in relation to issues of leadership and management, these subvert collaboration, co-learning and joint problem solving. A central focus in discussion concerned the management of change as professional groups and agencies move from mono-professional and single subject disciplinary practice towards integrated services underpinned by collaborative working.

In April 2007 the seminar series participants returned to Aberdeen for the fourth and final meeting in the series: *Future school services, 'global solutions'*. In the final meeting we drew together issues from earlier seminars, exploring narratives of interprofessional identification and gave consideration to the institutional conditions necessary for transprofessional learning. Issues of interprofessionalism, interagency working and of children's public services transformations in the UK countries were located within an analysis of the discourses and practices of school workforce modernisation and transformation in South Africa, New Zealand and Australia. Examining the effects of matters of professional agency and institutional cultures for working relations among professionals in future schools, the seminar questioned whether there are 'global solutions' that could take full account of the different historically contingent social and cultural conditions in specific institutional, regional and national contexts.

In keeping with the aim of the seminars, this collection is intended for practitioners, managers and leaders, academics and policy-makers in the fields of education health and social care across the UK nations and in other countries who are interested in thoughtfully presented and challenging analyses that critique fundamental issues for all involved in recent developments in children's services restructurings.

INTRODUCING THE CHAPTERS

Each of the four sections of the book is prefaced by a comprehensive introduction and overview of the contents of the chapters that follow and so the outline of the chapters given here is concise. Part One of the book considers the research and policy discourses of service integration, interprofessional and interagency working. This first section is introduced by Michael Cowie who takes as his starting point the notion that, at least in terms of policy, the 'introduction of collaboration is seen as unproblematic'. Cowie then goes on to show how the chapters that follow in Part One each illustrate ways in which the nature of collaborative working is not unproblematic. In chapter one, *Learning how to collaborate? Promoting young people's health through professional partnership in schools*, Janet Shucksmith, Kate Philip, Jenny Spratt and Cate Watson offer an examination of how different professional groups claim expertise on the basis of different types of knowledge. They argue that the knowledge used by others at professional boundaries challenges the previous bases of teacher professionalism, but such challenges may be viewed as openings for the fruitful reconstruction of teachers' practices. In her chapter, *Joining up working: Terms, types and tensions*, Elspeth McCartney outlines, classifies and discusses a number of models of speech/language therapist and teacher co-working and goes on to contend that in practice the emphasis may need to be on 'good enough' models of working together. In the concluding chapter in Part One, *After the break? Interrupting the discourses of interprofessional practice,* Julie Allan considers the ways in which policy discourses already inscribe expectations for interprofessional practice and proceeds to uncover the effects of such policy discourses for both beginning and established teachers.

Each of the chapters in Part Two examines how service integration is operating in practice in the Scotland, Northern Ireland and England policy contexts. Roy McConkey sets the context for the three chapters that follow in this section. Noting that the opening years of the twenty-first century have seen a broadening of a previous focus on learning and teaching with the introduction of new imperatives for education and other children's services to review how they work together, McConkey describes how each of the chapters in section two draw on experiences from Scotland, Northern Ireland and England to examine the practical issues involved in service integration and, strikingly, goes on to identify 'a number of icebergs' that may 'threaten the integration agenda on its maiden voyage'.

Ian Menter's chapter, *Service integration in schools: The Scottish scene and the implications for teachers*, draws in part on a study of teachers' working time in

Scotland following the implementation of the 'McCrone report' and the impact of this on moves towards establishing integrated children's services in schools. He illustrates how there is evidence of both convergence and divergence of Scottish policy and practice with parallel developments in other parts of the UK. Menter argues for greater conceptual clarity around the notion of integrated services and calls for a major research agenda, including critical discourse based analyses, to unpack and examine the discourses and practices of children's services in Scotland and beyond.

In their chapter, *Communicating, co-ordinating and connecting: Integrated service provision in Northern Ireland,* Anne Moran, Lesley Abbott and Una O'Connor describe moves towards the integration of services in a very fluid national context of evolving child centred social and educational policy and practice developing alongside major reviews of education and overall public administration. Moran and colleagues conclude that the development of genuinely integrated partnerships amongst education, health and social services in the Northern Irish extended schools initiative is recognised as a constituent feature of both educational policy and overall public services reform.

In the final chapter in Part Two, *Every child matters: The implications for service integration in England,* Gillian Pugh examines the main recent policy thrusts driving children's services transformations in England. Reporting the huge and ambitious nature of the 'Every child matters: Change for children agenda', the author reframes the question of joined-up working as a means to an end for children and not an end in itself and suggests strategies for improving integrated working amongst professionals.

Part Three of the book focuses on leading and managing collaborative practice. Deirdre Martin's introduction to Part Three opens with the premise that leaders of integrated or 'extended' schools must now engage with the challenges and opportunities of moves towards integration to well position the institutions and organizations they lead for future success. Outlining for the reader the theoretical orientations of Vygotsky and Engeström in relation to learning and learning in work organisations such as integrated schools which inform the chapters by Warmington *et al.* and Hartley which follow, she notes that the theme which cuts across those papers and the chapter by Brown is that of 'distributed leadership at system and multiagency levels'. Highlighting issues raised by the three chapters relating to professional discourses, practices, knowledge, skills, beliefs and identity that underlie the nature of professionalism, Martin concludes by proposing that such questions merit further study and constitute a necessary and timely research agenda for the current moment of school and service integration.

The opening chapter in this section, *Learning leadership in multiagency work for integrating services into schools* by Paul Warmington and colleagues emerges from earlier work of this group in an Economic and Social Research Council (ESRC) study: *Learning in and for Interagency Working. Examining the learning in practice of professionals and organisations.* Warmington and colleagues identify a need to access horizontal learning and distributed, multiagency expertise across sectors, and argue that vertical learning needs to be fostered between the strategic and operational levels of practice. They conclude that it is through professionals learning to negotiate the intersections of vertical and horizontal learning that future practitioner learning and flexible and responsive action are promoted and supported.

The next chapter by David Brown, *Leadership and capacity in the public sector: Integrated children's services and schools*, provides an account of the challenges to leadership arising from the recent radical reform of children's services in England as a consequence of the wide ranging *Every Child Matters* agenda. As Executive Director of Children's Services in Walsall, Brown explores the challenges and opportunities for leaders arising from the plethora of systemic and organizational complexities involved in such comprehensive public sector transformation. His analysis of cross agency 'system leadership' in the new economy of the children's public sector leads him to conclude on a philosophical note that future leaders will need to establish their own 'moral compass'.

In *Education policy and the 'inter'-regnum*, David Hartley reflects critically on public services policy discourses and terminology in the current moment. Critiquing examples of the proliferation of prefixes – inter, trans, multi and so forth, he reframes the notion of 'inter' as a new 'reigning philosophy' or 'inter'-regnum. Hartley considers how, taken together, these strands constitute a new network regime of governance that complements those of markets and hierarchies. He suggests that 'inter' forms of governance have emerged from previous education discourses of the market and consumer choice associated with new public management, as apposite 'solution spaces' in the 'new capitalism' work order of affinity, and as discourses and practices that are intellectually well supported by a number of theoretical strands in marketing, organisational learning and activity theory.

Part Four broadens the conceptualisation and contextualisation of the themes developed to examine future school services and explore questions of 'global solutions'. Audrey Hendry's introduction *Future school services, 'global solutions,* contextualises the papers in section four of the book. Recognising that, for some, the issues raised may seem far removed from day-to-day work of practitioners in schools, Hendry challenges readers to be open to looking differently at problems and looking in different places for solutions. She argues that it is through a wider conceptualisation and contextualisation of the issues that a clearer grasp of the challenges of integrated services and insights into best ways to now adapt and transform services to children will be gained.

In chapter ten, *Modernising and remodelling schools: Are there 'global solutions' to transforming the school workforce?*, Graham Butt and Helen Gunter present findings from research concerning the impact of the National Agreement for workforce modernisation, change and remodelling in England. Drawing on case study evidence from children's services reformations in South Africa, New Zealand and Australia, Butt and Gunter unpack the background, underlying assumptions and drivers for reform and explore the processes of restructuring in England and other places. Their analysis elucidates the nature of what is important in the work of children's professionals and points to the danger of organisational approaches to children's workforce remodelling and modernisation that focus on structures and management rather than on more student and practitioner focused perspectives of learning and teaching and care. At issue in 'modernised education', they contend, is what is at its centre – structures or students.

In her chapter, *Mythical spaces and social imaginaries: Looking for the global in the local in narratives of (inter)professional identification,* Cate Watson applies the theory of discourse of Laclau and Mouffe to explore the relationship between local personal narratives, global institutional discourses and the professional identifications they engender. She offers a microanalysis of a narrative fragment from research with beginning teachers to uncover how institutional identifications are manifested in and through narrative. Concluding that the political moment is revealed in the microanalysis of discourse, Watson calls for mappings of the 'mythical spaces' and 'imaginary geographies' of schools and argues for the construction of new imaginaries of interprofessional practice that do not seek superficial consensus, but are more firmly based on 'contested dissensus'.

The final chapter in the book, *The conditions for inter-professional learning: The centrality of relationship,* addresses the four themes discussed in the preceding chapters: changing children's services; possibilities for new relationships; the institution and operation of new professional norms and networks; and practitioners' constructions of new professional identities. Jon Nixon takes as his point of departure the assumptions that institutional well being is dependent not only on structures and systems, but on institutional culture and practitioners' relationships, and that global solutions must take full account of regional and institutional social relations and be locally grounded. Nixon highlights the need for a new alternative language to that of market-management to talk about professional practice and offers a deliberately oppositional language of 'hope', 'friendship' and 'virtue'. The chapter and book ends by offering a number of suggestions regarding the conditions for the redefinition of professional identities and interprofessional working relations if these were constituted in terms of 'virtuous friendship', as they surely must be if we are to take forward seriously the notion of working together for better outcomes for children.

Joan Forbes
School of Education
University of Aberdeen
UK

EDITORS' NOTE

In a collected work like this it is perhaps inevitable that author preferences for particular spellings and use or not of the hyphen will emerge. We have decided to accommodate these differences rather than to impose a uniformity which would perhaps imply the acceptance of a 'one size fits all' philosophy that we are very far from espousing. We hope the reader will not find this approach irksome.

CONTRIBUTORS

Lesley Abbott's work focuses on special educational needs and inclusion issues. She was awarded the Brian Simon Fellowship by the British Educational Research Association in 2006-07. Dr Abbott was a co-researcher (with Professor Anne Moran) for a project funded by the Department of Education on Developing Inclusive Schooling in Northern Ireland.

Julie Allan is Professor of Education and Deputy Head of Department at the Stirling Institute of Education, University of Stirling, Scotland. She directs the Professional Doctoral Programme, teaches on the undergraduate teacher education programme and is involved in research on inclusion, disability, children's rights and social capital. Her recent book, *Rethinking Inclusion: The Philosophers of Difference in Practice,* is published by Springer.

Apostol Apostolov worked as a research officer on Professors Harry Daniels and Anne Edwards' ESRC funded *Learning in and for Interagency Working Project,* 2005-2007.

David Brown is Executive Director of Children's Services in Walsall which includes responsibility for 120 schools, social services for children and young people's services. He is an Honorary Research Fellow at the University of Birmingham and his most recently published work is with Professor Alma Harris on Executive Leadership in schools. Prior to taking up his current post he was Executive Headteacher of two comprehensive schools in Birmingham including his substantive Headship and he led a multi-racial community school for seven years.

Steve Brown is a Professor in the School of Management, University of Leicester. His interests include psychology; processes of collective and recovered memories; organisational communication; children's welfare services and practices; and elderly care settings.

Graham Butt is currently Director of Academic Planning and Deputy Head of School at the School of Education, University of Birmingham. As a Reader in Geography Education Dr Butt's research interests are predominantly in the areas of geography education, assessment in geography and teacher workload. The role of the Teaching Assistant in helping to alleviate teacher workload has become a recent focus for his research.

Michael Cowie is based at the Centre for Educational Development at the University of Edinburgh. Dr Cowie's development work, research interests and publications centre on headteacher preparation and development and school management and governance.

Harry Daniels is Director of the Centre for Sociocultural and Activity Theory Research at the University of Bath. Professor Daniels is the author of *Vygotsky and Pedagogy* (Routledge Falmer) and editor of *An Introduction to Vygotsky* (CUP).

Anne Edwards is Director of the Oxford Centre for Sociocultural and Activity Theory Research at the Department of Education, University of Oxford. Professor Edwards' research lies in the area of learning and practice with a particular interest in individual and organisational learning.

Joan Forbes is Director of Research at the School of Education, University of Aberdeen. Her research interests focus on practitioner relations and professional knowledges and identities in schools and children's services. Dr Forbes is currently principal organiser of an ESRC funded research seminar series: *The effects of professionals' human and cultural capital for interprofessional social capital.*

Helen Gunter is Professor of Educational Policy, Leadership and Management in the School of Education at the University of Manchester. Her particular interest is in the history of knowledge production in the field of educational leadership, and she has undertaken work around mapping theory and research. She is currently completing an ESRC funded project on knowledge production and school leadership in England in the first decade of New Labour. She has written a range of books and articles, and her most recent books are: *Leading Teachers* (Continuum) and, co-edited with Graham Butt, *Modernising Schools: people, learning and organisations* (Continuum).

David Hartley is Professor of Education at the University of Birmingham. Prior to joining the University of Birmingham he was Professor of Educational Theory and Policy at the University of Dundee. His recent books include: *Teacher Education: Major Themes in Education,* in five volumes (edited with Maurice Whitehead) (Routledge); *Re-Thinking Teacher Education: Collaborating for Uncertainty* (with Anne Edwards and Peter Gilroy) (Routledge); and *Re-Schooling Society* (Falmer).

Audrey Hendry has recently taken up post as a Quality Improvement Officer with Aberdeenshire Council. Prior to this appointment she worked within the School of Education at the University of Aberdeen where she held a senior lecturer post. Audrey Hendry's research interests are in the area of service integration. Currently she is conducting research into leadership within integrated community schools. Previously, Audrey Hendry was a primary Head Teacher.

Jane Leadbetter is Tutor in Educational Psychology at the University of Birmingham. Her interests include applications of sociocultural and activity theory research in professional settings.

Bob Lingard, previously Andrew Bell Professor of Education at The University of Edinburgh, is now a Professorial Research Fellow in the School of Education at The University of Queensland. His most recent books include: with Wayne Martino and Martin Mills, *Educating Boys: Beyond Structural Reform* (Palgrave, 2009), with Jon Nixon and Stewart Ranson, *Transforming Learning in Schools and Communities* (Continuum, 2008), with Jenny Ozga, the *RoutledgeFalmer Reader in Educational Policy and Politics* (2007) and with Debra Hayes, Martin Mills and Pam Christie, *Leading Learning: Making Hope Practical in Schools* (Open University Press, 2003) and *Teachers and Schooling Making a Difference* (Allen and Unwin, 2006). His research interests include education policy, school reform and gender and schooling.

Deirdre Martin is a Senior Lecturer in Education at the University of Birmingham. Dr Martin's interests include speech and language difficulties and organisational learning in the implementation of 'joined up' working among professionals working with children at risk.

Elspeth McCartney teaches and researches in the field of childhood speech and language impairment and therapy at the University of Strathclyde. Dr McCartney has employed a variety of methods, from scholarly analysis and critique to full-scale co-professional clinical trials and the construction of materials, to foster service development for school-aged children with language difficulties in schools.

Roy McConkey is Professor of Learning Disability at the University of Ulster, Northern Ireland; a post jointly funded by the Eastern Health and Social Services Board. A psychologist by training and a native of Belfast, he has previously held posts at the University of Manchester, in Dublin and in Scotland. He has worked in the field of intellectual disability for over 30 years and has authored, co-authored and edited over 15 books, and published over 100 book chapters and research papers in learned journals. He has acted as a consultant to various United Nations agencies and International NGOs. This work has taken him to some 20 countries in Africa, Asia and South America.

Ian Menter is Professor of Teacher Education and Deputy Dean of the Faculty of Education at the University of Glasgow. His main research interests are teachers, teacher education and education policy making. He has undertaken studies funded by a number of bodies including the ESRC, the Scottish Government and the (English) National College for School Leadership. He is a former President of the Scottish Educational Research Association.

David Middleton is an Honorary Reader in Psychology at the University of Loughborough. His research interests include work based learning in multiagency service provision for young people; social practices of remembering and forgetting in organisational settings; parent-professional communication in neo-natal intensive care.

Anne Moran is Dean of the Faculty of Social Sciences at the University of Ulster and former Head of the School of Education. Her research interests are inclusive education and teacher education and she has contributed significantly to policy formulation and development in Northern Ireland (NI) in both these areas. In the sphere of teacher education she is a current co-grant holder for an ESRC TLRP project entitled *Values-based Teacher Education* (with Smith, McCully and Clarke) and a consultant to a research seminar series entitled *Learning to Teach in Post-devolution UK* (with Professor Ian Menter as the principal applicant). Prior to that she was awarded (with Dr Lesley Abbott) a research grant from the Department of Education to undertake research on Developing Inclusive Schooling.

Jon Nixon is Professor of Professional Education and Dean of the Faculty of Education at Liverpool Hope University. He has previously held Chairs at the University of Sheffield (where he continues to hold an Honorary Chair in Education), the University of Stirling, and Canterbury Christ Church University. His most recent publication is *Towards the Virtuous University: The Moral Bases of Academic Practice* (Routledge, 2008).

Una O'Connor's interests focus on responses made by society to inclusion and social inclusion, in particular parental concerns about the statutory arrangements for pupils with special educational needs. Dr O'Connor has reviewed community relations in schools in Northern Ireland (NI) and has completed a four year evaluation study of local and global citizenship for the Council of the Curriculum Examinations and Assessment in NI (2007).

Kate Philip is a Senior Research Fellow in the Rowan Group at the University of Aberdeen and was originally a community education worker. Dr Philip also worked in health promotion before establishing an academic career as a researcher on young people's issues.

Anna Popova worked as a research officer on Professors Harry Daniels and Anne Edwards' ESRC funded *Learning in and for Interagency Working Project*, 2005-2007.

Gillian Pugh retired in 2005 as Chief Executive of Coram Family, the leading children's charity which aims to develop and promote best practice in the care and support of very vulnerable children and their families. She is an advisor to the Department of Children, Schools and Families in England and is currently working with the Local Government Association to support the implementation of the new children's agenda through the *Narrowing the Gap* project. Gillian is Chair of the National Children's Bureau, a member of the Children's Workforce Development Council, and is on the Board of the Training and Development Agency for Schools. She is visiting Professor at the Institute of Education, an advisor to the House of Commons Select Committee for children, schools and families, and chairs the advisory group for the two year national review of primary education. She was awarded the DBE in 2005 for services to children and families.

Janet Shucksmith is Professor in Public Health at the University of Teesside, having previously worked in both Education and Sociology. She has varied interests in relation to young people's heath and wellbeing and is particularly interested in the way schools are used as sites for health promotion and surveillance.

Jenny Spratt is a Research Fellow in the Rowan Group at the University of Aberdeen. Her origins as an educationalist have expanded into a strong interest in how health issues are handled with young people in the school setting.

Paul Warmington is a Senior Lecturer in Education at the University of Birmingham. Dr Warmington's research interests include widening participation, work-related learning, media coverage of education and critical understandings of race, class and education.

Cate Watson lectures in inclusive practice and research methodology at the University of Aberdeen, and is Depute Director of Research in the School of Education. Dr Watson has research interests in pupil mental health and wellbeing and in the development of professional and institutional identities. Her most recent publication is *Reflexive Research and the (Re)turn to the Baroque* (Sense).

MICHAEL COWIE

PART ONE
RESEARCH DIRECTIONS IN THE DISCOURSES OF INTERPROFESSIONALISM

Interagency networks of professionals in education, health and social work, with multiagency teams collaborating in more meaningful ways than previously found in schools are central to a new and different approach to schooling in the UK. Improved co-ordination of existing services is seen as unlikely to be enough and it is argued that collaborative working requires to be guided by a set of integrated objectives, led by staff skilled in and committed to integrated approaches and set within an integrated management structure. Within this structure the introduction of collaboration is frequently seen as unproblematic.

But the chapters in this section, however, illustrate that the nature of collaborative working is certainly not unproblematic. The piece by Janet Shucksmith, Kate Philip, Jennifer Spratt and Cate Watson emerges from an empirical study previously undertaken for the then Scottish Executive Education Department (SEED) on how behavioural issues are dealt with in schools and the extent to which these might be caused by mental health problems of children and young people. The focus of this chapter is the nature of the collaborative partnerships formed by teachers and schools with other agencies and professional groups and the extent to which teachers were prepared to collaborate and share knowledge and skills with other professionals. Based on a wide range of interviews and six detailed case studies of the experiences of different schools and interventions, Shucksmith and her colleagues highlight some of the difficulties involved in effecting integration. Most schools exported problems off site or offered integrated services on site, utilising another agency or professional group and devolving specific authority to that agency or group. Because the structures that were put in place to support the services were not integrated, most teaching staff were not exposed to the ways of working of other professionals. Very few used integrated service teams to develop practice in innovative ways.

Shucksmith *et al.* point out that much of the literature on collaborative working rests on an easy assumption that through some form of osmosis consensual solutions will emerge if professionals from different fields are brought together. This assumption neglects issues to do with identity, power and status in particular contexts and how these considerations may influence the extent to which

J. Forbes and C. Watson (eds.), Service Integration in Schools, 1–4.

professionals are willing to learn from those in other fields and collaborate with them in integrated ways.

This chapter analyses data gained in the case studies and uses Lam's (2000) typology of knowledge as an heuristic tool to explore and explain the readiness of teachers to collaborate and share knowledge and skills with other agencies and professional groups. What is implicit in the typology is that some forms of knowledge are regarded as being of a higher order than others, with 'embrained' knowledge (abstract, theoretical knowledge) and 'encoded' knowledge (which fortifies professional competence) valued more than 'embodied' and 'embedded' knowledge (the individual and collective forms of tacit knowledge). However, analysis of the interview data suggests that the forms of knowledge most valued by teachers are the 'craft skills' developed through reflection on experience over time. This leads Shucksmith and her colleagues to conclude that the value teachers place on 'embodied' and 'embedded' forms of knowledge is an integral part of their professional self-identity. Their findings suggest that co-working challenges the authority and autonomy of teachers in quite fundamental ways and that initiatives are unlikely to succeed if their aims are not in touch with teachers' needs and do not connect with their 'embodied' and 'embedded' knowledge.

Embedded knowledge involves shared norms and professional routines and when it comes to collaborative working Shucksmith *et al.* suggest that teachers may feel uneasy at the boundaries of communities of practice where there may be divergence in interaction with professionals using other forms of knowledge.

However, the chapter ends on an optimistic note, with reference to the interplay between agency and structure and to contemporary thinking on how professional knowledge is constructed through the tensions and discontinuities of lived experience, raising the possibility that one response of teachers to the challenge to their professional identity may be to 'reinvent their professionality and practice'.

Elspeth McCartney also tries to get a better understanding of what is involved in interagency working by considering how speech and language therapists (who, as she says, have already 'been around the block' in terms of co-working) operate in schools. McCartney first describes and summarises some of the models of co-professional working found in the literature. Four dimensions are used (who works with the child; egalitarian relationships; supportive relationships and who sets targets). As McCartney points out, no model is intrinsically better or worse than any other and different models can be used in different contexts.

The 'consultancy model', where speech and language therapists advise teachers on language teaching procedures, is the most prevalent model in the UK. The limitations of this model are discussed, as are some of the reasons for its continued use. Despite the policy imperative for integrated service delivery and a generally more propitious systems environment, a range of systemic factors continues to impair co-professional working. Drawing on examples raised by speech and language therapist students, as well as examples gathered in research with teachers in schools, McCartney highlights the interactive relationship between social structure and organizational culture.

In exploring some of the functional differences and limits to co-professional working, the chapter reviews key issues and provides illustrative examples of 'culture clashes'. This highlights what speech and language therapists can and cannot do as employees of the National Health Service and regulated by the Health Professions Council, and McCartney contrasts this with Learning Support teachers who can work with all pupils. Other issues discussed include the limitation placed on the ability to be flexible caused by heavy case loads, measures of success and the influence of different research paradigms, and the right of children not to accept the service offered by speech and language therapists.

McCartney suggests some practical measures that could be taken to improve roles and relationships within existing structures and suggests that some reconfiguring within new structures would be helpful, but she also argues that there are some immutable differences between the Health and Education services, which means that convergence of the two services is unlikely. She also points out, however, that immutable differences in professions need not prevent the co-working necessary for understanding the perspectives of others.

Julie Allan provides a philosophical basis for considering the implications of policy imperatives. She first considers the discursive aspects of policy; how people are constructed through policy and how this works on people in their particular professional contexts. The reader is reminded of the political nature of the policy making process and that policy texts are not the rational documents they may appear to be, but Allan's main focus is on policy as discourse and how policy discourses constrain inter-professional practice.

As with other contributions in this collection, this chapter also questions the presumption that enjoinders to collaborate will be productive. Allan argues that collaborative working both among teachers and with others needs to be learned and developed over time because complex relationships are involved. She also points out that government policy itself is not entirely 'joined up,' with some policies encouraging practice which runs counter to the collaborative policy imperative.

The chapter draws on the work of Derrida (1994) and Deleuze and Guattari (1987, 1994) ('philosophers of difference') and challenges the prevailing policy discourse. Allan argues that the certainty and closure of official policy documents on professionalism and inter-professionalism can be interrupted by thorough analysis (deconstruction) to expose double contradictory imperatives (aporias) that pull teachers in different directions. Allan goes on to argue that deconstruction of policy texts should be explored in preparing teachers because until these aporias are opened up they will be a source of confusion and uncertainty. Although disruptive, Allan argues that deconstruction should be seen as a positive and empowering process because it is in the areas of uncertainty where choices have to be made that student teachers could be opened to inventing new practices and be more disposed to collaborate with other teachers and other professionals.

Allan also argues that if existing understandings and ways of behaving are to be changed teacher education needs to be 'deterritorialized' and that such ruptures would encourage more creative thinking and productive learning. Part of this process, she argues, would involve losing aspects of what is currently undertaken in teacher education, allowing more scope for interprofessional work.

The attractions of disrupting conventional knowledge about teaching and learning through 'rhizomic wanderings' are also discussed, with student teachers supported in creating new knowledge and in becoming the kind of teachers they themselves want to become.

Allan points out that if professionals are to engage in collaborative work then it makes sense that space is needed within pre-service training for people from different professions to learn together and engage with each other, and that this should continue through on-going continuous professional development, with more specific focus on the development of interdisciplinary working practices and space provided for professionals to recover some lost ground. She also argues that collaboration may not only improve practice but also enable 'rhizomic inter-dependency,' which would support and encourage teachers and other professionals to challenge existing ways of doing things and find creative solutions for themselves. But first, Allan argues, it is important to recognise the nature of the contradictory demands on teachers before rupturing the processes of teacher education and professional development. What is required is to create opportunities for teachers and others to find creative solutions to the challenges they face which are likely to be more productive than imposed plans.

Taken together, the chapters in this part of the book provide empirical, practical and theoretical perspectives on the nature of collaborative working and demonstrate how problems inherent in the micro realities of implementing a national policy initiative have been ignored or neglected by policy makers. In particular, the contributions point to the need to take account of the concerns of individuals and professional groups, the interrelationships of the people involved and the operational assumptions that influence how they approach their work. If individuals working in different public services are to work together in more coordinated ways to achieve the aims of integrated service provision, the contributions here suggest that more consideration will need to be given to the beliefs, values and assumptions that guide teachers and other professionals and the means by which these are developed, influenced and shared.

Michael Cowie
Moray House School of Education
University of Edinburgh
UK

JANET SHUCKSMITH, KATE PHILIP, JENNIFER SPRATT AND
CATE WATSON

LEARNING HOW TO COLLABORATE? PROMOTING YOUNG PEOPLE'S HEALTH THROUGH PROFESSIONAL PARTNERSHIP IN SCHOOLS

INTRODUCTION

This chapter emerges from an empirical study undertaken in 2004/5 for the then Scottish Executive Education Department (SEED) which looked at how schools were responding to the increasing problem with behavioural issues in children and the extent to which these might be the result of mental health problems.

For schools to take on a significant role in the promotion of mental health requires a change in the way schools understand and respond to issues surrounding 'mental health'. However, Weare (2004) argues that concepts of 'mental health' are not well understood in school, having belonged until recently within a medical discourse. Moreover, she suggests that schools frequently fail to see the relevance of mental health to learning, arguably their central concern. This may in part be related to the unfamiliarity of the language and the tendency for the term 'mental health' to be conflated with 'mental illness' since schools *are* familiar with the language of social and personal development and the importance of self-esteem in learning - both important components of mental health and well-being.

A key element of the study reported here was an observation of the extent to which schools were using collaboration with other agencies and professional groups to improve or extend their ability to deal with the new responsibilities being required of them by a raft of government policies emphasising the need for integrated working, user-led services and so on. This chapter reports on the patterns of service response to the new challenge, and the extent to which teachers seemed ready and willing to collaborate with other professional partners, and to share knowledge and skills in this new area of responsibility. Lam's (2000) typology of different types of knowledge, showing the preferencing of some forms of knowledge over others, is used as an initial framework to help understand how professional groups compete for power in the school setting in ways which may hinder collaboration and restrict professional learning. From this perspective it appears that professionalism is constructed not through bureaucratic diktat, but rather through a struggle from within the cracks, crevices and contradictions of practice. A question remains as to whether the teaching profession can reinterpret

J. Forbes and C. Watson (eds.), Service Integration in Schools, 5–22.

such challenges to their authority and autonomy as opportunities to reinvent their professionalism and practice.

BACKGROUND

Recognition of the extent of children's needs in respect of mental health is just beginning to emerge:

> It has only recently become clear that mental ill health among children and adolescents is not confined to only a small proportion of young people, but is surprisingly common. Although mental disorders may not constitute catastrophes that disrupt young people's lives and futures, they cause much suffering, worry and disturbance and they can be precursors of severe disorders in adults. (World Health Organisation, 2004, no pagination)

Worldwide, measures of child and adolescent mental health vary and are influenced by social and cultural factors. There is also a lack of consensus or shared understandings as to meanings (Rowling, 2002). However, the World Health Organisation (2003) reported recently that in many countries 25% of adolescents show symptoms of mental disorder. The Mental Health Foundation estimates that 20% of children and adolescents are experiencing psychological problems at any one time (Target & Fonagy, 1996, cited by MHF website). Bayer and Sanson (2003) within the Australian context discuss the difficulties of estimating the prevalence of childhood emotional problems but suggest that 'up to one young person in five from the general population has an emotional disorder at some time in their childhood' (p. 8). They suggest that this may be an underestimate and moreover that the prevalence may be greater among those born more recently, implying that the problem may increase in the future.

In the UK research indicates a decline in the mental health of children and adolescents over the last 25 years (MHF, 1999). However, as West and Sweeting (2003, p. 399) point out, 'conclusive evidence on the issue is actually in exceedingly short supply'. One of the reasons for this lies in the methodological difficulties associated with researching this area. Recent research by Collishaw, Maughan, Goodman, and Pickles (2004) draws on data from three large-scale national longitudinal surveys over a period of 25 years between 1974 and 1999. Findings indicated increases in conduct problems across all social groups and family types for both boys and girls, more especially for what they termed 'non-aggressive' (stealing, lying, disobedience) than for 'aggressive' conduct problems (fighting, bullying). Their findings indicate that emotional problems ('misery, worries, fearful of new situations') remained stable between 1974 and 1986 but have increased in the period 1986 to 1999, again for both boys and girls. The authors also suggested a link between conduct problems in adolescence and multiple poor outcomes in adulthood. While the research has attempted to overcome some of the limitations of previous studies in this area, for example using comparable measures of mental health over the period of investigation, the findings should still be interpreted with caution.

While the term 'mental health' and 'mental health problem' are terms used within health services, schools have, since the Warnock Report (Department of Education and Science, 1978), tended to use the term 'emotional and behavioural difficulties' (EBD) or 'social, emotional and behavioural difficulties' (SEBD) to refer to a range of difficulties that can create barriers to children's learning. The definition is, however, problematic. SEBD is a non-normative construct, and as a label can be arbitrarily bestowed (Daniels, Visser, Cole, & De Reybekill, 1999). SEBD covers a continuum of behaviour and 'there is often considerable uncertainty about the boundaries between "normal" misbehaviour, emotional and behavioural difficulties, and mental illness' (Atkinson & Hornby, 2002, p. 4). Conflation of constructs such as 'SEBD', 'disaffection' and 'disruption' highlights the confusion and indeed the value laden-ness of terms used to describe difficulties that impact on behaviour.

Better Behaviour Better Learning (SEED, 2001a) recognises that there is no agreement on the meaning of the term 'SEBD' and adopts an inclusive definition:

> Whether a child 'acts out' (demonstrates bad behaviour openly) or 'acts in' (is withdrawn), they may have barriers to learning which require to be addressed. Children 'acting out' may be aggressive, threatening, disruptive and demanding of attention – they can also prevent other children learning. Children 'acting in' may have emotional difficulties which can result in unresponsive or even self-damaging behaviour. They can appear to be, depressed, withdrawn, passive or unmotivated; and their apparent irrational refusal to respond and cooperate may cause frustration for teachers and other children. (p. 13)

Atkinson and Hornby (2002, p. 4) suggest that a distinction needs to be drawn between 'occasional withdrawn or disruptive behaviour on the one hand and a continuum comprising EBD, mental health problems and disorders on the other', otherwise the child's problems may be dealt with inappropriately. Criteria for determining the distinction between 'occasional withdrawn or disruptive behaviour', EBD, mental health problems and mental health disorders depend on such factors as the severity and the persistence of the problem, its complexity, the child's developmental stage, and the presence or absence of protective/risk factors and presence or absence of stressful social and cultural factors. However, in all these cases the mental and emotional well-being of the child is likely to be compromised. It is necessary to recognise that this may occur either as the result of some long-standing diagnosed mental health problem such as conduct disorder, attention deficit hyperactivity disorder (ADHD), anxiety or depression or it may arise as the result of, or be complicated by, adverse psychological events. Events such as bereavement or divorce, or life situations that give rise to stress (for example, being homeless, subject to racial or sexual harassment, being bullied) may in themselves be part of the warp and weft of growing up but, coming on top of each other or of other life events, may trigger more deep-seated difficulties.

7

The Scottish policy context

Policies in Scottish education now recognise the necessity for schools to deal with issues of children's mental well-being. In Scotland, since 2007 all schools have been officially designated as 'Health promoting schools' (Schools (Health promotion and nutrition) (Scotland) Act 2007). Recent legislation on supporting children in schools broadens the previous definition of 'special needs' and shifts to a more inclusive focus of 'additional support needs' (Education (Additional Support for Learning) (Scotland) Act 2004). This encompasses any issue which could create a barrier to learning, whether long or short term, and arising from any cause.

The report of the Discipline Task Force (*Better Behaviour – Better Learning*, SEED, 2001a) and the more recently published *Better Behaviour in Scottish Schools. Policy update* (SEED, 2004b), make a clear link between learning and behaviour and recognise that promoting better behaviour in schools requires the engagement of pupils and parents. These two reports also acknowledge that both pupils and staff require adequate support in order to make schools safe and well-managed learning environments.

Recommendations for the development of support for pupils are contained within the National Review of Guidance 2004 (*Happy, Safe and Achieving their Potential: A standard of support for children and young people in Scottish schools*, SEED, 2005a). This report emphasises the importance of partnerships in developing pupil support. The *Review of Provision of Educational Psychology Services in Scotland* (Scottish Executive, 2002b) addressed concerns about the recruitment, training and role of educational psychologists. The report recommended that educational psychologists develop a greater role in the provision of integrated services for children and families; and in working in a consultative capacity with schools.

In addition to these policy instruments related specifically to education, there has been a range of health and social care policy responses that relate to the support of children's mental well-being in schools. The report, *For Scotland's Children: Better Integrated Children's Services* (Scottish Executive, 2001), sets out the inequalities faced by Scotland's children and puts forward the agenda for the development of integrated service provision to ensure the best start in life for every child. If every child does matter, there is much to do and both the targeted and universal services that children and their families come into contact with must address better the picture presented here.

The *National Programme for Improving Mental Health and Well-being: Action Plan 2003-2006* (Scottish Executive, 2003) identifies the development of mental, emotional and social health and well-being in schools as a priority area and builds on the recommendations of the 'SNAP' report (*Needs Assessment Report on Child and Adolescent Mental Health*, Public Health Institute of Scotland, 2003). This report emphasises the right of children and young people to be heard and their capacity to be engaged in the process of developing effective ways of promoting mental and emotional health; the importance of removing the stigma associated with mental ill-health; and the need to integrate promotion, prevention and care. As part of this programme, a draft consultation was issued in December 2004 (*Children and Young People's Mental Health*, Scottish Executive, 2004).

It's Everyone's Job to Make Sure I'm Alright was produced as a report by the Child Protection Audit and Review (Scottish Executive, 2002a). The review gives a comprehensive overview of services involved in child protection and emphasises the role of schools and other agencies and the need for 'joined up' responses to ensure children's protection. The report makes the link between child abuse/neglect and mental health problems which may manifest themselves as behavioural problems in school. The drive for the development of integrated children's services has been brought together in the policy document *Getting it right for every child* (Scottish Executive, 2006) 'which sets out reform of services for children in three areas – practice change, removing barriers and legislation' (p. 2).

Taken together, these key reports and policy guidelines constitute a commitment on the part of government to develop 'joined up' responses to social injustice and exclusion. The role of the school within the community, providing a range of integrated services is central to this vision. However, it is apparent that different agencies and professionals have different perspectives about what 'joined up' means. The development of integrated assessment frameworks is an essential step in developing 'joined up' approaches (Gibson, Baldwin, & Daniel, 2005).

METHODS

The study reported here did not attempt to make any assessment of the prevalence of mental health-related behaviour problems encountered in Scottish schools, but concerned itself rather with the extent to which schools had in place a culture or ethos which recognised mental health issues as lying at least in part within the professional remit of teachers. Since teachers and schools could hardly be expected to deal in isolation with such issues, a key question was to what extent they had formed collaborative partnerships with other agencies or service providers to help them address these issues.

The study encompassed three main phases of activity: a literature review; a mapping and scoping study to explore the extent of provision of services across all areas of Scotland; and then a more intensive look (through a set of in-depth case studies) at ways in which schools were rising to the challenge of addressing the mental health and well-being agenda with which they were newly charged.

The scoping study comprised a series of telephone interviews undertaken with local authority personnel (particularly educational psychologists and those with responsibility for pupil support) and local health board personnel in all local authority and health board areas in Scotland. In total, 67 interviews were carried out, using a structured framework similar to that developed in the Department for Education and Science report on Child and Adolescent Mental Health Services (CAMHS) work in schools (Pettitt, 2003). Additional stakeholder interviews included representatives from:

- Statutory organisations outwith the school system who work to promote mental health and well-being in young people or would have this as part of a general social care remit, e.g. social work, community development and youth workers in specialist settings (for example, alternatives to school projects), community psychiatric nurses, school nurses, early years workers;
- Representatives of children's voluntary organisations and charities concerned specifically with mental health or who have expertise with key groups of 'vulnerable' children;
- Representatives of mental health support groups and parent organisations;
- Those working in national level agencies on mental health and/or behaviour issues, e.g., NHS Scotland, Health Promoting Schools unit.

These interviews, undertaken throughout Scotland, were semi-structured, recorded and transcribed. Most were undertaken by telephone for reasons of economy and time, but where possible, face-to-face interviews were conducted.

Case studies of the experience of individual schools/interventions formed an integral part of the field work for this project. Undertaking such work involves an in-depth approach to data collection (Yin, 2003) that gathered the views of all stakeholders in a setting, including teachers, managers, parents, pupils and extramural staff concerned with mental health or behaviour issues. Case study involves the compilation of data from a variety of sources and in a variety of formats, allowing – from the triangulation of perspectives – a view to emerge of the features of the setting, along with an analysis of those responses to problems which may hold promise for sustainable good practice in the field and which may be transferable to other practice situations.

Six case studies were undertaken. Case studies were selected from a total sampling frame derived from the stakeholder survey and interviews, and using theoretical parameters or typologies derived from the literature review. These were derived in discussion with SEED in order to ensure that the work was as focused as possible on the issue of interest.

The case studies selected were:

- **ASSIST** (Aberdeenshire Staged Intervention Supporting Teaching) – an initiative to support classroom teachers dealing with low-level disruption.
- **The Place2Be** – a UK charity providing therapeutic and emotional support to children in primary schools in Edinburgh.
- **Newbattle Integrated Community School Team** – this had developed from the New Community School pilot initiated in 1997 and was based in an area of Mid-Lothian which included areas of poverty and social exclusion. An integrated team headed up by a manager and including a range of professionals was based near a large secondary and worked closely in the school and feeder primaries.
- **East Renfrewshire Multidisciplinary Support Team** – a well-established Integrated Community School team which included a youth counsellor and a

social worker, and demonstrated a commitment to individual and community well-being.

- **Clydebank High School Support Services Team** – an extended team in which pastoral care, learning support and behaviour support staff had been amalgamated, together with a group of pupil and family support workers.
- **The North Glasgow Youth Stress Centre** – a voluntary organisation working directly on mental and emotional well-being and behaviour with young people in three secondary schools and community settings.

Field work consisted of a concentrated site visit over a period of one week, with some follow-up interviews by telephone to confirm detail. The following types of data were collected: documentary material relating to the intervention (funding plans, minutes of meetings, letters to parents etc.); ethnographic observation data collected on site and recorded as field notes; semi-structured interviews at individual and group level with those delivering and managing the intervention, collaborating partners in other services, children and young people in receipt of the intervention, parents and carers, and ancillary staff (classroom auxiliaries, guidance staff).

Interviews with professionals were conducted as one-to-one or, where the school timetable allowed, as paired or group interviews. The format was semi-structured, allowing for freedom of response from the participants, and enabling the interviewer to probe more deeply into areas of interest or concern to the participants. Parents were offered the choice of group or one-to-one interviews, to allow those who felt the issue too sensitive for wider discussion to express their views in confidence. The inclusion of some group interviews also allowed for collection of data from a larger number of participants.

Group interviews were conducted with children and young people. The emphasis was on the use of child-friendly methods, which focused discussion on vignettes which presented scenarios featuring fictional children. In this way pupils were invited to discuss issues relating to emotional and mental well-being in the abstract, only disclosing personal information if and when they chose to do so. This technique was used to avoid drawing children into any discussions which might cause distress.

Data from the case studies were synthesised to produce richly textured accounts of action in practice.

LEARNING TO COLLABORATE

Before moving to examine the results emerging from the empirical work we pause here to explore the framework that has enabled us to begin interrogating the data.

The policy agenda that encourages co-working can be seen (in Foucauldian terms [Foucault, 1991]) as one aspect of a governmentality agenda (i.e., part of the formal and informal processes through which populations are governed). Apart from direct regulation, populations are governed more indirectly through processes operating through agencies, programmes, tactics and technologies. The negotiation of professional knowledge and expertise, and the recognition of its value lie at the heart of governmentality.

Lam's (2000) typology looks at different types of knowledge and at the preferencing of some forms of knowledge over others and helps us understand how different forms of power are negotiated. His typology is presented in the following table:

Table 1. Lam's (2000) typology

Embrained knowledge	Abstract, theoretical	Linked to professional bureaucracies – external bodies define standards of knowledge
Encoded knowledge	'information'; does not allow for practical knowledge	Linked to 'machine bureaucracy' – allows standardisation and control; knowledge which fortifies professional compliance
Embodied knowledge	Individual; tacit; practical	e.g., an experienced mother's way of handling a crying child
Embedded knowledge	Collective form of tacit knowledge; based on shared norms, routines	e.g., the 'craft' aspects of classroom teaching

People move between different knowledges in their practices (see Brownlie & Howson, 2006) but it is also clear that in a co-working situation, different professional groups can call on different types of knowledge to validate their claims to expertise. How powerful each of these groups is will be significant in deciding how valid are their claims to expertise in working on mental health care. Thus if community-based workers are described as 'specialists' in the field, they are accorded kudos but this may be perceived as less valid than medicalised specialist knowledge.

Education has struggled to produce an evidence base to support practice and policy, but there are clearly aspects of all these types of knowledge in the work of the teacher. We can look at the work of educational theorists such as Basil Bernstein, Jerome Bruner and others as providing examples of embrained forms of knowledge. However, whilst most teachers will have studied these theories in initial training, it would not be an exaggeration to say that they are rarely explicitly referred to thereafter. (Perhaps we should here make a distinction between teachers' embrained knowledge about teaching and learning and their embrained subject-specific knowledge which is particularly required by teachers in the secondary sector.)

Forms of encoded knowledge, as defined by Lam, are also evident in teachers' practice. Recent examples might relate to government edicts concerning 'synthetic phonics' in the teaching of reading, and the introduction of the 'literacy and numeracy hours' in England. The rationale for these innovations is often shaky – policy-based evidence rather than evidence-based policy being the order of the day – but standardisation is the goal and compliance is enforced.

Teachers are not alone in highlighting the other important types of knowledge in their practice – the 'craft' aspects of classroom work, which are so much harder to teach in the abstract. In this respect they are not very far different from the craft qualities of the doctor whose 'bedside manner' and ability to empathise with patients may be critical to reaching an appropriate diagnosis. Embedded /embodied knowledge is clearly required for classroom management, behaviour management and generally forming positive relations with pupils, and, although it has a basis in theoretical training, it is generally acknowledged to be honed considerably by practical experience, and by observing experienced practitioners.

In negotiating the role of different partners within systems of collaborative working it would seem likely that their understanding of one another's perspective and the complicated rituals involved in the dance to accommodate other people's ways of working owes something to the forms of knowledge which are preferenced in different situations. Thus, in dealing with children's routine 'bad' behaviour *en masse*, as in the case of dealing with rowdy behaviour in a corridor, for example, teachers' embedded knowledge might seem the most legitimate and useful. In a different situation where a single child's violent or erratic behaviour was self-evidently the result of a form of post-traumatic stress disorder, as in the case of a refugee child arriving from a war-torn area of Africa for example, the educational psychologist's embrained knowledge is likely to be deferred to in choosing a treatment option.

In being asked to deal with mental health issues teachers may feel de-skilled, not only because they do not possess the embrained knowledge about mental health that the psychologist or mental health nurse might have but also because the issue may demand individual or one-to-one ways of working which lie outside the embodied and embedded craft skills of many teachers who habitually deal with children en masse or in groups. There is perhaps also an argument that embodied and embedded knowledge is harder to change. Embrained knowledge can be altered, through exposure to new and convincing forms of evidence, through debate or training and reading, but practical dispositions are harder to change (see our earlier article on Bourdieu and the role of *habitus*, Spratt, Shucksmith, Philip & Watson, 2006). It is these practical aspects of teaching that teachers are most fiercely protective of, and claim that other workers don't and cannot understand.

Some over simple assumptions are threaded through the literature on collaborative working which suggest that pulling representatives from different professional groups together to deliver services for children will result in a blurring of professional boundaries, the production of a utopian blend of capacities and insights in which dedicated professionals will come together to share their perspectives and arrive at a consensual resolution as to the best way forward.

13

However, the extent to which collaborative working will result in some form of osmotic learning between professional groups – to produce utopian 'learning communities' – must be affected by the willingness of different partners to appreciate and value the knowledge base from which the others work. Implicit, if not explicit, in Lam's typology is a ranking of knowledge types, where – context aside – encoded knowledge trumps embodied knowledge or embedded knowledge by a long shot.

How willing would teachers be to learn from professional colleagues brought in to work alongside them? Sullivan and Skelcher (2002) suggest that assessment of partners' capacity to learn should be incorporated into any evaluation of collaborative working. Wight and Buston's (2003) study of teachers exposed to a new training on sexual health (SHARE) showed their reluctance to change and learn. The authors conclude that learning is less likely to occur (and innovations therefore more likely to fail) when the goals of the intervention do not overlap with teachers' previously perceived needs, particularly if these goals involve adopting a theoretical approach unrelated to their existing repertoire of teaching skills and tactics. Teachers in their study showed a singular lack of interest in the intended mechanism of behaviour change (based on a form of embrained knowledge) and were only really interested in facets of the scheme that added to their embodied or embedded teaching knowledge.

There is no reason to think that teachers are the only professional group that operate in this manner. A group of clinical epidemiologists who introduced Evidence Based Practice into medicine at McMaster University in Canada (clearly an attempt to base practice on embrained or perhaps encoded knowledge) have had 10 years to review their original work and now conclude (Guyatt, Meade, Jaeschke, Cook & Haynes, 2000, p. 954) that for general practice doctors in the community:

> Habit, local practice patterns and product marketing may often be stronger determinants of practice [than research evidence]. Controlled trials have shown that traditional continuing education has little effect on combating these forces and changing doctors' behaviour. On the other hand, approaches that do change targeted clinical behaviours include one-to-one conversations with an expert, computerised alerts and reminders, preceptorships, advice from opinion leaders, and targeted audit and feedback. Other effective strategies include restricted drug formularies, financial incentives, and institutional guidelines.

We now explore the data generated in the scoping studies and more particularly the case studies to examine whether Lam's typology offers a way of understanding teachers' reactions to new challenges to their professional remit and identity.

RESULTS

Patterns of ownership

The data demonstrate that co-working was being used to deliver a range of different or additional services in both universal and targeted ways. A crude description of the range is that children with difficult behaviour arising out of mental health problems were being dealt with in three main ways. Schools would either:

- **Export problems** off-site by referring troubled or poorly behaved children off for expert services delivered elsewhere or into containment schemes;
- **Import skills** into schools to solve problems of mental well-being/indiscipline, but devolve authority to another agency or professional group;
- **Retain ownership** of 'problem' in school, importing skills and personnel, but using these in integrated service teams to develop new approaches that are embedded in school life.

In practice there was considerable overlap between these categories. In addition, the tendency to see the categories as transitional (with a gradual move towards greater ownership of mental health/discipline issues by schools) may be misleading. Essentially, however, the typology is useful in forcing consideration of the extent to which schools are prepared to locate mental well-being/discipline issues in the school environment as well as in the child and his/her family background and to put in place structures which support young people, remediate problems and which operate preventatively.

The first of the three actions above obviously denies any 'ownership' of the problem, implies lack of skills in dealing with such issues and also perhaps a lack of willingness to learn. Both local authorities and health boards worked hard to stop schools shipping problems off-site. For some children with severe/enduring problems, access to specialist help will always be necessary, but is seems unlikely that Scottish schools in particular will be able for much longer to evade responsibility for CAMHS tier 1 activities (services provided by practitioners who are not mental health specialists working in universal services; this includes GPs, health visitors, school nurses, teachers, social workers, youth justice workers, voluntary agencies). Taking on the new challenge will necessitate a change of mindset and language, the development of new skills and the establishment of new structures within school.

A number of schools, already moving fast towards offering integrated services on site, were importing skills. Within this category, however, some bought in other services, but many seemed reluctant to take co-ownership of the problems, which meant little or no integration of work between professional groups. Parallel rather than integrated structures were put in place and the possibilities for collaborative working or learning from one another's practice were limited to a few members of staff only. This second model was by far the most common – offering additionality, rather than genuine integration.

15

Of the third model we saw precious few examples. The road to full integration and whole school working is, we suspect, a long and meandering one, involving full-scale review of structures, ethos and relationships inside and outside school. What new skills or new knowledge might teachers require to get them to the stage where they are able to be full participants in an integrated service delivery offered to young people with mental health problems?

New knowledge; new skills?

What opportunities were made in schools for learning to take place regarding the need for new skills to tackle new responsibilities? In-service training is the obvious place to look, but from most accounts given to the researchers, it appeared that issues of mental well-being were largely presented as part of an optional or extended menu. The implication of this is that not only were such opportunities brief but that it is likely to leave the issue of dealing with the topic to an (already involved) minority:

> *In-service days are usually planned like years in advance and you'll get phone calls, 'We'd like you to come along and do an input on mental health'. 'Very good and how long would you like this session to last?' 'Oh, we're thinking about 45 minutes.' 'Right... ok.' So that is one of the challenges and one of the barriers. We do appreciate that time is precious for them but there is no way that you can do it justice [in that time] at all. (Voluntary sector representative)*

> *We just ignore that side... leave that to the pastoral people... 'that's your job, you can go and do all that'... Probably we're so flaming busy delivering a curriculum that it's not the kind of thing that I would seek out on the CPD catalogue, you know. (Principal teacher)*

Perhaps if opportunities to learn new skills formally are few, there is a lot of informal learning going on through working in proximity to one another? Unfortunately data from this study show that, even leaving aside the cases of overt hostility and 'trial by fire', there was a general and studied indifference between teachers and their professional colleagues (mostly on the part of teachers) with relatively little leakage of professional learning, dispositions and attitudes between teachers and others.

We found some indication that this was being tackled head on in some authorities by the deliberate establishment of 'mentoring' schemes, aimed at building capacity. Thus in Glasgow a team of peripatetic teachers had been trained to work with schools, both with pupils and teachers, to develop their understanding of mental health issues. Also within Glasgow we found a number of health development workers assigned to school clusters with a remit which deliberately included capacity building for other staff. One of these workers commented on the uphill struggle she faced in her role:

It's early stages and you have to have the same person in post to actually become ingrained into the education system. And for them to begin to value what you put in ... it doesn't happen overnight. They still do see people like me as an add-on, not part of the bigger picture. (Health development officer)

People like us

Many teachers feel strongly that they can only learn from 'people like them' who work within the same environment and face similar problems, e.g., they feel that the problems facing a class teacher are not the same as those facing people working one-to-one with children.

Teachers don't like it when experts come in and tell them what to do but don't get their hands dirty with the pupils. (Education authority health staff tutor)

What we have here is a conscious valorising of the embodied and embedded forms of knowledge in Lam's framework.

You can talk professional development all you like, but if it is done in an intellectual way people find it hard to take it on board in terms of their own practice. You would always hope that children and young people wouldn't suffer a significant emotional and mental health issue, but it's difficult for staff to understand these issues if they haven't experienced it. I think staff develop a better understanding if they have seen a case and experienced the interagency working. (Head of service)

In Wight and Buston's (2003) evaluation of a programme of training for teachers asked to deliver a new sex education programme, they found that this preferencing of embodied knowledge continued despite all attempts to drive forward a model of teaching action based on encoded knowledge. They comment:

... there was little evidence that the third objective of the training, to improve teachers' understanding of the theoretical rationale for this behavioural change programme, was achieved. This seemed to be of little concern to the teachers: when interviewed they rarely referred to the behavioural change objectives of the programme...and only one referred to its theoretical basis. (p. 540)

Ten years before them, Brown and McIntyre (1993) had come to the same conclusion, namely that the poor level of success of many classroom innovations was due in large part to teachers' perceptions that the innovations were impractical. In terms of our analysis here, no amount of theoretical or empirical proof that method A was most effective could trump teachers' embodied and embedded knowledge of how to run a classroom.

For the innovation to be 'practical', however, it would have to be so clearly superior to the established practices, and so certainly achievable and safe, as

17

> to justify the abandonment of the extensive repertoire of teacher tactics, and the even more extensive craft knowledge about when to use what tactics, that each teacher had built up over the years. (Brown & McIntyre, 1993, p. 116)

Rather than seeing this as an indication that teachers are somehow stubborn, subversive and work at 'lower' levels than other professional groups, it may be useful to see the problem as one where, in teachers' eyes, embodied or embedded knowledge is implicitly valued above embrained and encoded knowledge. Where researchers are in the habit of developing curriculum or classroom innovations without taking into account the professional knowledge and understandings of teachers, there is bound to be a disjunction or a lack of 'buy-in' by the profession.

It may be useful to digress briefly here to look at Wenger's work (2000) on 'communities of practice', in which the author reflects that 'knowing is a matter of displaying competencies defined in social communities' (p. 226). He claims that knowing involves two components: the competence that our communities have established over time (i.e., what it takes to act and be recognised as a competent member); and secondly, our ongoing experience of the world as a member. These chime with Lam's embedded and embodied knowledge types respectively. Wenger goes on to describe how communities of practice define competence by combining three elements; *joint enterprise* (a collectively developed understanding of what the community is about); *mutuality* (interaction with one another, establishing norms that reflect these interactions; and a *shared repertoire* (communal resources, languages, routines, tools, stories). One suspects that it is these elements that take so long to develop even after policy diktat brings professionals together under one roof. Importantly, Wenger warns that communities of practice should not be romanticised, and notes that they can 'learn not to learn' (p.230). To grow and make progress they need to recognise and address gaps in their knowledge, develop mutuality through enhancing social capital and trust and also develop a degree of self-awareness.

A key notion in the communities of practice literature is that of boundaries. The boundary around a community of practice might be fluid and unspoken, but it is nevertheless real. The learning that takes place inside the boundary is quite different from that which takes place at the boundary, which is often a site of contestation and colonisation. Inside the boundary there is a convergence of competence and experience - this is a comfortable place to be. At the boundary there is a divergence. As Wenger (2000, p. 233) says: 'A boundary interaction is usually an experience of being exposed to a foreign competence'. In terms of Lam's model, this will often be a challenge to the embedded and embodied knowledge that teachers feel comfortable with by professionals using encoded or embrained forms of knowledge.

A recent review (Brown & White, 2006) highlighted the fact that the process of moving towards more integrated services for children does not presume the emergence of a 'melting pot' workforce where individual professional skills are lost or melded. Instead they point to evidence (Rushmer & Pallis, 2002) that suggests that the most successful collaborations are where boundaries are clear rather than blurred and the individual contribution made by different agents is recognised.

DISCUSSION

The drawing into schools of other professional groups offers the chance to build capacity on this issue within the teaching group and to provide for young people additional and different services from those which teachers can offer. An overview provided by this empirical study would indicate that we have the latter but not the former in most instances. Additionality has been achieved, but it may take time to build capacity in this way.

Why is it so difficult to effect integration and build capacity? From the current project we have seen that because ways of working are often parallel rather than truly integrated, many staff are still not exposed to other professionals and their ways of working. Moreover, school leaders are not exposed to the same degree of training/exposure on multi-agency working and so real institutional support may not be there for workers at the practice level.

This chapter offers a tentative exploration of why teachers are resistant to changing practice. Lam's framework gave us an initial template within which to start exploring the different kinds of knowledge that teachers value, and the way this embrained and embedded knowledge is valorised and seen as central to their identification of themselves as teachers. The valorisation of these forms of knowledge may also act as a way of resisting the governmentality agenda, whereby governments increasingly try to rule education through centralised and encoded knowledge (see Flynn, 2002).

Recent writings about professional knowledge suggest that it is constructed and/or sustained through the working out of tensions at different levels of experience (Stronach, Corbin, McNamara, Stark & Warne, 2002). This situational and constructivist view of professional knowledge, as Gleeson and Knights (2006) point out, contrasts sharply with the more disembodied cognitive conceptions of the professional as the harbinger of esoteric knowledge or competencies (Eraut, 1994). Parallel research, for example, in medicine, nursing health, the probation service, all indicates the ways in which professional identity and knowledge are constructed through the micro-politics of the workplace.

Gleeson and Knights (2006) feel that this perspective draws attention to the ways in which professionalism is constructed not through bureaucratic diktat, but rather through a struggle from *within* the cracks, crevices and contradictions of practice. Such a perspective is essentially an optimistic one, emphasising the role of agency rather than that of structure. Reflexive interpretation of professional change by professionals, according to Stronach *et al.* (2002), allows a group like the teaching profession to reinterpret challenges to their authority and autonomy as opportunities to reinvent their professionality and practice.

According to Martin and Wajcman (2004) it is through such living tensions that a multiplicity of professional roles and identities are experienced and developed. The ambiguities and tensions, the disruptions and discontinuities of lived

19

professional experience will stimulate creative, pragmatic and potentially innovative practice. It is to be hoped that this innovative practice does indeed come about as a consequence of service integration in schools and that it is ultimately to the benefit of young people with mental health problems needing attention and support.

ACKNOWLEDGMENTS

The authors gratefully acknowledge the financial support of the Scottish Executive Education Department who commissioned the original piece of research, and also the Scottish National Programme for Improving Mental Health and Well-being which gave an additional grant that has allowed a longer period of dissemination.

REFERENCES

Atkinson, M., & Hornby, G. (2002). *Mental health handbook for schools.* London: Routledge.

Bayer, J.K., & Sanson, A.V. (2003). Preventing the development of emotional mental health problems from early childhood: Recent advances in the field. *International Journal of Mental Health Promotion, 5*(3), 4-16.

Brown, S., & McIntyre, D. (1993). *Making sense of teaching.* Buckingham: Open University Press.

Brown, K., & White, K. (2006). *Exploring the evidence base for integrated children's services.* Edinburgh: Scottish Executive Education Department.

Brownlie, J., & Howson, A. (2006). 'Between the demands of truth and government': Health practitioners, trust and immunisation work. *Social Science and Medicine, 62,* 433-443.

Collishaw, S., Maughan, B., Goodman, R., & Pickles, A. (2004). Time trends in adolescent mental health. *Journal of Child Psychology and Psychiatry, 45*(8), 1350-1362.

Daniels, H., Visser, J., Cole, T., & De Reybekill, N. (1999). *Emotional and behavioural difficulties in mainstream schools.* London: Department for Education and Employment.

Department of Education and Science (1978). *Report of the Committee of Inquiry into the Special Educational Needs of Children and Young People* (Warnock Report). London: Department of Education and Science.

Eraut, M. (1994). *Developing professional knowledge and competence.* London: Falmer.

Flynn, R. (2002). Clinical governance and governmentality. *Health, Risk and Society, 4*(2), 155-173.

Foucault, M. (1991). Governmentality. In G. Burchell, C. Gordon, & P. Miller (Eds.). *The Foucault effect: Studies in governmentality* (pp. 87-104). Chicago, IL: University of Chicago Press.

Gibson, P., Baldwin, N., & Daniel, B. (2005). *Integrated assessment framework for children. Evaluation report for SEED.* Available at:
http://www.south-ayrshire.gov.uk/news/2005/publications/Assessment%20Report.pdf

Gleeson, D., & Knights, D. (2006). Challenging dualism: Public professionalism in 'troubled' times. *Sociology, 40*(2), 277-295

Guyatt, G.H., Meade, M.O., Jaeschke, R.M., Cook, D.J., & Haynes, R.B. (2000). Practitioners of evidence based health care. *British Medical Journal, 320,* 954-955.

Lam, A. (2000). Tacit knowledge, organizational learning and societal institutions – An integrated framework. *Organizational Studies, 21,* 487-513.

Martin, B., & Wajcman, T. (2004). Markets, contingencies and preferences. *Sociological Review, 52*(2), 240-264.

McCartney, E. (2006). Joining up working: Terms, types and tensions. In J. Forbes (Ed.), *The research and policy discourses of service integration, interprofessional and interagency working: ESRC seminar 1 Proceedings* (pp. 33-51). School of Education, University of Aberdeen, *Research Paper 14.*

Mental Health Foundation (1999). *Bright futures. Promoting children and young people's mental health*. London: Mental Health Foundation.

Mental Health Foundation (2001). Available at: www.mentalhealth.org.uk.

Pettitt, B. (2003). *Effective joint working between child and adolescent mental health services (CAMHS) und schools*. RR 412. London: DfES.

Public Health Institute of Scotland (2003). *Needs assessment report on child and adolescent mental health*. Edinburgh: NHS Scotland.

Rowling, L. (2002). School mental health promotion: Perspectives, problems and possibilities. *International Journal of Mental Health Promotion, 4*(4), 8-13.

Rushmer, R., & Pallis, G. (2002). Inter-professional working: The wisdom of integrated working and the disaster of blurred boundaries. *Public Money and Management, 23*(1), 59-66.

Scottish Executive (2001). *For Scotland's children. Better integrated children's services*. Edinburgh: Scottish Executive.

Scottish Executive (2002a). *'It's everyone's job to make sure I'm alright.'* Edinburgh: Scottish Executive.

Scottish Executive (2002b). *The review of provision of educational psychology services in Scotland*. Edinburgh: Scottish Executive.

Scottish Executive (2003). *National programme for improving mental health and well-being: Action plan 2003-2006*. Edinburgh: Scottish Executive.

Scottish Executive (2004). *Children and young people's mental health: A framework for promotion, prevention and care. Draft Consultation*. Edinburgh: Scottish Executive.

Scottish Executive (2006). *Getting it right for every child: Draft Children's Services (Scotland) Bill Consultation*. Edinburgh: Scottish Executive

Scottish Executive Education Department (2001a). *Better behaviour, better learning*. Report of the Discipline Task Group. Edinburgh: SEED.

Scottish Executive Education Department (2001b). *A teaching profession for the 21st century: Agreement reached following recommendations made in the McCrone Report*. Edinburgh: SEED.

Scottish Executive Education Department (2003). *Moving forward: Additional support for learning*. Edinburgh: SEED.

Scottish Executive Education Department (2004a). *Being well, doing well: A framework for health promoting schools in Scotland*. Scottish Health Promoting Schools Unit. Edinburgh: SEED.

Scottish Executive Education Department (2004b). *Better behaviour in Scottish schools. Policy update*. Edinburgh: SEED.

Scottish Executive Education Department (2004c). *A curriculum for excellence. The Curriculum Review Group*. Edinburgh: SEED.

Scottish Executive Education Department (2004d). *Support in school: The views of harder to reach groups*. Edinburgh: SEED.

Scottish Executive Education Department (2005a). *Happy, safe and achieving their potential: The report of the National Review of Guidance 2004*. Edinburgh: SEED.

Scottish Executive Education Department (2005b). *Ambitious, excellent schools*. Edinburgh: SEED.

Spratt, J., Shucksmith, J., Philip, K., & Watson, C. (2006). Interprofessional support of mental well-being in schools: A Bourdieuan perspective. *Journal of Interprofessional Care, 20*(4), 391-402.

Stronach, I., Corbin, B., McNamara, O., Stark, S., & Warne, T. (2002). Towards an uncertain politics of professionalism: Teacher and nurse identities in flux. *Journal of Education Policy, 7*(1), 110-138.

Sullivan, H., & Skelcher, C. (2002). *Working across boundaries – Collaboration in public services*. Basingstoke: Palgrave Macmillan.

Weare K. (2004). The international alliance for child and adolescent mental health and schools (INTERCAMHS). *Health Education, 104*(2), 65-67.

Wenger, E. (2000). Communities of practice and social learning systems. *Organization, 7*(2), 225-246.

West, P., & Sweeting, H. (2003). Fifteen, female and stressed: Changing patterns of psychological distress over time. *Journal of Child Psychology and Psychiatry, 44*(3), 399-411.

21

Wight, D., & Buston, K. (2003). Meeting needs but not changing goals: Evaluation of in-service teacher training for sex education. *Oxford Review of Education, 29*(4), 521-543.

World Health Organisation (2004). *Pre-conference on mental health of children and adolescents,* Luxembourg, 20-21 September. Available at:
www.euro.who.int/mentalhealth/ChildAdolescent/20040917_1 (1709/2004, 2004).

World Health Organization (2003). Meeting of WHO Task Force on Child and Adolescent Mental Health, Heidelberg, Germany, 9-10 July 2003. Available at:
http://www.euro.who.int/InformationSources/MtgSums/2003/20031001_4?PrinterFriendly=1&

Yin, R. (2003). *Case study research: Design and methods* (3rd ed.). London: Sage.

Janet Shucksmith
School of Health and Social Care
University of Teesside
UK

Kate Philip, Jennifer Spratt and Cate Watson
School of Education
University of Aberdeen
UK

ELSPETH McCARTNEY

JOINING UP WORKING: TERMS, TYPES AND TENSIONS

INTRODUCTION

Terms for models of co-professional working are at times used interchangeably in policy documents, but definitions for 'named types' do exist. The models that may be used are influenced by the structures within which staff work and the ease with which co-professional contact can be made. Integrated services will require to make decisions about the models they intend to foster, but resource limits will play a part. In this chapter questions concerning the effects of specific models of co-practice, the implications for practitioners and the ways in which schools need to reconfigure to include professionals from other agencies are illustrated with reference to the work of speech and language therapists (SLTs) in schools in the United Kingdom as they seek to provide 'front-line delivery' of service. This is an illuminating example for several reasons. SLTs have already 'been around the block' with respect to their structural involvement in schools. Until 1974 therapists who provided services to schools were employed by education authorities. Since that date the vast majority have worked in the health service, and are now Allied Health Professionals (AHPs), regulated by the Health Professions Council. Their current involvement in schools is therefore an example of cross-sector or interagency working, where new structures are only now developing which aim to foster co-professional working.

SLTs' work in school has been subject to considerable research and evaluation over time. (For Scotland, see Reid, Millar, Tait, Donaldson, Dean, Thomson & Grieve, 1996, and HMI, 1996; for England and Wales, Law, Lindsay, Peacey, Gascoigne, Soloff, Radford, Band & Fitzgerald, 2000, Law, Lindsay, Peacey, Gascoigne, Soloff, Radford & Band, 2002, and Lindsay, Dockrell, Mackie & Letchford, 2002, 2005a; for Northern Ireland, Northern Ireland Commissioner for Children and Young People, 2005.) Their role is specifically discussed in relevant education acts and codes of practice across the UK. SLTs are professionally committed to basing their services within schools and to planning jointly with education professionals (Gascoigne, 2006, p. 17; Royal College of Speech and

J. Forbes and C. Watson (eds.), Service Integration in Schools, 23–36.

Language Therapists, 2005, p. 25) to provide services as an integral part of a child's school life (Royal College of Speech and Language Therapists, 2006, p. 224). Their focus on language and communication fits with the centrality of the language curriculum in schools, and large numbers of children have additional learning needs with a language and communication basis. As Forbes (2006) notes, a specific focus on SLT-education relationships has now been subsumed into wider policies of service integration. As these are being formulated it may be worth revisiting this relatively well-explored example to shed light on issues that affect interagency working between education and the other services in general, and health services in particular.

This chapter therefore considers the variety of ways in which co-professional working can operate, how SLTs and teachers currently operate and why this is, and considers future options for integrated services.

MODELS OF WORKING TOGETHER

It is worth considering what models of co-professional working are available. Several are described, usually defined from the perspectives of the professionals involved.

Terminology is problematic and terms are used differently across policy documents and within the literature. For example, 'multidisciplinary' appears in both *For Scotland's Children* (Scottish Executive, 2001) and *Every Child Matters* (Department for Education and Skills, 2003) in what is probably a common usage to describe the situation where a number of different professionals are involved. *For Scotland's Children* lists education, social work and health staff (p. 74) and then community education, mental health and housing management staff (p. 85) as forming multidisciplinary teams. *Every Child Matters* uses 'multi-disciplinary' for co-working amongst education, social care and health services (p. 60), and later amongst health visitors, nursery nurses and community development workers (p. 93). However, *Supporting Children's Learning: The Code of Practice* (Scottish Executive, 2005, p. 135) retains the term multidisciplinary for instances where professionals from different disciplines within the same agency work together, such as an SLT with a health visitor. Where the professionals come from different agencies the term 'interagency' is used, and by this definition a teacher and SLT working together would not be described as a multidisciplinary pairing.

'Collaboration' is another term that has received several definitions. Williams and Salmon (2002) use the term generically when discussing all aspects and styles of joint working practice. However, Kersner (1996) discussing SLTs in schools follows Conoley and Conoley (1982) in retaining 'collaboration' to describe situations where individuals join in an egalitarian partnership to achieve a mutually determined goal. Marvin (1990) uses the term to describe teachers and SLTs engaging in informal networking who have a shared responsibility for children and DiMeo, Merritt, and Culatta (1998) use collaboration only where there is trust, mutual respect and personal support, free and honest discussion and shared responsibility for planning.

Where terms are used differently and are also in common usage it is unlikely that their meanings can now be constrained - document-specific definitions and glossaries are probably the best that can be expected. However, it is worth attempting a classification to consider and gain some clarity about dimensions considered relevant by those describing co-professional practice.

Writers have tended to classify models of co-professional working using four aspects: first, who works with a client to carry out planned activities, usually designed to meet health or learning targets; second, how egalitarian and third, how supportive are professional relationships, and last who agrees targets, here used as shorthand for any agreed end. These will be considered in turn in relation to professional working with school pupils, leaving aside for the moment considerations of how children and their families also are involved in agreeing and meeting targets.

Who works with the child
Professionals may work either directly with a child or indirectly, where learning activities are delivered by others (and so these terms are used from the professional's point of view). 'Others' can include professionals or assistants such as SLT assistants, classroom assistants or learning support assistants. Where implementation is through an assistant a professional retains responsibility and accountability for the assistant's performance: otherwise much responsibility for implementation lies with the professional undertaking the activities.

Egalitarian relationships
Some inequalities are formalised within job descriptions, such as that between a professional and an assistant or a professional and a manager. Here good relationships can be formed, but by definition not egalitarian relationships. Co-professional work often involves professionals who have nominally equal status in that neither is 'the boss of' the other in formal employment terms, and each has their own area of knowledge and expertise to share. Working together with equals should be a key feature in co-professional work, although in practice some may prove to be more equal than others.

Supportive relationships
Supportive and trusting relationships and mutual respect can arise or not irrespective of how egalitarian a relationship is – it is possible to trust, respect and receive support from an assistant or boss and to mistrust an equal. This dimension is concerned with inter-personal comfort and rapport.

Who sets targets
Where nominally equal professional relationships pertain, ways of setting targets have been used to distinguish models of working. McGrath and Davis (1992) distinguish 'multidisciplinary' models that involve professionals setting targets independent from 'interdisciplinary' models where targets are set and agreed jointly. In both cases learning activities are often delivered by professionals

25

separately. Mackey and McQueen (1998) use the term 'transdisciplinary' to reflect joint goal-setting where the resulting learning activities are delivered by the professionals together, with considerable role-release as every member of the team contributes to holistic learning experiences as the need arises. The Royal College of Speech and Language Therapists (RCSLT) (Gascoigne, 2006, p. 16) regards transdisciplinary models as central to work with children within integrated teams.

NAMED TYPES

Considering these dimensions allows us to chart some of the types of co-professional working that have been described. Figure 1 summarises some of the types noted in the literature. In each instance some information is shared, and used to influence future decision-making: 'expert' models where one professional works quite independently are omitted. Figure 1 uses only three dimensions, but Marvin (1990) and DiMeo et al. (1998) would add the dimension of positive interactions through relationship building to interdisciplinary and transdisciplinary types to form 'collaborative' models.

Targets agreed jointly:	Activities delivered by:	Nominally egalitarian relationships:	Named variety:
No	Each professional separately	Yes	Multi-disciplinary[1]
Yes	Each professional separately	Yes	Inter-disciplinary[1]
Yes	Professionals working together	Yes	Trans-disciplinary[2]
No	Professionals working together	Yes	Co-teaching[3]
No	Assistant	No	Expert-aide or Transfer[4]
No	Another professional	Yes	Consultancy[5]
Yes	Another professional	Yes	Co-operation[6]

Figure 1. 'Named Types' of professional co-working — 1 McGrath & Davis (1992); 2 Mackey & McQueen (1998); 3 Creese (2002); 4 Cunningham & Davis (1985); 5 Law et al. (2002); 6 McCartney et al. (2006).

There is nothing intrinsically better or worse about any type of co-working, and each model may be used successfully in some contexts. (The somewhat anomalous situation where professionals in formally egalitarian relationships deliver activities together without planning targets jointly is found in a study by Creese, 2002, describing how teachers specialising in English as an additional language co-taught with secondary school subject teachers, concentrating on language issues. The pairs had not consistently planned together, and in this example were all teachers rather than coming from different professions. Creese's example is not an entirely happy one – the relationships became less than egalitarian in practice – but the named type of working is not dissimilar to that used successfully within many higher education post-graduate tutorials.) Some types, however, share more dimensions considered to be positive than others, particularly joint target-setting and working together, and much writing is from professionals celebrating the achievement of closer working relationships in terms of professional satisfaction (Miller, 2002) and (more rarely) child benefits (Wren, Roulstone & Parkhouse, 2001). These two aspects should probably be kept separate – there is to my knowledge no strong evidence that closer working relationships that benefit staff also benefit children, despite a common (and commonsense) assumption that it does. Different types may also have different 'transaction' costs (Hudson & Ranade, 2003), the time spent meeting, agreeing, planning and working together as well as maintaining relationships, and so different staffing implications.

Closer interactions may flourish where there is continuity of staffing, joint responsibility, and time to plan and discuss together. For example, Wright (1996) reports that the more SLTs and teachers had opportunities to collaborate the more they valued it, and that working in close proximity helped information exchange. DiMeo et al. (1998) note that building a collaborative working relationship is like building a personal friendship, requiring time to develop and sustain, and so it is not reasonable to expect SLTs or teachers to achieve collaboration with all professionals with whom they interact. Williams and Salmon (2002) suggest that working together is facilitated where teams can anticipate long-term relationships amongst members, with stability in the appointment of key individuals, and with regular contact sustained.

Such facilitative factors should be considered when building new integrated services, if an aim is to develop closer partnerships. However, at present they do not commonly pertain, and the current situation reflects their absence.

WHAT CURRENTLY HAPPENS IN THE UK?

Types of co-professional working encountered in practice reflect the opportunities afforded to professionals. McCartney, Ellis, and Boyle (2006) discuss how SLTs' and teachers' desire to develop language skills in the social and educationally rich classroom environment has coincided with SLTs' need to offer service to a large number of children with limited staff resources. This has led to widespread, although not exclusive, use of consultancy models of SLT service delivery (Law et *al.*, 2000), where SLTs provide teachers with advice and guidance on language teaching procedures to be implemented by school staff.

Consultancy approaches are not particularly close models of collaboration, and their widespread adoption has received critical comment. Law *et al.* (2002) recognise the assumed learning benefits for children who undertake language work in their classroom, but also that severe service capacity limits have motivated the move towards consultancy services as 'a pragmatic solution to the problem of coverage' (p. 154). Lindsay *et al.* (2002) make similar points, questioning whether consultation approaches have become the method of choice for professional or pragmatic reasons (p. 200). Law *et al.* (2002, p. 158) note that the consultancy model relies heavily on the availability and commitment of educational staff with whom to consult, and that there are low numbers of staff with specialist language skills in schools, running the risk that activities recommended by an SLT may not be implemented systematically in the classroom. McCartney, Boyle, Ellis, Turnbull and Bannatyne (2004) found this fear was justified, in that language intervention activities shown to be effective in developing expressive language for children with language impairment when delivered by SLTs or SLT assistants (Boyle, McCartney, O'Hare & Forbes, 2006) were less effective when delivered by classroom staff. This appeared to be related to the amount of time children spent on the activities, which was less than in the Boyle *et al.* (2006) study and which varied considerably across schools. SLTs can advise, but if classroom staff cannot deliver language activities consultation approaches may not result in particularly effective experiences for children.

The Royal College of Speech and Language Therapists (Gascoigne, 2006) have also registered concerns about consultancy approaches, stressing the need to replace the term with a more accurate description of the service being delivered, and to uncouple consultancy used to enhance a child's levels of activity and participation from resource issues:

> Unfortunately, where models involving the delegation of tasks and programmes to others have been perceived as resource saving strategies, the positive reasons for such approaches have been lost. (p. 18)

McCartney *et al.* (2006) suggest some ways of developing and improving the consultancy model, but this is hardly service-integration utopia. The SLT will still tend to be seen as an 'outside expert', advising teachers on what to do rather than developing partnerships that draw together the specialist knowledge of each profession. Teachers may feel pressurised or coerced into carrying out language activities, or into allocating tasks to their classroom assistant without feeling confident about their ability to supervise appropriately. The SLT's priorities may clash with the teacher's. Misunderstandings may arise, and synergy may not be achieved.

Why is this situation continuing?

Given that 'better' ways of working together exist, it is worth considering what has led to consultancy models being set up and sustained in mainstream schools. Hopes for language learning and generalisation and limits of staff to carry out direct work have been raised as factors initiating consultancy approaches, but other factors are also relevant. As McCartney (1999) discusses, health and education services are radically different organisations, giving rise to systemic factors which tend to hinder co-professional working. These will be considered using the systems headings presented by McCartney but in reverse order.

It is particularly encouraging that the systems environment in which services operate has become publicly friendly to interagency service development, although the opinions of staff and service users about integrated services will require to be continually monitored. Processes of planning for and delivering learning activities remain similar in health and education, involving the setting up and reviewing of co-ordinated support plans and statements of special educational need; devising and delivering individualised education programmes; and children monitoring their own learning. Limits to co-working remain chiefly around structures and functions. Structures that should facilitate co-professional working are now developing, such as integrated community schools, community health partnerships, children's services commissioners and aligned budgets. These are not as yet fully in place, and the continuing structural split between SLTs as health employees and education services has implications for models of co-professional working in terms of the different functions or goals of service that pertain.

Functional differences and limits to co-professional working

SLTs conform to highly determined health service philosophies and policies and their resulting procedures. Current key issues are reviewed here, and illustrative examples of 'culture clashes' raised by SLT students or collected during research with classroom teachers are presented. SLT remains a commissioning service, offered only to targeted children where a specific need arises. SLTs also must prioritise such needs against the competing needs of other children for a similar service, taking into account both the potential benefits to be gained by the child and the costs of providing the service. This contrasts with education services who have to meet the needs of all children in their care, and who cannot take resources into account as a prime determinant of service provision. Working only with selected children who have been accepted onto a case-load explains why an SLT cannot just 'take a look while they are in' at a child who is causing concern to a school: a clash that can be highly annoying to teachers.

As National Health Service (NHS) employees SLTs may work only with children who are referred, accept service and join the 'case-load'. This has implications for ways of working in schools. As it is highly unlikely that all children in a class, particularly in a mainstream school, would be on an SLT case-load, types of co-working are limited. In particular, classroom-based group work

29

carried out by an SLT or team teaching between an SLT and a teacher will be difficult to implement: the SLT has no 'right' to interact with children in the class who are not on the case list and cannot include them in groups along with a child who is (although the class teacher may do so if they consider it in the interests of all children). Lindsay, Dockrell, Mackie and Letchford (2005b) found examples of joint SLT-teacher implementation of programmes and of SLTs offering direct support to children in curriculum subjects like science in specialist provision such as language units, but it would be most unusual to find this in mainstream provision, which is of course the default placement option for children in the UK. This contrasts with education employees, for example learning support teachers, who form part of a school's repertoire of learning and teaching resources, and can work with all children. This difference explains why SLTs are surprised (and a bit shocked) when parents do not know that their child is working with a learning support teacher.

Selecting children also means that SLTs have to have clear standards of what will constitute 'case status', as they have a public health service responsibility to maintain equality of access to service (even and particularly where service is insufficient). SLT services therefore continue to spend time managing fair access to services, and attempting to construct equitable decision-making frameworks. This can compete with time taken to actually deliver services (and can cause problems – cf. Puttick, 2006) but is a corollary of selection, to prevent arbitrary or biased decision-making or services going to those who make greatest demands. Prioritisation parameters are not easy to construct and can be used to limit access to service (McCartney, 2000), and can upset schools, which offer services to all enrolled children. Determining who should receive intervention can lead SLTs to spend a lot of time re-assessing and updating rather than 'getting on with' intervention – which can also annoy teachers who tend to assess children 'on line' while teaching.

Selecting children for service is ongoing in a context where there have been few attempts to plan a workforce sufficiently large to meet demand, unlike the planning undertaken to secure teacher numbers. Some workforce planning has begun in England in respect of AHPs (NHS Workforce Review Team, 2005) and has recorded low numbers of SLTs, who remain a shortage profession (Home Office, 2004) so that services struggle with high demand compared to staff resources. For example, Law et al. (2000) suggested that a case-load of around 40 children per SLT would be manageable in a school context, but Law et al. (2002) reported the average primary school case-load for children with speech and language needs as 123. There is therefore considerable overload on individual SLTs and pressure on services to be as fair and efficient as possible. Large case-loads also mean that SLTs run rigid timetables and cannot adapt to rapid short-term changes. This can frustrate teachers who want to liaise, and also SLTs if their work in schools is disrupted by other school activities. This is reportedly not a rare occurrence.

SLTs must ensure that confidentiality is assured, and information on children, families and services can only be transferred in pre-agreed circumstances, and with their consent. This explains why a teacher wanting to build up their personal skills and knowledge cannot visit to watch an SLT working with a child who is not the teacher's direct responsibility – or at least not without extensive discussion and agreement by all parties.

The health service is concerned with intervention and with 'what works' in a highly deterministic way. This affects the research designs used to measure 'outcome'. These are more complex than is sometimes realised, and are concerned not only with success but with the opportunities lost by offering or withholding service, and of the potential harm that can be caused by inappropriate interventions. Acceptable evidence of 'good outcomes' can reflect many aspects of health and wellbeing, and can relate to personal opinion, quality of life and evaluation of services received as well as measures of functioning. The aim is to perfect procedures and optimise interventions and to base procedures on the best evidence available. This has differences with the research paradigms developing in education (Furlong & Oancea, 2005), particularly with respect to the idea of how far one can remove context from learning (McCartney, 2004).

Individual SLTs are therefore being judged against different research criteria from schools. NHS concentration on interventions and effects can mean that SLTs are puzzled by arguments for social inclusion framed only in terms of a child's rights and not as a matter of providing 'best' educational outcome. An understanding of research as an iterative investigative process involving trials and control of extraneous factors can mean that SLTs are unimpressed by policies that impose one educational approach (such as the use of synthetic phonics) upon children and their teachers without definitive randomised controlled trials (RCTs).

On the other hand, SLT services along with other health services are not compulsory. Unlike schooling which is unavoidable for children within prescribed age bands, each 'episode' of SLT intervention has to be agreed to by a child's parents, and by the child themselves from the point at which they have the capacity to understand the implications of the decision. For example, no research study concerning primary school age children would be funded that did not include procedures for obtaining the formal consent of each child, and extensive attempts must be made to ensure each child has understood and agreed to participate. A child can also leave such a study at any time, without giving reasons. A child's right to accept or reject SLT service can cause clashes with schools, particularly towards the end of primary school, when competence to make an informed decision about therapy can often be assumed, but where a statutory language curriculum still exists.

Given these factors, working together in the classroom and transdisciplinary approaches would be a very difficult to operate, and a consultancy model or at best a co-operative model is almost inevitable in mainstream schools, despite their limitations. This is less a decision about optimal co-working than the result of an absence of opportunity to make alternative decisions. It appears to be the best that can be done in the circumstances.

RECONFIGURING SERVICES AND PREPARING PROFESSIONALS

We are currently working in a context where new services are being developed, and where the hope and expectation is that they will improve children's health, social and emotional development and their ability to learn. It is worth thinking forward to how services can be improved, and better meet these ends.

Considering the issues discussed above it seems to me there are some things that can be done to improve roles and relationships within existing structures, and to 'work' the prevalent consultancy model in a more productive way. There are also some things that new services could envisage changing, and some features that will probably not change and have to be recognised and lived with.

Reconfiguring within existing service structures

Suggestions for changes within existing services are based partly on recent research (Boyle *et al.*, 2006; McCartney *et al.*, 2004, 2005a) which surveyed and talked to classroom teachers in mainstream schools and SLTs about their experiences of working together, as part of larger studies concerned with models of service delivery and cost-benefit analyses.

Co-working can be helped by explaining the factors that lie behind unexpected cross-professional clashes as they arise. For example, teachers can be told that referrals are needed: they tend not to know this. However, they can also be told that SLT services will happily accept referrals from teachers with parental agreement (although headteachers tend to get a bit twitchy about this). Explaining professional assumptions before surprises occur is even better. Notions of consent, confidentiality, ethics, competition for service, efficiency and outcomes are perfectly comprehensible to both health and education staff, but they often require to be pointed out. Some SLT services have developed useful documents for schools explaining such factors.

Explaining, agreeing and committing to roles and responsibilities when using some version of a consultancy model, and recording what happens, is discussed at length in McCartney *et al.* (2006). Their model envisages that the considerable transaction time requirements needed for discussion, joint target-setting, and differentiated activities are built into such agreement. Existing monitoring and audit procedures that evaluate interagency work can be used to track how agreements are implemented.

Although this would be a step forward, this model probably places insufficient emphasis on the processes of learning to work together, and of learning how to do a new job, and on the feelings of uncertainty that can arise when coping with understandings one knows to be less than expert. Pre-service AHPs and pre-service teachers are now meeting with 'other' professionals to investigate co-working, and there are some in-service opportunities, but the issues remain new and challenging to many professionals. More training opportunities would help.

There are also issues about the inclusion of 'visiting' services that are only just emerging. Boyle *et al.* (2006) asked SLTs and SLT assistants who had been delivering services in schools to 119 children three times per week over 15 weeks how welcomed they felt by the schools. Schools for 69% of the children made SLT/Assistants feel welcome or very welcome, for 27% of children schools made SLTs feel fairly welcome, and for 3% they were not very welcome (with 1% no response). Comments on 'very welcoming' schools included 'I was shown the staffroom, instructed to make coffee if I wanted to. The headteacher was often around and had informal talks'. Feelings of being 'not very welcomed' resulted when, for example, 'They never remembered I was coming'. Monitoring such factors and discussing the reasons behind such variation is probably needed before mutual trust and respect can be considered.

Configuring within new structures

New services should consider their functions in order to set up structures. For example, if transdisciplinary working were considered desirable new services could move SLTs into the position now occupied by learning support staff who may work with children in addition to those on a defined case-load, although the views of parents and children about the value of this should be canvassed, and the need for parental permission considered. This would open up new types of co-working such as classroom-based group work including SLTs. It would need careful management with issues of confidentiality as probably the major sticking point, and issues of best use of staff time would no doubt arise.

New services could, as Williams and Salmon (2002) suggest, aim to make and sustain long-term professional relationships and key appointments, rather than relying on short-term projects as has been common. This would make efforts to foster team-building worthwhile. Appointing individuals specifically responsible for managing and championing service integration and maintaining co-working (Ranade & Hudson, 2003) would be appreciated, preferably if these individuals were accessible and relatively local.

New structures to plan SLT and other AHP services to meet the expected demands would be very helpful. Workforce planning is already carried out for schools, and although not perfect provides a rough-and-ready match of staff numbers to children and classes. At present AHP planning is at a much more rudimentary stage, with limited agreement about the job to be done and who is going to do it. The background question is whether supported assistants could contribute to the provision of the same service just as effectively but more cheaply. And transferring skills to support workers is a main way in which SLT and other AHP services are being extended at present (McCartney *et al.*, 2005b), with similar moves in schools. New structures that could reach principled decisions about such matters and determine appropriate staff numbers could remove the need to limit practice to meet resources.

Immutable differences?

This leaves out certain aspects of difference where I can foresee very little chance of convergence between health and education, even within new services. A major instance is research, which I perceive to be a very sticky sticking point indeed. I see no way in which the evidence-based health service will accept the models of research being codified in education at present – they are too far away from the complex models currently in use. Whether education will bend towards health service models is also doubtful – a randomised control trial of the literacy hour profiting from large numbers, assured 'compliance' and 'manualised intervention' seems unlikely, although without such studies policy decrees cannot be challenged. Perhaps the best solution is to explain the differences that pertain in the two services and ensure that professionals understand the paradigms that operate, and the limits to evidence that each produces.

But we can cope with diversity

New structures tend to want to set up teams by bringing a range of professionals 'in-house', and as stated there can be advantages. However, this cannot extend indefinitely – working with those not in the core team will often be needed, with 'outside' expertise required. Given this, even immutable differences between professions need not stop co-working. People need to work together specifically to gain access to the perspectives of others. A unifying culture is not essential – if teachers want to work with other teachers or other kinds of teachers they may do so. Where they want an SLT's perspective, they need a real SLT, including (most of!) their professional baggage. Explaining one to the other can be helpful, as suggested, but there is no need to construct some complex hybrid before co-working can take place. It is precisely the differences between professions that are relevant.

REFERENCES

Boyle, J., McCartney, E., O'Hare, A., & Forbes, J. (2006). *An RCT and economic evaluation of direct versus indirect and individual versus group modes of speech and language therapy for children with primary language impairment.* Final Report to the National Co-ordinating Centre for Health Technology Assessment.

Conoley, J.C., & Conoley, C.W. (1982). *School consultation: A guide to practice and training.* Oxford: Pergamon.

Creese, A. (2002). The discursive construction of power in teacher partnerships: Language and subject specialists in mainstream schools. *TESOL Quarterly, 36*(4), 597-616.

Cunningham, C., & Davis, H. (1985). *Working with parents: Frameworks for collaboration.* Buckingham: Open University Press.

Department for Education and Science (2003). *Every child matters.* London: DfES.

DiMeo, J.H., Merritt, D.D., & Culatta, B. (1998). Collaborative partnerships and decision making. In D.D. Merritt & B. Culatta (Eds.), *Language in the classroom.* San Diego, CA: Singular.

Forbes, J. (2006). Types of social capital: Tools to explore service integration? *International Journal of Inclusive Education, 10*(6), 565-580.

Furlong, J., & Oancea, A. (2005). *Assessing quality in applied and practice-based educational research: A framework for discussion.* Available at: www.bera.ac.uk/pdfs/Qualitycriteria.pdf (Accessed: 18.06.2008)

Gascoigne, M. (2006). *Supporting children with speech, language and communication needs within integrated children's services.* RCSLT Position Paper. London: RCSLT.

HMI (1996). *The education of pupils with language and communication disorders*. Edinburgh: Scottish Office Education & Industry Department/HMSO.

Home Office (2004). *Work permits UK*.
http://www.workingintheuk.gov.uk/workingintheuk/en/homepage/workpermits/applyingforawork/b usinessandcommercial/howdoimakeanapplication/shortageoccupations/healthsector.html (Accessed 05/07/2005.)

Kersner, M. (1996). Working together for children with severe learning disabilities. *Child Language, Teaching and Therapy, 12*, 17-28.

Law, J., Lindsay, G., Peacey, N., Gascoigne, M., Soloff, N., Radford, J., Band, S., & Fitzgerald, L. (2000). *Provision for children with speech and language needs in England and Wales: Facilitating communication between education and health services*. DfEE Research Report 239. Norwich: HMSO.

Law J., Lindsay, G., Peacey, N., Gascoigne, M., Soloff, N., Radford, J., & Band, S. (2002). Consultation as a model for providing speech and language therapy in schools – A panacea or one step too far? *Child language, Teaching and Therapy, 18*, 145-163.

Lindsay, G., Dockrell, J. with Mackie, C., & Letchford, B. (2002). *Educational provision for children with specific speech and language difficulties in England and Wales*. Coventry: Centre for Educational Appraisal and Research.

Lindsay, G., Dockrell, J., Mackie, C., & Letchford, B. (2005a). Local education authorities' approaches to provision for children with specific speech and language difficulties in England and Wales. *European Journal of Special Needs Education, 20*(3), 329-345.

Lindsay, G., Dockrell, J., Mackie, C., & Letchford, B. (2005b). The roles of specialist provision for children with specific speech and language difficulties in England and Wales: A model for inclusion? *Journal of Research in Special Educational Needs, 5*(3), 88-96.

Mackey, S., & McQueen, J. (1998). Exploring the association between integrated therapy and inclusive education. *British Journal of Special Education, 25*(1), 22-27.

Marvin, C. (1990). Problems in school-based language and collaboration services: Defining the terms and improving the process. *Language, Speech and Hearing Services in Schools, 25*, 258-268.

McCartney, E. (1999). Barriers to collaboration: An analysis of systemic barriers to collaboration between teachers and speech and language therapists. *International Journal of Language and Communication Disorders, 34*, 431-440.

McCartney, E. (2000). Include us out? Speech and language therapists' prioritisation in mainstream schools. *Child Language, Teaching and Therapy, 16*, 165-180.

McCartney E. (2004). 'Hard health' and 'soft schools': Research designs to evaluate SLT work in schools. *Child Language, Teaching and Therapy, 20*, 101-114.

McCartney, E., Ellis, S., & Boyle, J. (2006). Support your local co-op: Developing co-operative approaches to speech and language therapists and teachers supporting children with language impairment. In J. Forbes (Ed.), *Proceedings of the research seminar: Children's services integration in Scottish schools* (pp. 7-23). School of Education, University of Aberdeen, *Research Paper 13*.

McCartney, E., Boyle, J., Ellis, S., Turnbull, M., & Bannatyne, S. (2004). *A survey and cohort intervention using indirect speech and language therapy for children with primary language impairment in mainstream schools*. Final report to the West of Scotland Research and Development Partnership, July.

McCartney, E., Ellis, S., Boyle, J., Turnbull, M., & Kerr, J. (2005a). *The development and validation of materials for use by classroom teachers working with children with primary language impairment*. Final report to the West of Scotland Research and Development Partnership, November.

McCartney, E., Boyle, J., Bannatyne S., Jessiman, E., Campbell, C., Kelsey, C., Smith, J., McArthur. J., & O'Hare, A. (2005b). 'Thinking for two': A case study of speech and language therapists working through assistants. *International Journal of Language and Communication Disorders, 40*, 221-235.

McGrath, J.R., & Davis, A.M. (1992). Rehabilitation: Where are we going and how do we get there? *Clinical Rehabilitation, 6*, 225-235.

Miller, C. (2002). Learning from each other: Practitioners in school-based support for children with language and communications needs. *Support for Learning, 17*(4), 187-192.

NHS Workforce Review Team (2005). *Workforce review 2006-7.* Available at: http://www.healthcareworkforce.nhs.uk/wrtworkforcereviews.html.

Northern Ireland Commissioner for Children and Young People (2005). *Northern Ireland Commissioner for Children and Young People's Overview of SLT provision in Northern Ireland 2004/ 2005: 2005.* Available at: www.niccy.org/uploaded_docs/Overview.PDF (Accessed: 3/06/2008).

Puttick, H. (2006). Children lose out on specialist support. *The [Glasgow] Herald*, 23rd January, pp. 4-5.

Ranade, W., & Hudson, B. (2003). Conceptual issues in inter-agency collaboration. *Local Government Studies, 29*(3), 32-50.

Reid, J., Millar, S., Tait, L., Donaldson, M.L., Dean, E., Thomson, G.O.B., & Grieve, R. (1996). *The role of speech and language therapists in the education of pupils with special educational needs.* Edinburgh: University of Edinburgh Centre for Research in Child Development.

Royal College of Speech and Language Therapists (2005). *Clinical guidelines.* Bicester: Speechmark.

Royal College of Speech and Language Therapists (2006). *Communicating quality 3: RCSLT's guidance on best practice in service organisation and provision.* London: RCSLT.

Scottish Executive (2001). For Scotland's children: Better integrated children's services. http://www.scotland.gov.uk/library3/education/fcsr-00.asp (Accessed: 05/07/2005.)

Scottish Executive (2005). *Supporting children's learning: The Code of Practice.* Edinburgh: The Stationery Office.

Williams, R., & Salmon, G. (2002). Collaborations in commissioning and delivering child and adolescent mental health services: Editorial review. *Current Opinion in Psychiatry, 15*(4), 349-353.

Wren, Y., Roulstone, S., & Parkhouse J. (2001). A model for a mainstream school-based speech and language therapy service. *Child Language, Teaching and Therapy, 17*, 108-122.

Wright, J.A. (1996). Teachers and therapists: The evolution of a partnership. *Child Language, Teaching and Therapy, 17*, 108-122.

Elspeth McCartney
Division of Speech and Language Therapy
University of Strathclyde
UK

JULIE ALLAN

AFTER THE BREAK? INTERRUPTING THE DISCOURSES OF INTERPROFESSIONAL PRACTICE

INTRODUCTION

Despite the abundance of calls within policies to undertake collaboration and 'joined up' working, we know very little about how this should be achieved and what might constitute good outcomes for children and families. The policies themselves provide little insight on the nature of interprofessional practice and their privileging of consensus among professionals creates closure. This chapter considers the ways in which expectations of both beginning and established teachers to engage in interprofessional practice are inscribed within formal policy discourses and the effects of these upon them. Drawing on some of the analytical devices of two key philosophers of difference, Derrida and Deleuze, I will explore how the discourses create aporias, or double contradictory imperatives, which pull teachers in different directions, territorialise difference between themselves and other professionals, and force them to maintain rigid knowledge and professional boundaries. Some new propositions are offered for consideration. These are 'new lines of flight' (Deleuze & Guattari, 1987, p. 9) which are aimed at interrupting the closure and exclusion contained in these discourses. They involve seeking recognition of the aporetic nature of the demands on teachers, rupture of teacher education and professional development processes, and repair, through more explicitly political forms of engagement within and across professions. I argue that the initiative for interprofessional practice might need to come from within teacher education, if it is to happen at all.

Policy discourses and the 'interprofessionals'

Policy is as much a mindset as a set of texts. It is recognised as an expectation, and even an imperative, as much as it exists in written form. It is presented as rational, coherent, explicit, yet it is 'unscientific and irrational' (Ball, 1990, p. 3) and is certainly opaque. Furthermore, its inherently political nature is downplayed, as is the way in which teachers, children and others are constructed *through* policy, becoming its effects, as for example those who undertake interprofessional practice. The consensus which is assumed to characterise the policy-making process is far, however, from the reality:

J. Forbes and C. Watson (eds.), Service Integration in Schools, 37–50.
© *2009 Sense Publishers. All rights reserved.*

> There is ad hocery, negotiation and serendipity within the state, within the policy formulation process ... The point is that quibbling and dissensus still occur with the babble of 'legitimate voices' and sometimes the effect of quibbling and dissensus results in a blurring of meanings within texts, and in public confusion and a dissemination of doubt. (Ball, 1994, p. 16)

Policies themselves are also transient, subject to shifting interpretations – indeed to 'interpretations of interpretations' (Rizvi & Kemmis, 1987, cited in Ball, 1994, p. 16) – and representations. As Ball (1994) notes, sometimes the policy texts are not read in the original but are mediated and delegitimised, for example by teacher unions. Even where they are read, however, this is done in a very particular way, with teachers' readings and reactions constructed for them by the very nature of the text and its positioning in relation to the teachers' professional contexts.

Ball (1994) helpfully distinguishes between policy as text and policy as discourse. As was seen above, the texts themselves are full of contradictions and contestations. As discourses, policies create effects through the way they speak of objects and of people. It is the discursive aspect of policy that is the most significant because it works on people in their local situations and masks its own effects:

> It changes the possibilities we have for thinking *otherwise*; thus it limits our responses to change, and leads us to misunderstand what policy is by misunderstanding what it does. Further, policy as discourse may have the effect of redistributing *voice*, so that it does not matter what some people say or think, and only certain voices can be heard as meaningful or *authoritative*. (Ball, 1994, p. 23; original emphasis)

As Brantlinger (2004) has observed, education policy has replaced theory as a source of guidance for practitioners and this forms the content of much of teacher education. At the same time as student teachers are required to buy into a version of teaching which encourages them to control students' behaviours by modifying their own, they are kept under a veil of uncertainty about whether they will 'make it' as teachers, by ensuring that their knowledge of teaching is always partial:

> Incompleteness, often valorized in textual politics as ambiguity which exposes the limits of the metaphysics of voice, in the discourse of corporate training (which in a way has colonized the discourse of education) becomes another tactic of control in human resource management. (Gregoriou, 2001, p. 230)

Student teachers are thus controlled by being perpetually in training (Derrida, 1992), never finished with education, in the sense of not yet having proved themselves as competent, and remain, according to Deleuze (1992, p. 3), 'in debt'. At the same time, the notion of a teacher as expert persists and forces beginning teachers to feign confidence in an effort to convince onlookers of their competence. Interprofessional working is, in this context, understood as an incapacity to go it alone; and so the kind of person who might be designated the 'interprofessional' is a shadowy character, not quite complete and what Burgess (cited in Deleuze, 2004,

p. 244) refers to as a 'tragedy of insufficiency – half an egg, not half a double yolk'.

The standards which new teachers must achieve before they are accorded the status of qualified status territorialise teaching and envelop them within rigid stratifications (Roy, 2003). These deny complex thinking and firmly entrench their novice and incompetent identities. The standards have been recognised as invalid indicators of good teaching generally (Mahony & Hextall, 2000; Smyth & Shacklock, 1998) and as part of the 'struggle over the teacher's soul' (Ball, 2003, p. 217). Furthermore, the higher education institutions (HEIs) in which teacher education takes place are driven by the standards agenda and managerialism and this creates exclusion (Allan, 2003; Booth, 2003). Within Scotland, the *Standard for Full Registration* (GTC, 2002a) to which beginning teachers have to aspire includes working co-operatively with other professionals and adults. To meet this particular element teachers merely have to demonstrate that they can 'create and sustain appropriate working relationships with other teachers, support staff and visiting professionals'. Such low expectations in relation to interprofessional practice, together with the scarce mention of other professionals, and even then only as generalised 'others', inevitably leaves the beginning teacher surmising that a lack of importance is given to this work and encourages a focus on the more singular aspects of professional practice. This othering of professionals with whom teachers are supposed to engage 'appropriately' which is seen in the *Standard for Full Registration* is continued in the *Standard for Chartered Teacher* (GTC, 2002b). However, in order to gain this enhanced status, teachers are expected to exert an 'influence' on these generalised others. This does not appear to be a positive kind of influence, in the way I will suggest teachers might be encouraged to initiate engagement with colleagues in other professions, but calls on teachers to act as exemplars, the details of which remain unspoken.

The policy imperatives for 'joined up working' (Makaraeth & Turner, 2002; Milne, 2005) thrust teachers together with professionals from health and social work and make them search for a common purpose. In the absence of a body of knowledge about how this should be 'done', we are forced to talk in clichés – joined up working, the 'whole' child and initiatives being rolled out – the last of which, as Daniels (2005) suggests, conjures up notions of laying carpets and ensuring all the bumps are ironed out. The language used in policy privileges consensus and creates closure. The Agreement reached following the McCrone Report, *Teaching for the 21st Century* (Scottish Executive, 2001) for example, talks of clarity, commitment, harmonisation, all of which seeks to erode differences between practitioners. Collaboration among teachers and with other professionals is a complex knot of relationships which has to be learned and worked at. It is an interesting presumption that by issuing an enjoinder to collaborate, and by placing people together, that the outcomes will be positive. Research by Forbes (2003) illustrates how teachers and speech therapists, espousing the value of, and 'doing', collaboration, frequently talked past one another and maintained their own work practice boundaries. In research on the New Community Schools initiative (Remedios & Allan, 2004), professionals from education, health and social work described a prolonged period of fighting for resources – territorialisation – for their own service or school, before they learned to make decisions collectively.

At the same time as policies explicitly espouse joined up working, others appear to create an imperative against it. The most recent example of this is the Education (Additional Support for Learning) (Scotland) Bill (2005), the legislation which introduced measures for the statutory assessment and support of children and young people. Leaving the confusion created by the tautological definition of Additional Support Needs aside, the legislation sought to distinguish between those who would be given a Co-ordinated Support Plan and those who would not on the basis of requiring to seek the support of professionals beyond those within the school. This 'negative ontology' (Baker, 2002) constructs interprofessional working as a last resort for schools rather than as something that would be sought to enhance practice. Of course, if Co-ordinated Support Plans become, like the Record of Needs, a much coveted resource pursued by astute schools and informed parents, we may see a proliferation of interprofessional practice.

PHILOSOPHY GOES PROFESSIONAL

How might the enormous constraints on interprofessional practice produced by the policy discourses be challenged? I am suggesting that some constructs of two key philosophers of difference offer some possible ways of interrupting the policy discourses. Deleuze and Guattari, Derrida and Foucault, along with Irigaray, Kristeva, Lyotard and others, have been recognised as philosophers of difference because of their concern with achieving the recognition of minority social groups and their attempt to formulate a politics of difference which is based on an acceptance of multiplicity (Patton, 2000). Each of these writers has in common an orientation to philosophy as a political act and a will to make use of philosophical concepts as a form not of global revolutionary change but of 'active experimentation, since we do not know in advance which way a line is going to turn' (Deleuze & Parnet, 1987, p. 137). Their work is a philosophy of affirmation which is a 'belief of the future, in the future' (Deleuze, quoted in Rajchman, 2001, p. 6) and is intended to lighten and provide release:

> To affirm is not to take responsibility for, to take on the burden of what is, but to release, to set free what lives. To affirm is to unburden: not to load life with the weight of higher values, but to create new values which are those of life, which make life light and active. (Deleuze, 1983, p. 185; original emphasis)

Nietzsche's notion of the creation of 'untimely' concepts is taken up by Deleuze and Guattari as depicting the kind of political work they see as important: 'acting counter to our time and thereby acting on our time and, let us hope, for the benefit of a time to come' (Nietzsche, 1983, p. 60).

A key role for philosophy, if it is to be put to work on inclusion, is in relation to language and the challenge here is complex. It involves, following Deleuze (1998, p. 107), making language stutter, creating 'an affective and intensive language, and no longer an affectation of the one who speaks'. This is no easy task, as it involves taking language out of its natural equilibrium where there is security with definitions and meanings, but Deleuze suggests this is essential in order to move forward:

> Can we make progress if we do not enter into *regions far from equilibrium?* Physics attests to this. Keynes made advances in political economy because he related it to the situation of a 'boom', and no longer one of equilibrium. This is the only way to introduce desire into the corresponding field. Must language then be put into a state of *boom,* close to a *crash?* (p. 109; original emphasis)

Derrida (1974, p. 5) contends that language itself has lost some of its meaning and significance:

> The devaluation of the word 'language' itself, and how, in the very hold it has upon us, it betrays a loose vocabulary, the temptation of a cheap seduction, the passive yielding to fashion, the consciousness of the avant-garde, in other words – ignorance – are evidences of this effect.

Disruptive work on language has the potential to create an inclusiveness and high degree of reflexivity because disjunctions that are created 'follow a rolling gait that concerns the process of language and no longer the flow of speech' (p. 110). The process of causing language to stutter also creates a silence:

> When a language is so strained that it starts to stutter, or to murmur or stammer ... then language in its entirety reaches the limit that marks its outside and makes it confront silence ... To make one's language stutter, face to face, or face to back, and at the same time to push language as a whole to its limit, to its outside, to its silence – this would be like the boom and the crash. (p. 113; original emphasis)

The key ideas of the philosophers of difference have been utilised to reframe the problem of inclusion and to attempt to reform teacher education (Allan, 2008). The particular 'conceptual *bits'* (Rajchman, 2001, p. 21; original emphasis) I want to consider here as having particular significance for interprofessional practice are Derrida's deconstruction, and, from Deleuze and Guattari, deterritorialisation and rhizomic learning.

Exposing aporias and deconstructing dogma

Deconstruction of the official texts on professionalism and interprofessionalism involves looking at how they get into trouble, come unstuck and contradict themselves. It is a kind of two-handed reading which looks for the *this* and the *that*, looks for the other in the text and discovers their 'scrupulous and plausible misreadings' (Spivak, 1996, p. 45). Deconstruction, which Critchley (1999, p. 41) describes as a 'philosophy of hesitation', is directed at decidability and closure, for

41

it is these which create injustices. Derrida regards the instant of the decision as 'a madness' (1990, p. 26), which is also profoundly irresponsible:

> When the path is clear and given, when a certain knowledge opens up the way in advance, the decision is already made, it might as well be said that there is none to make; irresponsibly, and in good conscience, one simply applies or implements a program ... It makes of action the applied consequence, the simple application of a knowledge or know how. It makes of ethics and politics a technology. No longer of the order of practical reason or decision, it begins to be irresponsible. (pp. 41-45)

The function of deconstruction is to interrupt closure and certainty within texts and to create undecidability about their meaning and intent. It opens up what Derrida calls aporias, double contradictory imperatives which pull the student teacher in different directions and create impossibilities for them. These might include, for example, acquiring and demonstrating the necessary competences to qualify as a teacher *and* understanding themselves as in an inconclusive process of learning about others; developing as autonomous professionals *and* learning to depend on others for support and collaboration; allowing children and young people to make decisions *and* ensuring that they do not make choices which will harm them.

These aporias, ambivalences and contradictions could be exposed explicitly to students, as part of the challenge of becoming a new teacher, rather than as a source of confusion or disconnectedness for them. Uncertainty, the greatest torment for the student teacher, could become an acceptable part of the process, with the moments of undecidability being where they learn to do their most effective work. Exposing these aporias within teacher education, rather than being disruptive and negative, in which the adjudication between imperatives has created chasms and impasses, could force students to invent new practices which always involve at least two ways.

They may be more willing and able to connect with other teachers and other professionals if they can read playfully those texts which simultaneously urge them to undertake joined up working and fragment their practice and their sense of professionalism. Deconstruction may also help student teachers to acquire a more realistic sense of their responsibilities than is conveyed in policy discourses.

The process of preparing student teachers to meet the Professional Standards for teaching might be undertaken in a way which still ensures these are achieved, but also alerts them to some of the limitations of these kinds of frameworks. Student teachers could be encouraged to wander through the Standards, reading them in terms of the kind of performances they command, to enact these reflexively and critique their own identity work in achieving the required levels of competence.

More generally, if students are encouraged to deconstruct inclusion policies, rather than absorb and replicate their content, they may become aware of the contradictions and inconsistencies inherent in them and recognise how aporias are disavowed and closed down. Students would be alerted to the way in which policies 'write the teacher' (Cormack & Comber, 1996, p. 119) in ways that are contradictory and oppositional (Honan, 2004) and which constrain teachers' actions:

> Such documents and their associated technologies, written for and about the teacher, construct authorised versions of the curriculum subject, teacher and student. These statements officially 'write' the teacher and the student – who they should be, what they are to do and say and when and how they must do or say it. (Cormack & Comber, 1996, p. 119)

Deconstruction of policy texts could help to disrupt some of the assumptions about the relationships between teachers and other professionals, policies and context and may make student teachers better placed to challenge some of the pronouncements. Recognition of how they are regulated, and thereby controlled, and of the process of producing an effective teacher who is an 'elastic or infinitely flexible and ultimately dutiful figure who can unproblematically respond to new demands' (Cormack & Comber, 1996, p. 121) may make the passage towards full teacher status less of an ordeal.

From content to expression: Deterritorialising teacher education

Professional training – of teachers, health and social workers and others – takes place in highly striated spaces in which the flow of students, through the building itself, through the curriculum and in relation to the actors, is intensively regulated. Deterritorialisation seeks to knock existing understandings and ways of acting into a different orbit or trajectory (Roy, 2004). Its purpose is to undo the 'processes of continuous control and instantaneous communication' (Smith, 1998, p. 264). It is a performative breaking of existing codes which is also a 'making' (Howard, 1998, p. 115). That is, it is an escape, but in a positive sense, so that new intensities open up:

> The result is a return to a field of forces, transversing the gaps, puncturing the holes, and opening up the new world order to a quite different and new world of the multiple. (pp. 123-124)

Deterritorialisation creates 'chaosmos' (Bogue, 2004, p. 1), a term coined by James Joyce and which Deleuze and Guattari (1994, p. 204) considered an apt account of the effects of deterritorialisation, 'composed chaos, neither foreseen nor preconceived'. It precipitates new ways of thinking and acting: 'Once one ventures outside what's familiar and reassuring, once one has to invent new concepts for unknown lands, then methods and moral systems break down' (Deleuze, 1995, p. 322). The potential areas for deterritorialisation cannot be specified; rather it is a case of being alert to opportunities to interrupt:

> This is how it should be done: Lodge yourself on a stratum; experiment with the opportunities it offers, find an advantageous place on it, find potential movements of deterritorialization, possible lines of flight, experience them, produce flow conjunctions here and there, try out continuums of intensities

segment by segment, have a small plot of new land at all times. (Deleuze & Guattari, 1987, p. 161)

Deterritorialisation has the potential to attack the rigid, striated – or territorialised – spaces of teacher education, replacing these with ones which are smooth and full of creative possibilities. Within these newly created spaces 'life reconstitutes its stakes, confronts new obstacles, invents new paces, switches adversaries' (Deleuze & Guattari, 1987, p. 500). These smooth spaces are depicted by Deleuze and Guattari (p. 413) as 'holey space', like Swiss cheese. Crucially, deterritorialisation takes us from communication – through 'order-words' (Deleuze & Parnett, 1987, p. 22), imperatives for others to act – to expression. The four strands of deterritorialisation, developed by Deleuze and Guattari (1987), could be undertaken as a collective task within HEIs or by individuals. The first of these, becoming foreigners in our own tongue, would involve scrutiny of the language used in lectures and materials, keeping an eye for where the language of special needs is prevalent and creating stutterings over words and expressions which have hitherto been familiar. Colleagues at my own HEI developed a game of 'bullshit bingo' in an effort to pick up and subvert jargon in their written work. A similar exercise could be usefully undertaken with the teaching materials used with students.

The refusal of essences or signifieds is an important second strand of deterritorialisation. Instead of attempting, in lectures and materials, to define the professional, we could point to what professionals do, and explore 'interstanding' (Taylor & Saarinen, 2004) between professionals. Creative subtraction involves identifying what not to do within the curriculum. Instead of responding to the latest government imperatives to insert more content by looking to see where it can be squeezed in, there could be a search for what might be removed or reduced. An invitation to lose aspects of what we currently do in the teacher education curriculum, in order to put some other things in, could be attractive. Interprofessional work could prove to be more appealing as an *instead of,* rather than an *add on.* This, of course, will not be easy as there will be opposition from those who insist that the items proposed for shedding should remain purely because they have always been there and are precious to the individuals who put them there in the first place.

The acceptance that there is no-one behind expression, the final strand of deterritorialisation, is a refusal to attribute blame or responsibility for content to any individuals and to encourage the contribution of new and untried ideas. Greater use of brainstorming sessions – or thought showers, as the new nomenclature goes – could enable staff in HEIs to roam through the kind of teacher education that they really want to do, and the kind of interprofessional relationships they wish to support, rather than what they feel constrained to do, then to ask themselves 'why not?' The ruptures provided by deterritorialisation may create opportunities for more productive learning.

Rhizomic learning

Adopting the rhizome as the means for learning, to be a teacher ruptures the interpretation of theory (Deleuze, 1995) and the arborescent nature of learning with clear lines of demarcation between teacher and taught and in relation to content. Such knowledge is always fractured and partial. The rhizome, instead, privileges experimentation and experience, taking the student teachers on, in Derrida's (1992) terms, an 'empirical wandering' (p. 7). The rhizome allows student teachers to invent themselves as the kind of teachers they want to become and instead of absorbing, and later replicating, content, student teachers would be involved in:

> experimenting with pedagogy and recreating its own curricular place, identity, and content; expanding its syllabi and diversify its reading lists; *supplementing* educational discourse with other theories; deterritorializing theory of education from course based to interdisciplinary directions. (Gregoriou, 2002, p. 231; original emphasis)

These rhizomic wanderings could help to disrupt conventional knowledge about teaching and learning. This would force the student teachers to question what they know themselves, to 'ask what determinations and intensities [they] are prepared to countenance' (Roy, 2003, p. 91) and to abandon ways of working that seem unreasonable. Student teachers' knowledge and understanding might be fashioned as a series of maps, 'entirely oriented toward an experimentation in contact with the real' (Deleuze & Guattari, 1987, p. 12). These maps do not replicate knowledge, but perform and create new knowledge. Reflexivity, which students are often demanded to practise but are rarely given guidance on how to, could be directed towards producing maps of their journeys as becoming teachers. During their placements, student teachers could be invited to produce maps of their school contexts and of their connections with other professionals.

Learning to be a teacher through the rhizome is not a journey towards a fixed end, as denoted by the standards, but wanderings along a 'moving horizon' (Deleuze, 2004, p. xix) which are documented visually. As well as creating new knowledge, these wanderings provide opportunities for student teachers to establish, in Rose's (1996) terms, new assemblages and new selves, as teachers:

> A rhizome, a burrow, yes – but not an ivory tower. A line of escape, yes – but not a refuge. (Deleuze & Guattari, 1987, p. 41)

Students' wanderings need to be supported and responded to in a way which does not entrench further their novice and incompetent identity and they need to be supported within the schools in which they carry out their teaching. As Lather (1991) reminds us, the undecidable is experienced by students as an ordeal and sustained as evidence of non-mastery, and Gregoriou (2004) warns that the rhizome might come to signify a sense of loss for students and produce anxiety:

> I'm confused, how does this fit in now, how is this going to be useful in my teaching, how do all these fit together ... why do we keep shifting from subject to subject ... why do we keep criticizing things ...? Whose book is

45

this rhizome of anxious quests? Is it less authoritative than any other textbook? (p. 238).

Yet Deleuze and Guattari (1987) contend that 'it is through loss rather than acquisition that one progresses and picks up speed' (cited in Roy, 2003, p. 56). Students' 'creative stammerings' (Deleuze & Guattari, 1987, p. 98), questions and searches for links, would be engaged with, rather than closed down as indicative of their failure to grasp content. It is in these spaces or schisms where complex thinking would take place and where 'a new experiment in thought could be inserted ... that might help teachers get an insight into the generative possibilities of the situation' (Roy, 2003, p. 2). The function of the teacher educator, in Deleuzian terms, is to create pedagogical spaces which are open and smooth, in contrast with the closed and striated spaces of conventional approaches.

There is a danger that students' wanderings may simply take them *all over the place* without any clear focus. Gregoriou (2004, pp. 237-238) describes a concern expressed by a university colleague to this effect:

> I have a student who has been trying to formulate the thematic for a paper for almost a semester now. She comes early in the semester with a very tidy and 'tight' proposal. Her heart is tight too, bound by stress and confusion. We discuss different options, different ways to go, various connections and inquiries to attempt. She starts to map various directions. She sounds exhilarated ... She comes back the next week with a completely different theme. She talks about ways to expand, settles down at a new thematic. I suggest a preliminary bibliography. She comes back, again excited to discover this new author ... She drifts again. Is this what following a 'line of flight' means? Is this rhizomatics? Is this growth? Am I going to grade this mapping of disparate things?

This particular example relates to written work rather than to the practice of teaching, but it highlights a major difficulty: how far should students be allowed to wander before being reined in and made to focus? The answer to this possibly depends on the nerve of the educators and their capacity to respond effectively to the students' wanderings – that is by staying with them. It also requires them to have a strong resolve and to resist the pressures of the 'marketable skills and anxious college graduates searching for that educational supplement that will bestow to them a competitive advantage' (Gregoriou, 2004, p. 238). Finally they need to be persuasive and assure their students that if they 'invest in encounters with ideas where novelty escapes codification, ownership and repetition' (p. 238), the returns will be rich. The possibility of active experimentation being a better – or at least more affirmative – route to both the standards and to the kind of teacher they want to become could be enough of a temptation.

The students' own desires could be foregrounded as part of their identity as becoming teachers. Instead of their status representing a lack of competence, they could be encouraged to articulate their trajectory – emotional as well as in terms of their acquisition of skills – towards the kind of teacher they want to become. The narratives of experienced professionals – from health and social work as well as from education – could be a valuable resource in helping student teachers to understand the fractured, partial and embodied process of becoming a professional and the centrality of desire in this. Student teachers could be encouraged to offer and compare reflections on the intensities of their experiences and their 'percepts' and 'affects' (Deleuze, 1995, p. 164), the way they come to think and live as teachers.

Collaboration and collusion

Pre-service training is an obvious place to initiate professionals into collaborative working across boundaries, by providing spaces, for example, for teachers, health professionals and social workers to learn and engage together. Continuing professional development (CPD) would enable this mutual learning and engagement to continue, with support for collaborative practices; whilst some CPD does this at present, it could be more explicitly focused on the development of interdisciplinary working practices. It is essential also that evidence of what 'good', rather than effective, collaborative practice looks like is documented and used to inform training and professional development. This involves finding out from the people who experience it what it means to them. Staff development for professionals, instead of being a content-driven attempt to skill them up in response to the latest government imperative, could provide a smooth space for them to pause, think and repair some of the damage they feel has been done to them.

Collaboration, as well as possibly improving practice, may offer teachers support in the form of rhizomic interdependency and this could be particularly valuable in relation to children and young people with behavioural problems. If these were addressed collectively, with an expectation that they are too difficult to be managed by any one teacher, there might be less of a sense that including troublesome pupils is an impossibility. The networks formed by teachers with colleagues and with other professionals could provide new smooth spaces for engagement and much needed solidarity to subvert the structures and regimes which control them and create barriers to inclusion – their own and that of children and young people in their class. This kind of collective transgression does not imply major revolt against the system, but finding creative ways of resisting pressures to do things in a certain way, making what Honan (2004, p. 278) calls 'agentic choices' and making the language used within their own school contexts stammer. Stress might be a chasm to be investigated and ameliorated through creative subtraction, asking what could be removed from professionals' working lives in order to remove or reduce stress. This 'condition', instead of being a malady which reduces individuals' capacities, could become the material for collaboration because its mammoth proportions and spread across the professions require a collective response.

JULIE ALLAN

Recognition, rupture and repair?

Change in the conditions within and across professions, as Roy (2003, p. 147) reminds us, is unlikely to be achieved through 'grand plans' but through 'combat', 'looking out for microfissures through which life leaks: "Imperceptible rupture, not signifying breaks" opens up these possibilities as stammerings, murmurs, decodings, and disorientations'. In other words, teachers and other professionals may find ways forward in those moments of undecidability when a new thought or a new kind of experiment emerges. These are likely to be not new in the sense of never having been seen before, but 'uncanny ... a thing known returning in a different form ... a revenant' (Banville, 2005, p. 10).

REFERENCES

Allan, J. (2003). Inclusion and exclusion in the university. In T. Booth, K. Nes, & M. Strømstad (Eds.), *Developing inclusive teacher education.* London: RoutledgeFalmer.
Allan, J. (2008). *Rethinking inclusive education: The philosophers of difference in practice.* Dordrecht: Springer.
Baker, B. (2002). The hunt for disability: The new eugenics and the normalization of school children. *Teachers College Record, 104*(4), 663-703.
Ball, S. (1990). *Politics and policy making in education.* London: Routledge.
Ball, S. (1994). *Education reform: A critical and post-structural approach.* Buckingham/Philadelphia, PA: Open University Press.
Ball, S. (2003). The teacher's soul and the terror of performativity. *Journal of Educational Policy, 18*(2), 215-228.
Banville, J. (2005). *The sea.* Basingstoke: Picador.
Bogue, R. (2004). Search, swim and see: Deleuze's apprenticeship in signs and pedagogy of images. *Educational Philosophy and Theory, 36*(3), 327-342.
Booth, T. (2003). Views from the institution: Overcoming barriers to inclusive teacher education? In T. Booth, K. Nes, & M. Strømstad (Eds.) *Developing inclusive teacher education.* London: Routledge Falmer.
Brantlinger, E. (2004). Confounding the needs and confronting the norms: An extension of Reid and Valle's essay. *Journal of Learning Disabilities, 37*(6), 490-499.
Cormack, P., & Comber, B. (1996). Writing the teacher: The South Australian junior primary English teacher, 1962-1995. In B. Green, & C. Beavis (Eds.), *Teaching the English subjects: Essays on English curriculum history and Australian schooling.* Geelong, Vic.: Deakin University Press.
Critchley, S (1999). *The ethics of deconstruction.* Edinburgh: Edinburgh University Press.
Daniels, H. (2005). *Young people at risk of social exclusion: Interagency working and professional learning.* Paper presented at the Participation, Inclusion and Equity Research Network, Stirling, 20 June.
Deleuze, G. (1983). *Nietzsche and philosophy.* New York: Columbia University Press.
Deleuze, G.(1992). *Postscript on the societies of control.* Available from http//www.n5m.org/n5m2/media/texts/deleuze.htm (Accessed 24/10, 2006).
Deleuze, G. (1995). *Negotiations.* New York: Columbia University Press.
Deleuze, G. (1998). *Essays critical and clinical.* London/New York: Verso.
Deleuze, G. (2004). *Difference and repetition.* London: Continuum.
Deleuze, G., & Guattari, F. (1987). *A thousand plateaus: Capitalism and schizophrenia.* London: The Athlone Press.

Deleuze G., & Guattari, F. (1994). *What is philosophy?* New York: Columbia University Press.
Deleuze, G., & Parnet, C. (1987). *Dialogues.* New York: Columbia University Press.
Derrida, J. (1974). *Of grammatology.* New York: Columbia University Press.
Derrida, J. (1976). *Of grammatology.* Baltimore, MD: John Hopkins University Press.
Derrida, J. (1990). Force of law: The mystical foundation of authority. *Cardoza Law Review, 11,* 919-1070.
Derrida, J. (1992). *The other heading: Reflections on today's Europe.* Bloomington, IN: Indiana University Press.
Forbes, J. (2003). *Teacher/therapist collaborations: Discourses, positionings and power relations at work.* EdD thesis, University of Stirling.
General Teaching Council for Scotland (2002a). *Standard for Full Registration.* Edinburgh: GTC.
General Teaching Council for Scotland (2002b). *Standard for Chartered Teacher.* Edinburgh: GTC.
Gregoriou, Z. (2001). Does speaking of others involve receiving the 'other'? A postcolonial reading of receptivity in Derrida's deconstruction of Timaeus. In G. Biesta, & D.Egéa-Kuehne (Eds.), *Derrida & education.* London: Routledge.
Gregoriou, Z. (2002). Performing pedagogy with Deleuze: The rhizomatics of 'theory of education'. In *Philosophy of Education Society of Great Britain Conference Proceedings* (pp. 227-237). Oxford: New College.
Gregoriou, Z. (2004). Commencing the rhizome: Towards a minor philosophy of education. *Educational Philosophy and Theory, 36*(3), 233-251.
Honan, E. (2004). (Im)plausibilities: A rhizo-textual analysis of policy texts and teachers' work. *Educational Philosophy and Theory, 36*(3), 267-281.
Howard, J. (1998). Subjectivity and space: Deleuze and Guattari's BwO in the new world order. In E. Kaufman & K.J. Heller (Eds.), *Deleuze and Guattari: New mappings in politics, philosophy and culture.* Minneapolis, MN/London: University of Minnesota Press.
Lather, P. (1991). *Getting smart: Feminist research and pedagogy within/in the postmodern.* New York: Routledge.
Mahony, P., & Hextall, I. (2000). *Reconstructing teaching: Standards, performance and accountability.* London: Routledge Falmer.
Makareth, C., & Turner, T. (2002). *Joined up working.* London: Health Visitors Association.
Milne, V. (2005). Joined up working in the Scottish Executive. *Research Findings No. 17.* Available from: http://www.scotland.gov.uk/Publications/2005/10/0693747/37483 (Accessed 3/5/2006.)
Nietzsche, F. (1983). On the uses and disadvantages of history for life. In *Untimely meditations.* Cambridge: Cambridge University Press.
Patton, P. (2000). *Deleuze and the political.* London: Routledge.
Rajchman, J. (2001). *The Deleuze connections.* Cambridge, MA: MIT Press.
Remedios, R., & Allan, J. (2004). *Evaluation of New Community Schools in Stirling.* Report to Stirling Council Services. University of Stirling.
Rizvi, F., & Kemmis, S. (1987). *Dilemmas of reform.* Geelong, Vic.: Deakin Institute of Education.
Rose, N. (1996). *Inventing our selves: Psychology, power and personhood.* Cambridge: Cambridge University Press.
Roy, K. (2003). *Teachers in nomadic spaces: Deleuze and curriculum.* New York: Peter Lang.
Roy, K. (2004). Overcoming nihilism: From communication to Deleuzian expression. *Educational Philosophy and Theory, 36*(3), 297-312.
Scottish Executive (2001). *A teaching profession for the 21st century: Agreement reached following recommendations made in the McCrone report.* Edinburgh: Scottish Executive.
Smith, D. (1998). The place of ethics in Deleuze's philosophy: Three questions of immanence. In E. Kaufman, & K.J. Heller (Eds.), *Deleuze and Guattari: New mappings in politics, philosophy and culture.* Minneapolis, MN/London: University of Minnesota Press.
Smyth, J., & Shacklock, G. (1998). *Remaking teaching: Ideology, policy and practice.* London: Routledge.

Spivak, G. (1996). Explanation and culture marginalia. In D. Landry, & G. MacLean (Eds.), *The Spivak reader: Selected works of Gayatri Chakravorty Spivak*. New York: Routledge.
Taylor, M., & Saarinen (2004). *Imagologies: Media philosophy*. London: Routledge.

Julie Allan
Institute of Education
University of Stirling
UK

ROY McCONKEY

PART TWO
CREATIVE TENSIONS IN SERVICE INTEGRATION

Arguably there have been more changes in education during the closing decades of the 20th century than in the previous 100 years. The first decade of the new century may even surpass that record but with a major change of emphasis. Hitherto the focus of transformation has been on pupil assessment, curricula reform and public inspections; all geared toward school improvement. These issues, and others like them, are likely to occupy the energies and efforts of school personnel for some years to come. Yet the turn of the century has seen a new set of demands being placed on schools. They are being encouraged to look outward and review how education integrates with other services provided to children and families. Of course this broadening of focus is long overdue and some might argue that it should have had precedence over the school reform agenda especially if, as a society, we are serious about helping the 20% of lowest achievers. The chapters in this section examine the practical issues involved in service integration in schools and draws on experiences from Scotland, Northern Ireland and England.

Ian Menter sets the context by reviewing the values inherent in the Scottish school system and the distinctive approach to the modernisation of education in Scotland. The Scottish Executive extolled the need for 'joinedupness' and instigated a major policy initiative around the concept of *Integrated Community Schools*, and this focus has continued under the present Scottish Government. A recurring theme in the evaluations of progress to date is the need for an appropriately skilled workforce, i.e. teachers with expertise in interprofessional and interagency working. Accepting this argument has major implications for the training of teachers and their career pathways.

Anne Moran and her colleagues explore the same theme within the Extended School initiatives that are beginning to emerge in Northern Ireland of which the inclusion of pupils with special educational needs is one aspect. Their research with school personnel found strong support for inclusive practice but coupled with the need for changed systems in which there was strategic leadership at the highest level; co-ordinated and co-located services at an operational level; and pre-service and in-service training for all staff. Moran and her colleagues conclude that sustained service integration requires 'economic, legal and political accountability as well as moral, social and educational responsibility'.

J. Forbes and C. Watson (eds.), Service Integration in Schools, 51–53.
© 2009 Sense Publishers. All rights reserved.

Service integration is probably more advanced in England than anywhere else in the UK countries. Pugh summarises the main policy thrusts in terms of services provided to children, with particular reference to the Children Act (2004) but commonly known as the *Every Child Matters: Change for children agenda.* Integrated working across the traditional 'silos' of education, social services and health is seen as the key to tackling intractable problems where uni-agency working has patently failed. Pugh describes in some detail the new systems and approaches that are a feature of service integration but cautions that as yet there is sparse evidence of a positive impact on children and families and whether the costs involved in creating strategic partnerships bring sufficient benefits.

The authors though have done us a further service beyond describing these integration initiatives. Their analyses identify a number of icebergs that threaten the integration agenda on its maiden voyage. For example:

- There are tensions between Government-led policy directives that focus on uniformity and the creation of local solutions that are tailored to local needs. The latter may be especially necessary in rural rather than urban areas; or in places with high immigrant or transient populations compared to settled communities.
- Issues of power and accountability need consideration, for example who line manages non-educational staff working alongside or within schools?
- Similarly, what are the mechanisms for creating sustainable joint funding of new initiatives?

But possibly the most challenging conundrum is how schools will manage the tension between achieving academic excellence and creating integrated children's services. As the three chapters acknowledge these two policy initiatives derive from different philosophies and values. To date, little attempt has been made to bridge them. It would be premature to say that it cannot be done, but tackling one on its own runs the risk of sinking the other. The trick may be to redefine school improvement in such a way that it embraces the goals of service integration. An obvious example is the development of partnership working with parents. Likewise, can all the parties engaged in service integration own the goal of improving educational achievement? One approach to gaining ownership of outcomes is to have a child-and-family-centred plan that is shared across agencies.

On the face of it then, it may be possible to achieve both types of outcomes for schools but it will require unprecedented creativity and energy within a range of systems to make it happen. One sure ingredient for success, however, is a willingness to learn from our endeavours – inadequate though they may be – and to critically analyse the factors that contribute to success and to failure. Hopefully, the research communities within higher education will contribute to this challenge.

That was the spirit within which the seminar series which gave rise to this book was conceived and, as you see, the first fruits are starting to appear. In the best of academic traditions, the knowledge and insights gained thus far are freely shared with others but it is with the hope that you, the reader, will ponder on your responsibilities to contribute to these endeavours. You'd be made very welcome!

Roy McConkey
Institute of Nursing Research
University of Ulster
UK

IAN MENTER

SERVICE INTEGRATION IN SCHOOLS: THE SCOTTISH SCENE AND THE IMPLICATIONS FOR TEACHERS

INTRODUCTION

While 'joined-up government' may remain an aspiration rather than an achievement of Labour, this does not detract from its power as a discourse, a discourse that has produced important shifts in the languages and practices of public management and a reshaping of the notions of leadership, strategy and organisational culture on which it draws. The influence of this on roles, relationships and flows of power and influence have an impact far beyond the life-cycle of a particular partnership. (Newman, 2001, p. 124)

The 'new Scotland' has a strong emphasis on social and educational inclusion. There is no doubt that certain aspects of social policy have become very distinctive. For example, we have seen distinctive policies developing in relation to care of the elderly, higher education funding and other areas too. In relation to schools, as we shall see, there is evidence of both convergence and divergence with other parts of the UK. In the particular case of service integration, we can note the continuing influence of Scottish educational traditions as steps are taken towards greater integration. At least three of these traditions are worthy of mention (although we should note some scepticism among some commentators, who suggest there may be a strong element of romantic mythology about them; see Humes & Bryce, 2003):

- The longstanding commitment to comprehensive education
- The belief in education as a tool of meritocracy
- The continuing commitment to public sector provision and a less mixed economy certainly than in England. (So for example, we see local authorities continuing to be very significant stakeholders in education.)

We can also note at the outset that the policy community and policy process in Scotland have been investigated in some depth in the pre-devolution era and the insights from studies such as those by Humes (1986) and by McPherson and Raab (1988), demonstrating a number of distinctive features, continue to appear to have considerable relevance, even under the new dispensation.

J. Forbes and C. Watson (eds.), Service Integration in Schools, 55–64.

The focus of this paper is mainly on teachers. I review what has been happening to them, their work, their relationships with other workers and the wider community, particularly over the last few years as, in similar ways to the rest of the UK, we see steps being taken towards integrated services, inter and multidisciplinary working. But as I examine these matters I also want to look at the influence of the new managerialism on the Scottish scene (Arnott & Menter, 2007). While these elements may be less overt than in England, they are certainly there.

TEACHERS IN SCOTLAND

Teaching has been going through a process of modernisation in Scotland as elsewhere. However, the Scottish approach to addressing the 'problem' has been quite distinctive. The 1990s was a period of considerable unrest among Scottish teachers. There was great disgruntlement over pay and conditions and a series of industrial disputes was indicative of the poor relationship existing between the unions and employers. Of course, there had been – and still to a large extent is – one very dominant teacher union in Scotland, the EIS (Educational Institute of Scotland), the membership of which consists of the great majority of teachers in the country (a point to which we shall return).

Following this period of disquiet, one of the first actions of the Scottish Parliament was, in good traditional social democratic style, to establish a committee of enquiry to consider teachers' pay and conditions. The McCrone Committee reported in 2000 (Scottish Executive, 2000) and recommended very significant pay rises, reduction of teachers' contact time within a 35-hour working week, the creation of Chartered Teacher status, the increased deployment of assistants to help with routine administrative tasks, a review of initial teacher education, as well as several other significant steps. In contrast to England where (then) Chancellor Gordon Brown insisted that teachers should only get 'something for something', Scottish teachers were given a good pay deal 'up front', as an act of faith in their willingness and ability to modernise and enter an era of 'new professionalism'. Performance management was hardly visible in all of this and in comparative work carried out with my English colleagues Pat Mahony and Ian Hextall, we contrasted the developmental approach towards modernisation in Scotland with the performative approach in England (Menter, Mahony, & Hexstall, 2004). But perhaps the most significant element of the McCrone settlement (Scottish Executive, 2001a) in terms of our interest in interprofessional collaboration, was the overt attempt to give teachers greater professional responsibility and autonomy in carrying out their work – for example the provision for off-site working – and the commitment to collegiality in schools.

Colleagues at Glasgow undertook a study of teachers' working time in 2005/06, commissioned by the Scottish Negotiating Committee for Teachers (Menter, Forde, Hall, McMahon, McPhee, Patrick & Devlin, 2006). Few of the teachers who took part in this study were entirely happy about their working experiences at this time – three or four years after the settlement. While there was general acknowledgement of the benefits of the pay settlement, there was a sense of disenchantment and dashed hopes about working time. In spite of the widely publicised view that teachers' work should be achievable within a 35-hour week, the average working week was closer to 42.5 hours for classroom teachers, with headteachers averaging over 50. When we explored the questions around autonomy and collegiality, a typical response was that there had been so many policy initiatives, and there was now so much bureaucracy involved in being a teacher, that very few had experienced any sense of greater professionalism over this period.

So the Agreement was not all that had been anticipated. In parallel to the implementation of the Agreement, some other steps around the modernisation of teaching were taking place. If we had not seen the language of performance management being deployed overtly in Scotland there were nevertheless significant elements of technical rationality being introduced, in particular through the creation of a series of standards. This process had started before McCrone had got under way in the introduction of competences and subsequently benchmarks into initial teacher education from 1993 onwards. This process was indeed similar to what was happening in England under the auspices of the Teacher Training Agency; however, in Scotland the process was one that was carried out by working parties comprising leading professionals, with very little overt political interference (by contrast with what was happening in England). Nevertheless, the broad outcomes were similar – a series of statements indicating what it was a teacher should know and be able to do in order to become qualified. But, as may be seen in an Anglo-Scottish comparative study carried out at the University of Paisley with Ian Smith and Estelle Brisard, the details of the outcomes were different. There was for example a greater commitment to explicit statements of value dispositions, including social justice and anti-discrimination, a greater commitment to a research underpinning of teaching and indeed to the need for an understanding of the theoretical basis for teachers' actions (Menter, Brisard & Smith, 2006a, 2006b).

Not everyone would agree on the relatively positive picture of Scottish teachers that I have painted. Not only do many teachers feel disgruntled. Some commentators think there has been a concerted attack on teachers. For example, Gatherer (2003, p. 1027) wrote:

> The last ten or fifteen years have seen continual attacks on their autonomy, combined with increasing requirements for the 'delivery' of externally prescribed curriculum content and teaching methods; and their confidence has been undermined by insistent monitoring of their teaching in accordance with control devices such as 'performance indicators'. It is no wonder that many deplore the 'de-professionalisation' and the 'de-skilling' which come from treating teachers as mere technicians rather than experienced professional educators.

Arnott (2005, p. 253) suggests that there is indeed similarity in the direction of policy on teachers in England and Scotland but that the mode of regulation is rather different. In contrasting the increased responsibilities of governing bodies in English schools with the school boards in Scotland, she writes:

Under the 2000 Standards in Scotland's Schools etc. Act, school boards were given statutory responsibility for school improvement. However, in reality it was the educational professionals at school and local authority level who were regarded as the key policy participants in the implementation of reforms rather than school board members.

Furthermore she points out that Scottish central direction is more likely to be provided by wide-ranging broad policy initiatives, such as the National Priorities for Education launched in December 2000:

– Achievement and attainment
– Framework for learning
– Inclusion and equality
– Values and citizenship
– Learning for life

In addition we may note that these have been followed more recently by the four 'capacities' that the Curriculum for Excellence (2004) is seeking to develop in learners:

– successful learners
– confident individuals
– effective contributors to society
– responsible citizens

So in summary what we have seen is a series of developments that have both been distinctive from other parts of the UK but yet share much of the same direction. Political intervention has been much less overt – although there have been just as many policy initiatives – but the policy community has been, at least on the face of it, a much more consensual one over recent years than was the case in England or indeed in Scotland during the 1990s. This relative harmony will not necessarily endure.

A less positive depiction of this scenario is to suggest that there is a deep conservatism within the education establishment in Scotland and here we would need to look at the extent to which the 1980s critiques emerging from the studies by Humes (1986) and McPherson and Raab (1988) still hold good. In their different ways these studies revealed a coterie of powerful people involved in the development of education policy, sharing an 'assumptive world' or indeed constituting a 'leadership class'. What might be characterised as a predominantly white elitist fraternity extended throughout the civil service into local authorities and the inspectorate and to a significant extent into the teaching profession itself. The General Teaching Council for Scotland, established in the mid-1960s, and the pre-eminence of the Educational Institute for Scotland (EIS), the major teacher union in Scotland, together acted to defend the teaching profession from the greatest excesses of Thatcherism[1] during the 1980s.

This undoubtedly oversimplified account of the modernisation of the teaching profession in Scotland provides a backdrop against which to review the impact of service integration.

MOVES TOWARDS INTEGRATION

I have already noted the strong commitment in Scotland to social and educational inclusion and these have both strengthened since devolution. But I have also noted the strong commitment to education as an instrument of opportunity. The longstanding myth of the 'lad o' pairts' is based on a view of education providing a means of social advancement, but this is through a focus on a traditional scholarship model of educational success. In other words, the 'bright' child who works hard and secures good exam results leading to entry into one of the ancient universities becomes the successful lawyer, minister or businessman (see Paterson, 2003).

While we can identify a number of individuals who have succeeded in this way, it is perhaps more apparent, post-devolution, the extent to which this is indeed a myth and that while such success is possible, there is still an enormous element of apparent failure or at least lack of success in Scottish education. Concern is frequently expressed about the persistently lowest achieving 20 per cent of secondary school pupils, for whom school appears to provide little avenue towards meaningful employment or further education. It is no surprise that the majority of this 20 per cent come from the poorest families and are concentrated in urban estates and economically inactive towns and villages scattered across Scotland.

The related points I am wanting to make here are, on the one hand, that there is a recognition that Scottish education has not been as successful as has sometimes been suggested and, on the other hand, there may be strong cultural barriers to change within the education system, given its underlying values of 'the democratic intellect' and meritocracy. There may be concerns about 'dilution' of quality and reduction of standards for example.

Turning now to service integration, Scotland can make some claims to have led the way in the integration of children's services. Although this is not the place to review the full history of the move towards integration, we should at least note the significance of the Kilbrandon Report in 1964 on the topic of juvenile justice (which led to the setting up of children's panels) for its assertion of the importance of ensuring effective relationships between the different services in juvenile justice (see Cohen, 2005). According to Cohen, it was Sam Galbraith, who became the first Minister of Education in the Scottish Parliament, who coined the term 'joined-up working', while he was still a Westminster MP. When the Scottish Executive Education Department (SEED) was established, it was not long before a Children and Young People's Group was established alongside the Schools Group (Cohen, 2005, p. 6).

There have been a number of major policy initiatives relating to service integration around schools and in what follows I suggest some of the implications of these policies for teachers. Drawing on Glaister and Glaister's (2005a) useful collection of articles and on a paper by Joan Forbes (Forbes, 2006), the key policy initiative to focus on here is what were initially the New Community Schools (NCS), launched in 1998 and later becoming Integrated Community Schools (ICS). But in a sense we could take just about any recent policy initiative – they all have aspirations to encourage 'joinedupness' and address the needs of those with the greatest obstacles to success. (For example: *Count Us In* (HMIe, 2002); Additional Support for Learning is the Scottish Executive's approach to special educational needs; *A Curriculum for Excellence,* Scottish Executive Education Department, 2004, seeks to promote the recognition of wider achievement.)

Glaister and Glaister (2005b, p. 8) quote an early statement by the Scottish Executive (2001b): 'Despite their different history, boundaries and legislative requirements, children's services – encompassing education, child welfare, social work, health, leisure and recreation services for children from birth to 18 years – should consider themselves as a single unitary system'. However, the extent of commitment by the Executive to this agenda has been questioned by Ferguson (2005, p. 228), who says 'Where the development of services has taken place... it has usually involved the diversion of spending into short-term initiatives, rather than into improving mainline services'. One of the major criticisms emerging from the early evaluations of NCS/ICS has been that integration is only really happening among senior and/or specialist staff. It is not touching the working lives of most teachers. (This may in part be because of the strong tradition of designated specialist guidance teachers in the Scottish school system.) If that is one common comment, the second one is that this is seen by most players as an education initiative rather than a genuinely integrated one. As Glaister and Glaister put it (2005b, p. 63): 'The extent to which the New Community School solution still results in a gravitational pull towards an over-emphasis on school education and curriculum rather than the wider aspects of community life, mental health and wellbeing remains to be seen'.

In this light it is interesting to note that a recent glossy document from the Scottish Executive Education Department (2006, p. 1), setting out the remit of the ICSs for those in local authorities and schools, says:

Alongside this education-led initiative and following the publication of *For Scotland's Children* in 2001 much has been done at both national and international level to improve planning and delivery of integrated children's services to improve the lives of children and young people. In this context, it is no longer appropriate to think of ICS as a separate school-based initiative and our aim is to learn from the experience to mainstream approaches to integrated service provision.

To achieve this, the same document suggests, one of the requirements is 'an appropriately skilled workforce'.

This was also recognised by Glaister and Glaister (2005b, p. 69), who say that the ICSs:

will increasingly require teachers to work across professional and agency boundaries. This is a significant shift for professional bodies from a tendency to focus on professional status and identity, heightening distinctiveness and difference, and protecting boundaries quite ferociously. The challenges of a future, in which shared curricula, shared training and even shared assessment feature in initial professional education, are just beginning to emerge.

Returning to the Executive's own document (Scottish Executive Education Department, 2006, p. 4), there is indeed a section there on 'Workforce Development' which includes the following comments on the skills required of teachers:

> Within education, Initial Teacher Education already refers to the integrated context in which teachers will be working. Some programmes and school experience placements enable student teachers to train and work alongside other professionals, but overall such opportunities are limited, especially within the one-year PGDE where time pressures are most acute. There is, however, considerable potential to improve the skills and competencies for integrated working in the induction year and thereafter through the new contractual commitment to continuing professional development

One or two cautionary notes should be stated. Firstly, a large number of additional development needs are being lined up for the induction year and for statutory continuing professional development (CPD). Secondly, when the opportunity to develop significantly the integrated services element of initial teacher education (ITE) was available during the second stage review of ITE by SEED, that reported in 2005 (Scottish Executive Education Department, 2005), it was not taken. Indeed, within the most innovative developments actually occurring in ITE in Scotland at present, there appears to be greater concern with conventional subject knowledge for primary teachers than for integrated or interprofessional working. Nevertheless it should be noted that the largest individual provider of ITE in Scotland does train social workers alongside teachers for parts of the early stages of their degree programme. To some extent this same tension – that between conventional academic excellence and addressing social/individual needs – may be worth exploring in the contrasts between ICS and a more recent school improvement initiative, namely Schools of Ambition (see Hulme & Menter, 2007).

We should also consider what has been happening about early years provision, given that so much of the modelling for integrated working and for the development of anti-poverty strategies emanates from that field. There does appear to be some continuing tension and/or confusion around early years strategy between Westminster and Holyrood (the UK and Scottish parliaments respectively), presumably because early years policy is not entirely a devolved matter but includes elements that are reserved. Certainly in the case of Sure Start, New Labour's flagship commitment to community development, tackling poverty and raising educational standards, there are versions of the programme in all four parts of the UK. But a Scottish perspective on such work does inevitably draw some stinging criticism:

... while the new-found emphasis on prevention in programmes such as Sure Start is ... welcome, this is a particularly narrow form of prevention which fits in well with a New Labour moral worldview which sees the roots of problems as lying with 'failing parents' rather than the effects of poverty and failing services. In general, the Executive has eschewed more macro-responses to the problem of child poverty. ... Moreover, against the commitment to pre-school care and education which programmes like Sure Start suggest, must be set the Executive's failure to intervene in support of several thousand poorly paid nursery nurses (whose professionalism and commitment will be central to the success of any pre-five strategy) in their long and bitter battle for a professional salary with (mainly Labour-controlled) local authority employers in 2004 (Ferguson, 2005, p. 228).

CONCLUSION: WHERE NEXT WITH SERVICE INTEGRATION IN AND AROUND SCHOOLS?

There is a lack of conceptual clarity at times in Scottish approaches to these matters. Conducting a review of 'Equality Initiatives in Scottish Education' for SEED during 2004/05 we found it very difficult to get a clear definition of 'equality' from the Executive and what aspects of social life the phrase was intended to cover. This may have related in part to the interface between equality and social justice, as Lohde (2005, pp. 190-191) indicates:

Social justice in the Scottish context is about extending opportunities to give everyone the chance of an equal outcome ... However, the social inclusion agenda is juxtaposed with an Equalities Strategy, which was adopted in 2000 and mainstreamed across the Executive's policy areas ... it is not clear how these two strategies intersect, compete or complement each other.

The integrated services agenda is certainly being taken very seriously in the new Scotland, but there is little evidence yet that the full implications for teachers and for teacher professionalism are being systematically addressed. A demonstration of both of these assertions can be found in the form of a literature review carried out by SEED and published in January 2006, on the 'evidence base' for integrated children's services (Brown & White, 2006). The main conclusion to this report is that 'a substantial evidence base on the *challenges, barriers* and key factors for success exists' (p. 3, my emphasis). There is indeed a paucity of research on actual provision of service integration. Citing a Hay Group report the authors say that:

While professional judgements are being seen as increasingly important, professionals are also being called to work in contexts outside their professional tradition. The resulting tension and conflict, ... is not being directly addressed. Instead incremental approaches such as the appointment of 'co-ordinators' or 'integration managers' are preventing professional barriers being broken down and often arbitrate between professionals rather than confronting them head-on. (Brown & White, 2006, p. 17)

If integrated working can be effective anywhere it should surely be possible in Scotland. With 32 local authorities and just seven providers of initial teacher education, a coordinated approach to developing this way of working for teachers should be feasible.

There is what one might describe as a progressive potential within these developments. As Newman points out, on the one hand: 'There have been problems of balancing the drive to create momentum for change through collaboration while continuing to deliver on mainstream performance'. On the other hand, 'Those with strong public service values that are viewed as aligned with Labour's policies tended to welcome what they perceived to be a shift away from New Public Management towards more positive frameworks of action' (Newman, 2001, p. 123).

Two key questions which emerge from this review of recent developments in Scotland are:

1. Can the traditional aspirations for educational excellence and the commitment to integrated service provision be accommodated within the same educational system? So much of the latter comes from a motivation which is concerned with inequality and disadvantage whereas the former comes from a simple meritocratic ideology that assumes that access to a national comprehensive educational system will provide every young person with a fair chance.

2. Once the first question has been answered, then what are the implications for professional roles for teachers and others. Should all teachers have a strong grounding in interprofessional working? Should there be specialists? Should there be teacher/social workers?

There is a major research agenda here, in Scotland as elsewhere. However, that agenda should not be only, or even predominantly, a 'what works' type of research agenda. It should include a strong element of critical analysis of the discourse surrounding these matters, to identify value bases, unintended meanings and unintended consequences of integrated service provision and lead to greater conceptual clarity as a backdrop for those who have responsibilities for working with young people whether within or outwith schools.

NOTES

[i] Margaret Thatcher, UK Prime Minister, 1979-1990.

REFERENCES

Arnott, M. (2005). Devolution, territorial politics and the politics of education. In G. Mooney, & G.Scott (Eds.), *Exploring social policy in the 'new Scotland'*. Bristol: Polity Press.

Arnott, M., & Menter, I. (2007). The same but different? Post-devolution regulation and control in education in Scotland and England. *European Education Research Journal, 6*(3), 250-265.

Brown, K., & White, K. (2006). *Exploring the evidence base for integrated children's services*. Edinburgh: Scottish Executive Education Department.

Cohen, B. (2005). Interagency collaboration in context. The 'joining-up' agenda'. In A. Glaister, & B. Glaister (Eds.) *Interagency collaboration – Providing for children*. Edinburgh: Dunedin Academic Press.

Ferguson, I. (2005). Social work and social care in the 'new' Scotland'. In G. Mooney, & G. Scott (Eds.), *Exploring social policy in the 'new Scotland'*. Bristol: Polity Press.

Forbes, J. (2006). *Redesigning interprofessionalism: Some possibilities using social capital*. Paper presented at ESRC Seminar on Social Capital, Professionalism and Diversity: Diversity and Professional Practice, University of Edinburgh, 27 September.

Gatherer, W. (2003). Scottish teachers. In T. Bryce, & W. Humes (Eds.), *Scottish education (2nd edition: Post-devolution)*. Edinburgh: University Press.

Glaister, A., & Glaister, B. (Eds.) (2005a). *Interagency collaboration – Providing for children*. Edinburgh: Dunedin Academic Press.

Glaister, A., & Glaister, B. (2005b). Space for growth. In A. Glaister, & B. Glaister (Eds.), *Interagency collaboration – Providing for children*. Edinburgh: Dunedin Academic Press.

Her Majesty's Inspectorate for Education (2002). *Count us in – Achieving inclusion in Scottish Schools*. Edinburgh: HMIe.

Hulme, M., & Menter, I. (2007). Research to support schools of ambition. *Education in the North, 15*, 47-50.

Humes, W. (1986). *The leadership class in Scottish education*. Edinburgh: John Donald.

Humes, W., & Bryce, T. (2003). The distinctiveness of Scottish education. In T. Bryce, & W. Humes (Eds.) *Scottish education (2nd edition: Post-devolution)*. Edinburgh: University Press.

Lohde, L. (2005). Child poverty and devolution. In J. Adams, & K. Schmueker (Eds.) *Devolution in practice 2006. Public policy differences within the UK*. Newcastle-upon-Tyne: IPPR North.

McPherson, C. & Raab, C. (1988). *Governing education: A sociology of policy since 1945*. Edinburgh: University Press.

Menter, I., Mahony, P., & Hextall, I. (2004). Ne'er the twain shall meet? The modernisation of the teaching workforce in Scotland and England. *Journal of Education Policy, 19*(2), 195-214.

Menter, I., Brisard, E., & Smith, I. (2006a). Making teachers in Britain: Professional knowledge for initial teacher education in England and Scotland. *Educational Philosophy and Theory, 38*(3), 269-286.

Menter, I., Brisard, E., & Smith, I. (2006b). *Convergence or divergence? Initial teacher education in Scotland and England*. Edinburgh: Dunedin Academic Press.

Menter, I., Forde, C., Hall, J., McMahon, M., McPhee, A., & Patrick, F., with Devlin, A. (2006). *Teacher working time*. Edinburgh: Scottish Negotiating Committee for Teachers.

Newman, J. (2001). *Modernising governance*. London: Sage.

Paterson, L. (2003). *Scottish education in the twentieth century*. Edinburgh: University Press.

Scottish Executive (2000). *A teaching profession for the 21ˢᵗ century* (McCrone Report). Edinburgh: Scottish Executive.

Scottish Executive (2001a). *A teaching profession for the 21st century: Agreement reached following recommendations made in the McCrone Report*. Edinburgh: Scottish Executive.

Scottish Executive (2001b). *For Scotland's children: Better integrated services*. Edinburgh: Scottish Executive.

Scottish Executive (2005). *Review of initial teacher education stage 2: Report of the Review Group*. Edinburgh: Scottish Executive.

Scottish Executive Education Department (2004). *A curriculum for excellence*. The Curriculum Review Group. Edinburgh: SEED.

Scottish Executive Education Department (2006). *Improving outcomes for children and young people – The role of schools in delivering integrated children's services*. Edinburgh: Scottish Executive.

Ian Menter
Faculty of Education
University of Glasgow
UK

ANNE MORAN, LESLEY ABBOTT AND UNA O'CONNOR

COMMUNICATING, CO-ORDINATING AND CONNECTING: INTEGRATED SERVICE PROVISION IN NORTHERN IRELAND

INTRODUCTION

This chapter describes the development and implementation of an integrated service agenda in Northern Ireland, within the ongoing context of a process of substantial educational review, including an overall review of public administration. The focus will be forward-looking, towards an evolving social and educational landscape that, more than ever, is explicitly child-centred, and where an emphasis on co-operative collaboration between professional agencies will seek to be of mutual benefit to both service users and providers. A notable feature of the review process has been the development of the extended (community) schools initiative that has been articulated as a constituent feature of educational policy and reform and that will provide a co-ordinated and connected service to meet the diverse needs of all children and young people.

To explore the philosophy and practice of integrated service provision it is, perhaps, worth re-visiting some key questions:

- Where has the integrated services agenda come from?
- Whose interest does it serve?
- What does it hope to achieve?
- Will it make a difference to children and their families?
- What are the challenges or barriers to success?

In addressing the issue of integrated service provision in Northern Ireland, it is proposed that, instead of an exploration based on a deficit model of implementation, consideration should be given to the development and promotion of professional capacity and capability building.

BACKGROUND

Recently, criteria for inclusive policy development have been judged according to their relevance, consistency and capacity to be internalised and applied to other policy areas. The emergence of collaborative service integration, therefore, has

J. Forbes and C. Watson (eds.), Service Integration in Schools, 65–76.
© *2009 Sense Publishers. All rights reserved.*

become a core feature of a synergised policy context in Northern Ireland. By definition, this context carries expectations for a service provision that is relevant, representative and accessible to all stakeholders. Extended schools represent a constituent professional investment in integrated service partnerships, and are commonly characterised by multi- and transagency interaction. The value of a connected and shared professional remit is widely recognised (Campbell & Whitty, 2002; Tomlinson, 2003). Recent research in the USA, for example, has illustrated the positive educational outcomes for children with special educational needs (SEN) when multi-disciplinary practice is in place (Lieber, Beckman, Hanson, Janko, Marquart & Horn, 1997).

Internationally, service integration has been articulated in successive policy documents. Recent evaluations of these have sought to identify initiatives that have successfully linked schools to health and social services for the holistic benefit of children and young people at risk (Organisation for Economic Co-operation and Development, 1996; Training and Development Agency, 2006). Significantly, the most successful examples of good practice have been explicitly child-centred. The child-centred approach increasingly has assumed a key position in educational and human development. Crucially, this perspective acknowledges the complexity and multifaceted nature of the wider societal environment that a child inhabits since, '... wherever children live in difficult circumstances, there is more similarity than dissimilarity in their plight' (Volpe, 1996, p. 4).

Successful service integration has been defined as the cumulative product of interdependent, equitable and trusting working relationships; a collective identity and common purpose; shared responsibility and accountability and a coherent design for school improvement (Brabeck, Walsh & Latta, 2003). Similarly, professional collaboration represents a reciprocal arrangement based on co-operative and co-ordinated communication. In recent years, the premise of collaboration has permeated personal and professional boundaries and has been defined by the mutuality of its partnerships. It follows then, that the premise of inter-collaboration has resonance at all strata of policy and practice – from those relationships between professionals, to those developed to include the voice and expertise of young people and their parents. Transdisciplinary partnerships and the opportunities they represent for the physical, emotional and social wellbeing of all children and young people, by default, also yield benefits for families and the wider community. Research evidence has illustrated that infrastructural networks of community/extended schools that actively engage with health, social care and community participation can increase not just academic achievement and school attendance, but also offer the affective benefits of improved confidence, self-esteem and autonomy (Dryfoos, 1994; Stallings, 1995).

Although it has been contended that transdisciplinary practice can be difficult to achieve, it is not an impossibility (Graham & Wright, 1999). Studies have shown that when a co-ordinated approach, with clearly defined responsibilities and communication is in place, good practice can be effectively implemented (Tomlinson, 2003). However, notwithstanding the composite merits of the integrated services that extended or community schools confer, it is an arrangement that is also a potential source of interprofessional conflict due to the separate and often duplicating operational protocols of those agencies involved (Kinder, Halsey, Kendall, Atkinson, & Moor, 2000; McConkey, 2005). The challenges to integrated services are most commonly attributed to issues relating to funding, territoriality and professional autonomy, particularly where rationalisation is interpreted as a mechanism for the depletion of resources (Organisation for Economic Co-operation and Development, 1996; Volpe, 2000). Disparities in the nature and quality of provision and support have inevitably led to stalemates where there is a 'blame culture' among agencies, poor communication within and across agencies, and no clear understanding of each other's roles and responsibilities (McConkey, 2005). The possibility of professional tensions, then, is a by-product that has to be acknowledged as a fundamental planning feature if the process of service integration is to be successful.

THE CHANGING POLICY CONTEXT IN NORTHERN IRELAND

A child-centred approach continues to underpin much policy reform in Northern Ireland. Recent and ongoing governmental and legislative changes in social and educational policy are likely to have far-reaching implications for the development of integrated service provision, especially in the context of a changing social and cultural landscape. Demographic trends have highlighted a decreasing pupil population, which is projected to decline further over the next five years (Department of Education, 2004). At the same time, the overall population in Northern Ireland has become characterised by increasing cultural diversity as greater numbers of people from ethnic minority groups enter the jurisdiction. It is inevitable that these factors will impact significantly on the composition and constitution of schools, as well as on the generic profile of the pupil population and its attendant needs.

Changes within the policy environment in Northern Ireland, where concurrent reviews of public administration and government departments have been undertaken, have been designed, in part, to address the dual contradiction of top-heavy bureaucratic infrastructures and a declining resource. Rationalisation has been undertaken as a means to redress an existing policy environment where, historically, service providers have often operated in isolation from each other, leading to the duplication of resources, unnecessary bureaucracy and an absence of a coherent and connected vision. Within the education sector, this has been most notable with the review of the schools' estate, the review of teacher education, the review of special education and inclusion – including the future role of special schools – and the establishment of a new Education and Skills Authority to oversee the development and delivery of educational provision in Northern Ireland (Department of Education Training Inspectorate, 2006; Office of the First Minister and Deputy First Minister, 2006b). A significant element of the revision of services for children is the transfer of strategic priorities into local action. This process, by necessity, requires the assimilation of strategic thinking in conjunction with transparent operational outcomes so that policy is translated into new, effective practice which is manifested through greater ownership by professionals.

Other concurrent changes will be equally far-reaching. The introduction of a common curriculum framework from September 2007 is intended to be strongly pupil-centred, with the needs of the individual child at its core (Department of Education, 2004). The revised curriculum will confer fixed expectations and accountability measures for the way in which schools fulfil their institutional responsibility to all pupils through their school development plans and self-evaluation strategies, as well as through individual Education Plans (EPs) and Pupil Profiles (Council for the Curriculum, Examinations and Assessment, 2004). In addition, the introduction of a collegiate system between schools – including the further education sector – the emergence of specialist schools and a review of the role of special schools will invariably contribute to the changing educational landscape in Northern Ireland (Department of Education, 2002, 2004, 2005; Department of Education Training Inspectorate, 2006; Office of the First Minister and Deputy First Minister, 2006b).

A new education framework in Northern Ireland

Education is, by default, inextricably linked to, and reflective of, cultural, social and political reform. Undeniably, then, the far-reaching changes currently being implemented within the education system in Northern Ireland are inherently linked to this culture of change. The next decade will inevitably see significant shifts in the composition and function of schools as well as in the manner in which pupils learn. This has been articulated in successive policy documents that have variously addressed the funding, administration, structure, management and constitution of schools, as well as specifying the curricular content, focus, priorities and methodologies by which children will learn. Perhaps a key priority has been a governmental commitment to the creation of an education environment that recognises the diversity of learners and that is designed to enable all children to succeed, irrespective of their differing abilities. It is an arrangement aimed to harness the potential and condense the collaborative expertise of teachers and other professionals so that, '... the development of learning and support arrangements in which specialists from health care, social services and education work collaboratively and in partnership with schools, should be a high priority in any future arrangements' (Department of Education, 2001, p. 89).

The organisation of a revised education environment, however, is not without challenge. Some commentary has critiqued the proposals as a rhetorical framework rather than an explicit and coherent plan. The visionary aspiration of a business plan for education has been qualified by a series of caveats, most notably in relation to the professional association between education, health and social services. Central to the operational priorities for integrated service provision is the premise of equitable representation by each agency, defined in a connected strategy that will seek to raise standards and school improvement for all, counteract educational disadvantage and link schools with their communities. It is clear that, individually and collectively, the proposed changes will have an impact on the design and nature of services for children and young people. With specific reference to children and young people, the response to these changes has been most explicitly articulated in a ten-year strategy that will operate from 2006-2016 (Office of the First Minister and Deputy First Minister, 2006a).

Children and young people: A ten-year strategy

The local response to address the needs of children and young people has been variously outlined in a series of policy documents that have reiterated the expectation of shared vision and strategy, integrated infrastructures and unified professional ownership (Department of Education, 2005; Office of the First Minister and Deputy First Minister, 2006a). The publication of a ten-year strategy and funding package for children and young people has been developed to meet the diverse needs of children and young people, and has a particular focus on the most marginalised and disadvantaged groups. The strategy represents a governmental commitment to respond to need in a way that meets the real and composite needs of children and young people. The proposals represent a policy response to the assertion that the various needs of children cannot be properly fulfilled by public service departments working separately.

One area where the limitations of less cohesive service provision have been conspicuous is that of special education. The current funding arrangement for special education provision is largely historical and is apportioned between the mainstream and special school sectors. Recent research has drawn attention to the separate nature of existing provision and has highlighted the incomplete and inefficient use of resources for children with special educational needs in Northern Ireland. Findings have included the priority recommendation for a clearly articulated vision that will cater effectively for diversity of need; central to this is the establishment of high quality multidisciplinary service provision through collaborative working arrangements between education, health and social services (Department of Education Training Inspectorate, 2006).

Developing inclusive schools

For schools in Northern Ireland, one of the most significant policy developments has been the new statutory arrangements for special education and the revision of the terms and conditions to identify and deal with disability discrimination (Department of Education, 2005; Disability Rights Commission, 2002). The profile of special education has been a component feature of overall reform and has been articulated in policy documents as a commitment to greater inclusive practice and a right for children and their parents to secure a placement in the mainstream environment (Department of Education, 2002, 2004, 2005; Department of Education Training Inspectorate, 2006). In addition, the arrangements for the revised curriculum have stipulated that pupils with SEN should have access to the same range of learning pathways available to other pupils (Department of

69

Education, 2004). This premise of equitable provision has been underpinned by a fundamental principle that the interests of the child should be at the heart of all decision-making and should be based upon informed choice by both pupils and their parents.

Initial Teacher Education: Preparing education professionals

The integral relationship between teaching, learning and policy development, and the realisation of sustainable service integration is, undeniably, an issue for teacher education. To date, in Northern Ireland, interdisciplinary partnerships between teacher education and other relevant professional areas have largely not materialised. A future challenge exists for teacher educators to reconsider their provision of pre-service and in-service programmes. A revised emphasis on the mutual benefits of collegiate relationships represents a key starting point; the premise of teachers working alongside other professionals to provide reciprocal insight and expertise has become an established feature of teacher training programmes elsewhere. It is an approach that has attached commensurate priority to the development of affective as well as technical skills. At the same time, recent research has also highlighted the strategic and intrinsic value of a multi-agency dimension in initial teacher education (ITE) provision, the key findings of which appear below (Moran & Abbott, 2006). The opportunity for a combined learning experience alongside social workers, nurses and allied health professionals has been advocated as an initial introduction to interprofessional development and as a potential template for a new form of 'public service' qualifications (Moran & Abbott, 2006). It is worth noting that, at a time when teacher competencies in Northern Ireland and other parts of the United Kingdom are under review, an opportunity exists to articulate a new agenda for teacher education which incorporates learning alongside other professionals. It is a position that has been already been highlighted by the Universities Council for the Education of Teachers (UCET), which has identified integrated support services as pivotal to the lives of children and young people. It is a position that, by necessity, will entail fresh scrutiny of the requirements for teacher education and induction, reconsideration of the balance between initial training and continuing professional development (CPD), and a coherent strategy to build principled capacity and ownership between education and other services (UCET, 2003). It is reasonable, therefore, to envisage over the next few years a process of incremental collaboration, which moves professional partnerships from the rhetoric of policy into practical action.

RESEARCH DESIGN AND METHODOLOGY

Contextualising the research referred to above (Moran & Abbott, 2006), this was a one-year study commissioned by the Department of Education in Northern Ireland, the focus of which was on educational inclusion. However, significant aspects of it related to the multi-agency provision of a range of services. A qualitative approach was used to obtain the views and experiences of 28 principals in the nursery (N), primary (P), post-primary (PP) and special sectors (S) (seven in each), and of a purposive sample of ten interagency personnel. The purpose of the one-to-one, semi-structured interviews was to gain insight into how schools attempt to promote and develop inclusion, how the different external agencies work with schools and with each other, and how each perceives the other in terms of collaboratively creating effective, child-centred, context-specific models of inclusive practice. In schools, the main aims were:

- to examine existing practices that increase the motivation, participation and achievement of children and young people;
- to identify cultures and conditions that promote enhanced opportunities and attainment;
- to evaluate ways in which support services for teaching, including levels of support from learning support assistants, could more effectively interface with schools and professionals from other agencies; and
- to identify barriers to pupils' participation and learning.

In relation to professionals from other agencies, the aim of the interviews was:

- to liaise with members of the Education and Training Inspectorate, local education authority support teams, Department of Health, Social Services and Public Safety personnel and Alternative Education Providers on aspects of current inclusive provision.

Findings

Teachers

The main features of a whole-school philosophy of inclusion identified by most principals were: catering for individual difference (all 28), and treating all children the same regardless of ability or socio-economic background (25: 6N, 5P, 7PP, 7S). Most mainstream schools in the study accepted the full range of special educational needs (20: 6N, 7P, 7PP), said to be on the increase. Inclusion meant valuing all pupils, involving parents and the community, and accepting children from different cultural backgrounds. It also extended to staff anticipating the later needs of pupils with SEN and encouraging other pupils to be accepting of disability. For special schools, inclusion could additionally mean preparing pupils for reintegration into mainstream schools and providing outreach support for their teachers. Some principals felt that special schools were still seen as segregated, attitudes towards children with learning difficulties and disabilities still had to change (including those towards special school staff themselves), and the part played by the special schools in enabling pupils to adjust to mainstream schooling needed to be developed much further.

Achieving effective inclusive practices, however, required collaboration between the different professionals, and between the different services and the schools. The main factors said to hinder the full development of inclusion, apart from this lack of collaboration, were the delays in children being seen by outside professionals, the delays in receiving appropriate and sufficiently frequent therapy, and the issues surrounding confidentiality and disclosure whereby schools did not always receive information from outside agencies. The relationship between schools and social services was less than favourable with a perceived unwillingness on the part of the latter to share information cited as the main drawback, and different agencies having competing agendas and values. It was pointed out by three nursery principals that they had to be highly proactive in seeking out agency support, highlighting, in particular, the need for much better lines of communication with health visitors for this sector. Four post-primary principals acknowledged the heavy workloads of the educational psychologists and the different therapists.

As to how support services could better support inclusion, there was consensus that much greater communication and connection between education, health and social services should be strongly encouraged. There should be earlier diagnosis and intervention, prompt provision of specialist, therapeutic support, and also continuity of support between the different phases of schooling. Overall, the goal should be a properly co-ordinated, joint approach to commonly identified problems, good communication and regular contact including the growth of mutual trust and respect, the pooling of expertise and other resources, and willingness to share information in pursuit of the child's best interests. There should be a conscious resolve to avoid a mindset of competing priorities and different agendas. Consideration should be given to joint training among professionals in education, health, and social services to enhance teamwork (learning to be a team member) and to promote real inclusion.

Interagency professionals

For their part, the interagency professionals (referred to as 'senior officers' to ensure anonymity in a disparate group) had varied roles, but all had a strong focus on the inclusion in compulsory education of children and young people who are marginalised for any reason, and who receive alternative educational provision. They endorsed the concept of inclusive education, but said that the reality was complex. They believed that every child had to be treated as an individual and, although acknowledging that most children and young people with special needs should be educated in mainstream settings, it was not felt that this was the most effective environment for those with severe learning difficulties. In keeping with the principals' views, there was support for the continued existence of special schools, and whilst a positive thrust was noted to include as many children as possible in mainstream education, it was thought imperative to reflect, continuously analyse and evaluate to ensure that society in the wider sense, schools and children were receptive to inclusion, and that the resources were there to support it.

Concerning the current effectiveness of inclusive provision by schools in Northern Ireland, senior officers' comments related both to teacher attitudes towards pupils with additional needs, and to the fragmented nature of therapeutic and other provision. Some ambivalence was noted, though, as teachers were thought to recognise the desirability and need to develop inclusive practices, but could be decidedly reluctant to cater for certain special needs, the area of greatest concern being emotional and behavioural difficulties (EBD), already highlighted by principals. Moreover, unlike most principals, the senior officers doubted that teachers properly understood the underlying rationale of inclusion, or that they had discussed it enough with colleagues. Additionally, the lack of early intervention and very late placement in alternative education had resulted in many young people having no sense of self-worth at the latter end of their formal schooling, presenting major challenges for those attempting to retrieve the situation. There was now more awareness, though, of what alternative education providers could do, but approaches to them had to be made much earlier and they needed sustained financial support to enable long-term planning and implementation of their programmes.

Specifically, the senior officers saw more effective inclusive schooling to lie in greater and more incremental financial investment in children with special needs by health and social services, as well as better assessment, greater interagency collaboration (to provide improved support for children with special needs in mainstream and be proactive in retaining them), equipping schools and teachers properly to cope with inclusion, and providing leadership at strategic level with uniform support for schools across the local education authorities. Further, there had to be a shift in mindset so that parents of children with learning disabilities were offered mainstream education as a first choice, and better treatment of parents during the statementing procedure, described as laborious, bureaucratic and demeaning, and resulting in mistrust of education (see also Allan, 2003).

A much greater shift would be to move towards the notion of full service schools, now well established in other parts of the United Kingdom, the United States and Scandinavia. In Sweden, for example, children are educated with peers and siblings regardless of impairment or disability and, to achieve this in Northern Ireland, once again leadership and a change in attitude were needed. This more socially inclusive concept of schooling incorporates a wider range of agencies in school-related activities (Campbell & Whitty, 2002): it embodies early intervention and avoids later, more serious problems. In this system special education is viewed as a 'service' not as a 'place' and the integrated services have a positive impact on teachers (Wang, Haertel & Walberg, in Campbell, 2002). Northern Ireland has a broad continuum of alternative and outreach provision for a very wide array of special needs, but it is not well enough funded and often comes too late in the pupil's career. Although the local education authorities were making positive contributions to alternative provision, there was no commonality of approach. Early intervention to counteract later, more serious problems with EBD required money and resources at the preschool stage, including the training of teachers and nursery assistants in this area.

Distinctly differing views emerged on the support from external agencies to promote inclusion, from 'pockets of excellence' to 'interagency collaboration to support schools is not working'. What worked was when agencies came together to address commonly identified problems, used a joint approach where staff co-operated, established good communication, used their collective initiative to think creatively, and shared resources, personnel and transport. The advantages of multi-agency working extended to the child, the organisation and the individual professional. For the child, there was better access to services, to education and early intervention, and to improved educational attainment. For the organisation, there were opportunities to broaden perspectives on inclusion, improve understanding of related issues, interact more positively with other agencies and share expertise. For the individual, there were the rewards of working with other professionals, having keener awareness of the issues surrounding the child or young person, and making better joint decisions.

From the evidence, the school principals were in synchrony with the outside professionals in support of inclusive practices, and both groups put up strong and convincing arguments for integrated service provision characterised by effective interplay between education, health and social services. Key defining characteristics put forward for a model of best practice included:

- explicit, strategic leadership at the highest level;
- the cultivation of a positive attitude among mainstream teachers towards the implications of the new legislation on special needs and disability;
- a child- and young person-centred approach that permeates all teaching and learning, and all service provision;
- co-ordinated, co-located services at operational level with teamwork and sharing of knowledge in equal measure;
- training at pre-service and in-service levels to include all staff.

CONCLUSIONS

It would appear, then, that the goal for the three main service systems of education, health and social services in Northern Ireland will be the development of genuinely integrated partnerships. The challenge will be the implementation of system change and greater inter-professional co-operation that will be sustainable from the early years of a child's education and the subsequent transitions, through school sectors from primary to post-primary and beyond. The emergence of service integration, however, carries a responsibility beyond general adherence to standardised rules and procedures; it also carries an expectation of accountability (Hogan, 1999; McCroskey, 1999). For this reason, recognition of the principled professional has assumed increasing currency within the agenda for change. Reflecting the above research findings, the establishment of multiprofessional teams who espouse a common purpose and shared vision is a central feature of integrated partnerships and a critical population by which to identify and measure the outcomes and impact of system change.

Research evidence has suggested that the most advanced example of interprofessional collaboration is to be found in full-service community schools

(Dryfoos, 1994). In Northern Ireland, the extended schools programme represents the current model for the integration of services. Although it presently exists as a pilot initiative, its ability to be sustained fiscally and practically as a long-term, venture have been challenged. If the aspiration of an extended schools programme is to achieve realistic longevity, there is a need for a sustainable approach that is responsive to the purposes and needs of all constituent groups. It is an imperative that is bound as much by economic, legal and political accountability as by moral, social and educational responsibility. Within Northern Ireland, a differentiated approach has been exemplified through various models of interagency collaboration that have been developed to meet the diverse contexts of schools and their communities (Together 4 All; One Stop Shop: Communities in Schools). Crucially, the success of these initiatives has required an integrated and shared vision, in place of the status quo of competing silos that formerly perpetuated selective rather than collective involvement.

REFERENCES

Allan, J. (2003). Inclusion in Scotland: Progress and prospects. *Tizard Learning Disability Review, 8*(1), 13-18.

Brabeck, M., Walsh, M., & Latta, R. (Eds.) (2003). *Meeting at the hyphen: Schools – universities – communities – professions in collaboration for student achievement and well being. 102nd Yearbook of the National Society for the Study of Education, Part II.* Chicago: University of Chicago Press.

Campbell, C. (Ed.) (2002). *Developing inclusive schooling: Perspectives, policies and practices.* London: Institute of Education, University of London.

Campbell, C., & Whitty, G. (2002). Interagency collaboration for inclusive schooling. In C. Campbell (Ed.), *Developing inclusive schooling: Perspectives, policies and practices* (pp. 99-119). London: Institute of Education, University of London.

Council for the Curriculum, Examinations and Assessment (2004). *Way ahead (post-primary): The revised curriculum and its assessment.* Belfast: CCEA.

Department of Education (2001). *Education for the 21st century. Report by the post-primary review body* (The Burns Report). Bangor: DE.

Department of Education (2002*). Review of post-primary education* (The Burns Report). Bangor: DE.

Department of Education (2004). *Future post-primary arrangements in Northern Ireland: Advice from the post-primary-review working group* (Costello Report). Bangor: DE.

Department of Education (2005). *Draft supplementary guidance to support the impact of SENDO on the Code of Practice on the identification and assessment of special educational needs.* Bangor: DE.

Department of Education Training Inspectorate (2006). *The future role of special schools.* Bangor: DE.

Disability Rights Commission (2002). *Code of Practice for schools – Disability Discrimination Act* (revised) 1995. London: DRC.

Dryfoos, J. (1994). Full-service schools: A revolution in health and services for children and families. In M. Brabeck, M. Walsh, & R. Latta (Eds.) (2003), *Meeting at the hyphen: Schools – universities – communities – professions in collaboration for student achievement and well being. 102nd Yearbook of the National Society for the study of education, Part II.* Chicago: University of Chicago Press.

Graham, J., & Wright, J.A. (1999). What does inter-professional collaboration mean to professionals working with pupils with physical disabilities? *British Journal of Special Education. 26* (1), 37-41.

Hogan, C. (1999). Vermont communities count: Using results to strengthen services for families and children. In M. Brabeck, M. Walsh, & R. Latta (Eds.) (2003) *Meeting at the hyphen: Schools – universities – communities – professions in collaboration for student achievement and well being. 102nd Yearbook of the National Society for the Study of Education, Part II.* Chicago: University of Chicago Press.

Kinder, K., Halsey, K., Kendall, K., Atkinson, M., & Moor, H. (2000). *Working out well: Effective provision for excluded pupils.* Slough: National Foundation for Educational Research.

Lieber, J.A., Beckman, P.J., Hanson, M.J., Janko, S., Marquart, J.M., & Horn, E.M. (1997). The impact of changing roles on relationships between adults in inclusive programmes for young children. *Early Education and Development, 8,* 67-82.

McConkey, R. (2005). Multi-agency working in support of people with intellectual disabilities. *Journal of Intellectual Disabilities, 9*(3), 193-207.

McCroskey, J. (1999). Getting to results: Data-driven decision-making for children, youth, families and communities (A what works policy brief). In M. Brabeck, M. Walsh, & R. Latta (Eds.) (2003), *Meeting at the hyphen: Schools – universities – communities – professions in collaboration for student achievement and well being. 102nd Yearbook of the National Society for the study of education, Part II.* Chicago: University of Chicago Press.

Moran, A., & Abbott, L. (2006). *The development of inclusive schools in Northern Ireland: A model of best practice.* Bangor: DE.

Organisation for Economic Co-operation and Development (OECD) (1996). *Co-ordinating services for children and youth at risk: A world view.* Paris: OECD.

Office of the First Minister and Deputy First Minister (2006a). *Our children and young people – Our pledge. A ten-year strategy for children and young people in Northern Ireland,* 2006-2016. Belfast: OFMDFM.

Office of the First Minister and Deputy First Minister (2006b). *Better government in Northern Ireland. Final decisions on the review of public administration.* Belfast: OFMDFM.

Stallings, J. (1995). Ensuring teaching and learning in the 21st century. In M. Brabeck, M. Walsh & R. Latta (Eds.) (2003), *Meeting at the hyphen: Schools – universities – communities – professions in collaboration for student achievement and well being. 102nd Yearbook of the National Society for the Study of Education, Part II.* Chicago: University of Chicago Press.

Tomlinson, K. (2003). *Effective interagency working: A review of the literature and examples from practice.* Slough: National Foundation for Educational Research.

Training and Development Agency (2006). (http://:www.tda.gov.uk/partners/futures)

Universities Council for the Education of Teachers (2003). *DfES Green Paper: Every child matters. Response from UCET.* London: UCET.

Volpe, R. (1996). The CIPP model and the case study approach. In P. Evans, P. Hurrell, R. Volpe, & M. Stewart (Eds.), *Successful services for our children and families at risk* (pp. 303-328). Paris: Organisation for Economic Co-operation and Development.

Volpe, R. (2000). *What have we learned documenting and evaluating school-linked services for children and youth at risk?* Pan-Canadian Education Research Agenda, Ottawa, April 2000.

Wang, M.C., Haertel, G.D., & Walberg, H.J. (2002). *Effective features of collaborative, school-linked services* (Publication Series No. 1). Mid-Atlantic Laboratory for Student Success. Philadephia, PA: Temple University.

Anne Moran, Lesley Abbott and Una O'Connor
Faculty of Social Sciences
University of Ulster
UK

GILLIAN PUGH

EVERY CHILD MATTERS: THE IMPLICATIONS FOR SERVICE INTEGRATION IN ENGLAND

INTRODUCTION

This chapter summarises some of the main policy thrusts in terms of children's services in England over the past ten years, and in particular the ambitious programme of reform underpinned by the Children Act 2004 but universally referred to as 'the Every Child Matters: Change for children agenda'. This is a huge and ambitious agenda, primarily intended to improve outcomes for all children and narrow the gaps between those who do well and those who do not. It requires a paradigm shift on the part of all those who work with and for children, young people and their families, and in some instances this will require integrating services that have previously been delivered in silos. But it is not mainly about service integration. Working in joined up ways is a means to an end, not the end in itself.

The concept of partnership or integrated working is a central feature of current policy and service delivery, being seen as the key way of tackling intractable problems that cannot be resolved by single agencies. Families, of course, see their lives in a single piece, rather than separate silos called 'health' or 'education' and have long argued for a more coherent response from service providers. But although a more integrated approach appears to be eminently sensible, it is not easy to achieve, and there is still not a great deal of research evidence on how to go about it, or whether it is effective in improving outcomes for service users.

BACKGROUND

Every Child Matters was published in September 2003 (HM Treasury) but there had been a number of initiatives introduced before this which laid the foundations for a new approach to providing services for children and young people, and which placed a strong emphasis on multi-agency working and prevention. Most notable amongst these were Sure Start and the Children's Fund, a brief summary of which will be provided here before outlining the development of *Every Child Matters*.

Sure Start had its origins in a Treasury-led cross-department review of services for children under eight, established within a few months of the Labour government coming into power in 1997. A number of people were invited to contribute papers to three Treasury seminars, and Pugh's paper pulled out a

J. Forbes and C. Watson (eds.), Service Integration in Schools, 77–92.

number of key themes: the risk and protective factors that impacted on a child's capacity to thrive, research on early brain development and the importance of the first two years of life, the long-term impact of high quality early education, the importance of parents and of styles of parenting – and the importance of bringing services together to respond holistically to the needs of children and families (Pugh, 1998).

In July 1998 the government announced a £540m Sure Start programme, to fund some 250 local programmes covering 150,000 children living in the most disadvantaged areas. Before any evaluation findings were available, this was very soon expanded to a further 250 areas. The senior Treasury official described it as

> a radical cross-departmental strategy to raise the physical, social, emotional and intellectual status of young children through improved services. It is targeted at children under four and their families in areas of need. It is part of the government's policy to prevent social exclusion and aims to improve the life chances of younger children through better access to early education and play, health services for children and parents, family support and advice on nurturing. It will be locally led and locally delivered, but will be based on evidence from the UK and elsewhere on 'what works', in terms of improving the life chances of children and their parents. (Glass, 1999, p. 257)

All local schemes had to provide core services (outreach and home visiting, support for families, support for play and learning experiences for children, community-based health care, and support for children with special needs) but in response to local need as assessed by the local partnership board. The local Sure Start partnership boards were required to include representatives of all relevant statutory services – education, social care and health – and the voluntary sector and were to include parents. Indeed parents were soon chairing some boards and were certainly well represented on many others. The range of staff employed in the multi-agency teams reflected the broad aims of the local programmes, and there were some imaginative examples of secondments and cross-agency leadership and management. A substantial evaluation programme was put in place (see National Evaluation of Sure Start, 2005a, 2005b), findings from which will contribute to the discussion later in this chapter. More recently government has announced a programme of children's centres which will build on and develop Sure Start local programmes (HM Treasury, 2004) but with overall control moving to local authorities.

The Children's Fund was financially a more limited initiative, but one that was made available to all 150 local authorities in England rather than being area based. The overall aim of the Fund, which has been available over an eight-year period from 2001-2009, has been the provision of preventive services for children aged five to 13 and their families. There has been an emphasis on joint working, with a local partnership taking responsibility for planning and delivering the services, often in collaboration with voluntary organisations. Projects have focused on community cohesion and have all involved multi-agency working, providing a range of services including support for parents, home-school liaison, information and advice services, advocacy support and home learning. The final evaluation report was published recently and will be drawn on in the later discussion (Edwards, Barnes, Plewis & Morris, 2006).

EVERY CHILD MATTERS: CHANGE FOR CHILDREN

The past nine years have seen a veritable blizzard of new 'joined up' initiatives and programmes in addition to Sure Start and the Children's Fund, amongst them a national childcare strategy, Connexions Services, bringing together education, support and advice for young people, New Deal for Communities and Neighbourhood Renewal funding, and Quality Protects, ring-fenced funding intended to improve the life chances of children looked after by local authorities.

But it is the Green Paper, *Every Child Matters* (HM Treasury, 2003), described by Tony Blair, the then Prime Minister, at its launch as the most important document relating to children for over 30 years, and the subsequent 2004 Children Act that are likely to have the greatest impact on changing the culture and organisation of children's services in England. The Green Paper was initially planned as a response to the report by Lord Laming into the death of Victoria Climbié in 2002 at the hands of two people who were supposed to be caring for her, the last in a long line of failures to work collaboratively to protect very vulnerable children (Department of Health and Home Office, 2003). Her case was known to social services, the health service and the police in two boroughs, but on ten separate occasions they failed to protect her, and no one took responsibility for her death. The government's initial concern following this appalling tragedy was to focus on children at risk, but after widespread consultation the report took prevention as its starting point and accepted the view that to support all children better through well coordinated mainstream services is more likely to benefit those in need and at risk than a separate child protection service. The five key themes of *Every Child Matters* are: a strong foundation in the early years; a stronger focus on parenting and families; earlier interventions and effective protection; better accountability and integration locally, regionally and nationally; and reform of the workforce.

The *overall aims* are summarised as improving outcomes for all children, and narrowing the gap between those who do well and those who do not; improving and integrating universal services; more specialist help to promote opportunity and prevent problems; reconfiguring services around the child and family; and sharing responsibility for safeguarding children. Targeted services were to be planned and delivered within a universal context.

The decision to focus on improving outcomes grew out of work on 'results based accountability' in the United States (see Friedman, 2005) and its implementation in some local authorities in England during the late 1990s and early 2000s (Utting, Rose & Pugh, 2001). Building on this work, the *Every Child Matters* agenda identified five main outcomes (and a host of additional sub outcomes):

- being healthy – enjoying good physical and mental health, and living a healthy life style
- staying safe – being protected from harm and neglect
- enjoying and achieving – getting the most out of life and developing the skills for adulthood
- make a positive contribution – being involved with the community and society and not engaging in anti-social or offending behaviour
- economic wellbeing – not being prevented by economic disadvantage from achieving their full potential in life.

The long-term vision emerged through the initial Green Paper and the subsequent implementation document – *Every Child Matters: Change for Children* (Department for Education & Skills, 2004). In terms of service provision this is seen as the development of integrated education, childcare, health and social care, including family support services for 0 - 19s through three main models: children's centres for children under five and their families; extended schools; and improved services for young people. There is also a focus on better support for parents, on appropriately qualified staff, and on more effective interplay between universal and specialist services.

The vision and the current implementation programme are extraordinarily ambitious, in that they require cultural and organisational change at every point of the system. At central government level most services for children and families had, by 2007, been brought within a Children, Young People and Families directorate, within the Department for Education and Skills, under the direction of a Minister for Children. This new department included social care and children looked after (transferred from the Department of Health), children affected by family breakdown (transferred from the Lord Chancellor's Department), family policy (transferred from the Home Office) and all early years services. But significantly it did not include schools (within the Department for Education and Skills but under a separate Minister), children's health or the youth justice system. (See Postscript to the chapter for more recent changes to policy).

In local areas, the existing administrative arrangements led by a director of education and a director of social services are being replaced with a single director of children's services, and an elected councillor with a brief for children and young people. The 2004 Children Act requires these changes, and also puts a duty on local authorities to promote cooperation between agencies to improve children's wellbeing and to work together to safeguard and protect the welfare of children; and allows for the pooling of resources.

The role of Children's Trusts

The means of delivering joined up services that meet the needs of children, young people and families and lead to improved outcomes is through Children's Trusts. These can best be illustrated through Figure 1 generally referred to as 'the onion diagram'.

Children's trusts as catalysts for local change

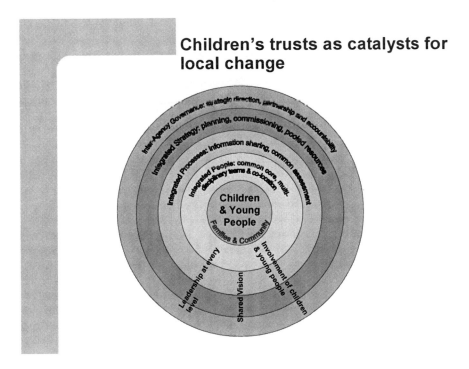

Figure 1. Children's trusts as catalysts for local change. (Source: Department for Education and Skills)

Children's Trusts are seen as the main catalysts for change.

The starting point is *children, young people and families*, living within local communities, and they are at the centre of the change programme. Services have to make sense to those who are using them.

The next layer is *integrated people* – professionals working together in multi-agency teams, including the Children and Young People's Partnership Board that drives the Children's Trust in each local authority, multi-agency panels and multi-agency teams including Sure Start, Youth Offending Teams, Child and Adolescent Mental Health teams, etc. These teams will often be co-located, sometimes based in schools, and increasingly there will be a lead professional taking responsibility for every child for whom additional support is required.

There is also an ambitious workforce reform programme (Department for Education and Skills, 2005a), led by the newly formed Children's Workforce Development Council, which is charged with working with others to create an Integrated Qualifications Framework. There are wide-ranging plans to ensure that the training of all staff who work with children, whether from a health, education, social welfare or youth justice background, includes a common core of skills and

81

knowledge – for example effective communication, child development, multi-agency working, safeguarding, sharing information and supporting transitions; and some new 'joined up' professional roles are emerging, such as the early years professional, and the pedagogue (drawing on European models – see Boddy, Cameron & Petrie, 2005).

The next layer is *integrated processes* – including a common assessment framework, a single data base of information on every child and young person and joint training.

Moving outwards again, though in reality this is the engine of reform, is *integrated systems* – a single system for assessing need, delivering a children's plan for the whole local area (through a Children and Young People's Partnership Board involving education, social care, health, police, probation, leisure and the voluntary sector), and jointly commissioned services through pooled budgets.

And finally, steering the whole agenda, is *interagency governance*, led within central government by the Minister for Children, Young People and Families, and at local government level by the director of children's services, a new position integrating the previous posts of director of education and director of social services.

To this must be added the *integrated inspection system*, whereby some ten inspectorates have come together to create a single framework for inspecting all children's services from schools to adoption agencies to youth offending institutions against the five *Every Child Matters* outcomes, with a key question at the centre – what does it feel like to be a child or young person using this service?

The planning structure for one local authority, Telford and Wrekin, is illustrated in Figure 2.

The legislative underpinning for this programme of change is the 2004 Children Act, which requires local authorities and other key agencies to work together to promote children's wellbeing, to set up a local Safeguarding Children's Board, to devise a single children and young person's plan, and to appoint a children's services director, and requires the integrated inspection framework to inform inspection of all children's services.

The key for ensuring that prevention remains central is the concept of 'joined up' mainstream services. For children under five, this is manifested in *children's centres*, currently numbering around 2,000 but with an expectation that there will be 3,500 by 2010 (HM Treasury, 2004). Children's centres are being merged with the Sure Start local programmes where they exist, and will include: early education and childcare places, in group settings, with childminders and at home; parenting and family support; health advice and information; preventative services to support additional needs, including outreach work in communities; and support for parents moving into training or employment. There are still issues about the affordability and sustainability of all day integrated early education and care. There is also an expectation that most provision will be in the private and voluntary sectors, and parents are still paying the vast majority of the cost (see Sylva & Pugh, 2005). But free nursery education for all three- and four-year-olds is being extended to 15 hours a week for 38 weeks of the year.

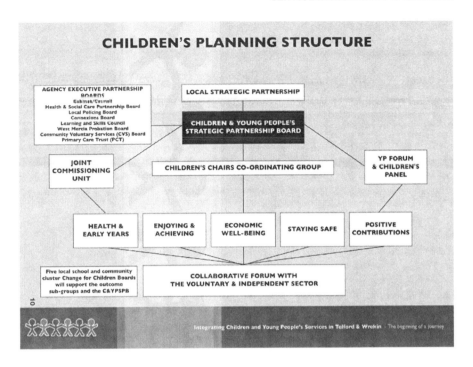

Figure 2. Children's planning structure, Telford and Wrekin Local Authority (as at 2006).

For school-age children, services are to come together around schools or clusters of schools, and by 2010 all schools are to become *extended schools,* offering a range of activities beyond the traditional school day (Department for Education and Skills, 20005b). Primary schools are to offer 'childcare' before and after school, and secondary schools are also to open before and after school offering music, sport and holiday activities. The 'core offer' (which may be offered by a cluster of schools working together) is to include high quality childcare, a varied programme of activities including homework clubs, sport, music, dance and drama, arts and crafts, etc, information and advice for parents, including parenting programmes and family learning, swift and easy referral to specialist health and social services, and wider community access to ICT, arts, sports and adult learning. Some 3,000 schools have met the challenge in the first year – about one in eight of all schools – and there are some challenging targets to ensure that all schools can be more responsive to the needs of children and families by 2010.

When *Every Child Matters* was published, there was a strong view that whilst its offer for children and families was good, it neglected the needs of young people. A youth Green Paper – *Youth Matters* (Department for Education and Skills, 2005c) – was published subsequently, which has four main strands. The main focus is on

83

things for young people to do and places to go – a requirement on local authorities to secure positive activities for all young people, with opportunity cards, and an opportunity fund. There is also an emphasis on encouraging young people to become volunteers; a new look at information, advice and guidance, giving schools and colleges a greater role in providing advice and guidance to young people; and targeted support for young people in trouble or with serious problems, bringing together current funding and support systems.

The most recent policy document has been the publication of a Green Paper focusing on the needs of children and young people not able to live with their birth families – *Care Matters: Transforming the lives of children and young people in care* (Department for Education and Skills, 2006a), and work is currently under way on a policy paper that reflects the needs of disabled children and their families.

WHAT DO WE KNOW ABOUT THE EFFECTIVENESS OF INTEGRATION?

As I have already indicated, the main purpose of the *Every Child Matters* reforms is to improve outcomes for children, not to integrate services. However, more coherent services, systems and processes are assumed to be a valuable means to this end, and it is important to assess the extent to which this move towards integration is impacting on children and families. It is early days in the implementation of the *Every Child Matters* agenda, but services such as Sure Start and early excellence centres (the forerunners of children's centres) have a longer track record. This section therefore draws on a range of evidence to look at the impact of integrated working.

There are many definitions of integration, but the following summary from Percy-Smith's overview of research into partnership working is perhaps the broadest in terms of the range of terminology that is used (2005, pp. 24-25).

Table 1. Terms related to 'partnership' (Percy-Smith, 2005, pp. 24-25)

Holistic government or governance	Integration and co-ordination at all levels and in relation to all aspects of policy-related activity – policy-making, regulation, service provision and scrutiny; mutually reinforcing means and objectives.
Joined up	Deliberate and co-ordinated planning and working which takes account of different policies and varying agency practice and values.
Joint working	Professionals from more than one agency working directly together on a project.
Multi-agency or cross-agency working	More than one agency working together; services are provided by agencies acting in concert and drawing on pooled resources or a pooled budget.

Multiprofessional or multidisciplinary working	Working together of staff with different professional backgrounds and training.
Interagency working	More than one agency working together in a planned and formal way.
Cross-boundary working	Agencies working together on areas that extend beyond the scope of any one agency.
Cross-cutting	Issues that are not the 'property' of a single organisation or agency – e.g., social inclusion, improving health.
Integration	Agencies working together within a single, often new, organisational structure.
Networks	Informal contact and communication between individuals or agencies.
Collaborative working or collaboration	Agencies working together in a wide variety of different ways to pursue a common goal, while also pursing their own organisational goals.
Co-operation	Informal relationships between organisations designed to ensure that organisations can pursue their own goals more effectively.
Co-ordination	More formal mechanisms to ensure that organisations take account of each other's strategies and activities in their own planning.

Outcomes for children and families

I will first of all look at what evidence there is on the impact on users, before looking at the evidence regarding the challenges and opportunities of working together for the staff involved.

The forerunners of children's centres were firstly – in the 1970s and 1980s – combined nursery centres. With a Labour government came 'early excellence centres', modelled on the best 'joined up' centres for young children and their families. Evaluation has now been suspended in response to changes in government policy, but the early evaluation findings were promising (Bertram, Pascal, Bokhari, Gasper & Holtermann, 2002). There were found to be substantial benefits for children, including enhanced social competence and cognitive development, delays or difficulties were identified early, and there was inclusion of children with a wide range of special needs. Families too benefited, reporting improvements in relationships and wellbeing, improved parenting skills, higher self-esteem and self-confidence, reduced isolation and – a key element of the government's anti-poverty strategy – increased access to employment and training. There were also felt to be benefits for the wider community in terms of greater social cohesion, and users were very positive about the quality and availability of services, which provided easy access and opportunities for personal development without the stigma so often associated with asking for specialist help.

The early findings from Sure Start have been widely discussed and often misreported as 'failure'. As far as impact is concerned (National Evaluation of Sure programmes showed greater benefit for those who were moderately disadvantaged than for those with less human capital, i.e., teen parents, lone parents and workless households. The programme was very flexible in how it was offered locally, and these early findings have led to stronger government guidance on how to reach and work with very troubled families, as well as a realisation of the importance of more intensive intervention in very disadvantaged communities (Department for Education and Skills, 2006b). The snapshot was also taken very early on in the life of a long term intervention, and there is plenty of evidence from local evaluation studies of the positive benefits for both parents and children.

Community variables have also been important in the evaluation of the Children's Fund, where positive outcomes were reported for children, young people and families receiving services, with success in meeting unmet needs at the level of individual children and families, but rather less success in addressing the community 'barriers' to social inclusion (Edwards *et al.*, 2006).

The first report from Ofsted on extended schools and children's centres was published in 2006 (Ofsted). Based on visits to seven children's centres, four secondary schools, eight primary or junior schools and one special school, the report states that it found that almost all the provision was effective in meeting the range of needs of children, young people and adults in the local community. The major benefits of extended services were the gains that children, young people and adults made in their self-confidence, improved relationships, raised aspirations and the development of more positive attitudes to learning.

The second year evaluation of full service extended schools (Cummings, Dyson, Papps, Pearson, Raffo, Tiplady & Todd, 2006) also provides evidence that such schools can have significant positive effects on children, adults and families, as well as providing benefits for schools (and, one might add, for children) in terms of improvements on performance measures, such as student attainment and exclusion rates, and increased intake numbers. The report also notes that full service extended schools were also able to take individuals through processes of change which re-engaged them with learning and had significant impacts on their life chances. This report, too, however notes that the positive outcomes of this work were not sufficiently widespread to transform whole communities.

And finally in this section the early findings from the research on pilot Children's Trusts, whose early findings point to the strong support that there is for the vision of *Every Child Matters* from children, families and professionals (National Evaluation of Children's Trusts, 2006). Realistically, significant improvements to outcomes will take time, but the report points to some positive measurable changes reported by professionals, such as innovative approaches to school inclusion which was correlated with a significant drop in pupil exclusions, and children at risk of harm or in need being identified earlier and dealt with more appropriately.

STRATEGIES FOR IMPROVING INTEGRATED WORKING AMONGST
PROFESSIONALS

The evidence from the studies cited above which relate to specific policy initiatives
also point to some clear strategies to improve integrated working for both senior
managers and front line workers. The *Every Child Matters* agenda is still relatively
new, and further studies are now underway – for example the Thomas Coram
Research Unit (Institute of Education, University of London) is looking at
interprofessional working in extended schools, children and family centres, and
Daniels, Edwards, Warmington, Apostolov, Brown, Leadbetter, Martin, Middleton
& Popova, (2006) are looking at interagency collaboration as part of a series of
wider Economic and Social Research Council (ESRC) studies. But there are also a
number of studies of multi-agency working predating the 2004 Children Act (see
for example Atkinson, Wilkin, Stott, Doherty & Kinder, 2002; Easen, Atkins &
Dyson, 2000; Frost, 2005; Percy-Smith, 2005; Robinson, Anning, Cottrell, Frost &
Green, 2004; Sloper, 2004; Statham, Cameron & Mooney, 2006; Webb &
Vulliamy, 2001). All of these studies are drawn on here in pulling out some of the
key messages about what facilitates partnership working, and what the main
barriers are.

Studies are united in pointing to the complexity and challenge of working
together and the time it takes to develop effective practice. There is remarkable
consistency amongst the studies as to what effective partnerships require in both
developing and delivering services through a partnership approach.

Developing partnerships and planning services

– Shared vision and purpose, and clear and realistic aims and objectives, which
  are understood and accepted by all agencies (Cummings *et al.*, 2006; National
  Evaluation of Children's Trusts; 2006; National Evaluation of Sure Start, 2005a;
  Percy-Smith, 2005; Robinson *et al.*, 2004).
– Strong and effective leadership and supportive management, with a multi-
  agency steering group (National Evaluation of Children's Trusts, 2006; Ofsted,
  2006; Percy-Smith, 2005; Robinson *et al,.* 2004).
– Careful planning to ensure long term sustainability, and an agreed timetable for
  implementation (Ofsted, 2006).
– Clearly defined roles, responsibilities and accountability, so that everyone
  knows what is expected of them and others (Frost, 2005; Robinson *et al.*, 2004).
– Commitment of staff at all levels of the organisation, and the involvement of
  front line staff in the development of the service.
– Developing common protocols for working together (Robinson *et al.*, 2004).
– A good communications strategy, with effective communication at all levels
  (Frost, 2005; National Evaluation of Children's Trusts, 2006; Robinson *et al.*,
  2004).

Delivering and ongoing management of services

- Time to build trust and develop respect within the team (National Evaluation of Children's Trusts, 2006; National Evaluation of Sure Start, 2005a; Percy-Smith, 2005; Robinson *et al.*, 2004).
- A lead co-ordinator, or project manager. Programme managers in Sure Start local programmes, for example, were crucial in holding together programme partnerships, and making collaborative service delivery successful. They were beneficial in incentivising the team and improving collaborative working (National Evaluation of Sure Start, 2005a) and this is reflected too in other studies.
- Adequate and shared resources. Studies of Sure Start programmes, Children's Fund projects and extended schools all make reference to the value of ear-marked funding (Edwards *et al.*, 2006; National Evaluation of Sure Start, 2005a; Ofsted, 2006).
- Recruitment of staff with appropriate experience and an enthusiasm for working collaboratively (Atkinson *et al.*, 2002).
- Joint training – important in developing a shared culture and developing trust and respect. This is also important for tackling issues such as managing change, working in new ways, and supporting the participation of children and young people (Percy-Smith, 2005).
- An organisational climate that allows for 'rule-bending' (Daniels *et al.*, 2006).
- Co-location often helps, though is not sufficient on its own (Robinson *et al.*, 2004; Vulliamy & Webb, 2003).
- Regular consultation with children and families to ensure that the services being provided are relevant and appropriate (Ofsted, 2006; Percy-Smith, 2005).
- Clarity on data collection and effective monitoring and evaluation of the service, in order to know whether the partnership is improving outcomes for children and young people.

Studies of multi-agency teams (e.g., Robinson *et al.*, 2004) point to the importance of valuing specialist expertise and celebrating professional diversity. The same study emphasised the importance of maintaining good personal relationships between team members and exploring the diverse perspectives of team members regardless of status. Working towards a shared language in team activities and service delivery was also important.

Challenges

The barriers to partnership working have been rehearsed over many years and most of them are the lack of the facilitating factors noted above. They include different status, pay and conditions between professional groups; different qualifications and training routes; different value bases, cultures, ideologies and traditions; lack of commitment and support from senior management; poor communication; lack of trust. There is an understandable tendency to see the world through your own professional spectacles, rather than being able to identify with the perceptions of either the service user or another professional. The tensions and contradictions are many and have been brought out in the studies cited above:

– The very considerable amount of time that it takes to get all the relevant partners on board (Cummings *et al.*, 2006).
– Constant reorganisation and uncertainty over funding (Percy-Smith, 2005).
– Frequent staff turnover, so that the approach is constantly having to be 'resold' (Percy-Smith, 2005).
– Difficulty in engaging with some partners in extended schools, and particularly in engaging with the most vulnerable and marginalised families, and involving them as local partners (Cummings *et al.*, 2006).
– The challenge of developing appropriate skills to work effectively with parents (National Evaluation of Sure Start, 2005a).
– The challenges of managing the size and pace of change and of changing the culture – people focusing on structural change instead of improving outcomes for children (National Evaluation of Children's Trusts, 2006).
– Tensions between long term approaches and the more immediate demands of the attainment agenda in schools (Cummings *et al.*, 2006).

Sloper (2004) notes that there is little empirical evidence on the effectiveness of methods to overcome barriers to change, but that there is evidence that shared learning in groups is effective in reducing interprofessional stereotypes and promoting better multi-agency collaboration.

IN CONCLUSION

There is considerable enthusiasm for the *Every Child Matters* agenda amongst the majority of professionals who are working with children and young people and a strong commitment to multi-agency working. Much has been achieved in a short time. Almost all local authorities have established Children's Trusts and appointed Children's Services directors well ahead of the government's timetable, and all have produced integrated children's services plans and begun to focus on the priorities for improvement in their area. Children's centres are being rolled out across the country, albeit with inadequate funding, and the development of extended schools is ahead of target, despite concern over the lack of resources and the overload on staff.

But three key challenges remain. The first is that despite the speed of change and the level of commitment, there is still too strong a focus on structures, processes and inputs, and too little understanding of whether these changes are making a real difference to children (Tiotto, Hutchinson & Pugh, 2006).

The second is that despite the growth of partnership working and a growing number of research studies, 'definitive answers to the central question of the impact of partnership working for children and young people are harder to find' (Percy-Smith, 2006, p. 321).

The research evidence also shows that, while partnership working is widely assumed to be a good thing, it can be difficult to put into practice successfully, 'It requires careful planning, commitment and enthusiasm on the part of partners and the overcoming of organisational, structural and cultural barriers and the development of new skills and ways of working' (Percy-Smith, 2006, p. 321). Given these challenges, it will be important to continue to monitor whether the costs involved in strategic partnerships bring sufficient benefits.

And thirdly, this is a bold vision and one which is tackling many complex and intractable problems. It will take many years to come to fruition. Is it sufficiently well embedded to withstand changes in the political system, or will a change of prime minister or political party or government require different priorities? Only time will tell.

POST-SCRIPT

This chapter developed from a presentation given in October 2006. Since then the *Every Child Matters* agenda has continued to move forward, receiving fresh impetus with the publication in December 2007 of *The Children's Plan: Building Brighter Futures* (Department for Children, Schools and Families, 2007). This wide ranging plan builds on the earlier reforms, with a stronger emphasis on supporting parents ('government does not bring up children – parents do') but also – of particular relevance here – reinforcing the central role of schools, both in improving outcomes for children but also as the focal point for integrated service delivery. Schools are seen as the heart of children's services, both for the education they provide and for their role in accessing other services and support – health and social care, support for parenting, access to more specialist services. Schools are seen as central to the Children's Trust and to the strategic plan for children's services; the Team Around the Child will be linked into schools; better access to Child and Adolescent Mental Health Services (CAMHS) and youth justice support is promised; and schools' contribution to children's wellbeing will be reflected in Ofsted inspections from 2009.

There is to be also a significant focus on early years, including enhanced workforce development for the sector, better joint working between the early years workforce and the workforce in schools, better transitions into primary schools, and a requirement to set up 0 – 7 partnerships locally, bringing together early years settings and primary schools. Recent figures also show that the development of children's centres in all communities is ahead of target, with nearly 3,000 now established.

Integrated working continues to be at the heart of the *Every Child Matters* agenda, and will impact on every single adult working with children, young people and their families, requiring a substantial cultural shift. A high quality workforce is seen as key to improving outcomes for children.

> Practitioners need to work together as an integrated workforce, characterised by professional respect and trust, cutting across service boundaries to fit services around the needs of children, young people and families. This will

involve working in teams made up of a range of people from different professional backgrounds. (Department for Children, Schools and Families, 2007, p. 153)

This does not mean that all teachers have to become social workers or vice versa. But it does mean that all professionals, including teachers, need to take account of children's well-being, and that all schools have in place systems for linking into other services for children with additional needs (Common Assessment Framework, lead professional etc).

The implications for the workforce are further spelt out in the latest government publication on the children's workforce – *Building brighter futures: Next steps for the children's workforce* (Department for Children, Schools and Families, 2008), which promises further investment in workforce reform, in developing integrated working, and in creating stronger leadership across the sector. A taskforce has been charged with creating and developing a vision for a workforce in 2020 that really will have a positive impact on outcomes for children, young people and families.

REFERENCES

Atkinson, M., Wilkin, A., Stott, A., Doherty, P., & Kinder, K. (2002). *Multi-agency working: A detailed study*. Slough: National Foundation for Education Research.

Bertram, T., Pascal, C., Bokhari, S., Gasper, M., & Holtermann, S. (2002). *Early excellence centre pilot programme*. Research Brief RB 361. London: DfES.

Boddy, J., Cameron, C., & Petrie, P. (2005). The professional care worker: The social pedagogue in Northern Europe. In J. Boddy, C. Cameron, & P. Moss (Eds.), *Care work: Present and future*. London: Routledge.

Cummings, C., Dyson, A., Papps, I., Pearson, D., Raffo, C., Tiplady, L., & Todd, L. (2006). *Evaluation of the full service extended schools initiative, second year*. Thematic papers RR 795. London: DfES.

Daniels, H., Edwards, A., Warmington, P., Apostolov, A., Brown, S., Leadbetter, J., Martin, D., Middleton, D., & Popova, A. (2006). Learning for interagency working. Working Paper, September. University of Birmingham.

Department for Children, Schools and Families (2007). *The Children's Plan: Building brighter futures* London: The Stationery Office.

Department for Children, Schools and Families (2008). *Building Brighter Futures: next steps for the Children's Workforce* London: The Stationery Office.

Department for Education & Skills (2004). *Every child matters: Change for children*. London: DfES.

Department for Education & Skills (2005a). *Children's workforce strategy*. London: DfES.

Department for Education & Skills (2005b). *Extended schools: Access to opportunities and services for all*. London: DfES.

Department for Education & Skills (2005c). *Youth matters*. London: DfES.

Department for Education & Skills (2006a). *Care matters: Transforming the lives of children and young people in care*. London: DfES.

Department for Education & Skills (2006b). *Sure Start children's centres: Practice guidance*. London: DfES.

Department of Health and Home Office (2003). *The Victoria Climbié Report of an Inquiry by Lord Laming*. London: HMSO.

Easen, P., Atkins, M., & Dyson, A. (2000). Interprofessional collaboration and conceptualisations of practice. *Children & Society, 14*, 355-367.

Edwards, A., Barnes, M., Plewis, I., & Morris, K. (2006). *Working to prevent social exclusion of children and young people: Final lessons from the National Evaluation of the Children's Fund.* RR734. London: DfES.

Friedman, M. (2005). *Trying hard is not good enough: How to produce measurable improvements for customers and communities.* Crewe: Trafford Publishing.

Frost, N. (2005). *Professionalism, partnership and joined-up thinking: A research review of front-line working with children and families.* Dartington: Research in Practice.

Glass, N. (1999). Sure Start: The development of an early learning intervention programme for young children in the UK. *Children & Society, 13*, 257-264.

HM Treasury (2003). *Every child matters.* London: HMSO.

HM Treasury (2004). *Choice for parents, the best start for children: A ten-year strategy for childcare.* London: HMSO.

National Evaluation of Children's Trusts (2006). *Managing change for children through children's trusts.* University of East Anglia.

National Evaluation of Sure Start (2005a). *Implementing Sure Start local programmes: An integrated overview of the first four years.* Report 10.London: DfES.

National Evaluation of Sure Start (2005b). *Early impacts of Sure Start local programmes on children and families.* Report 13. London: DfES.

Office for Standards in Education (Ofsted) (2006). *Extended services in schools and children's centres. HMI Report, 2609.* London: Ofsted.

Percy-Smith, J. (2005). *What works in strategic partnerships for children?* Barkingside: Barnardo's.

Percy-Smith, J. (2006). What works in strategic partnerships for children: A research review. *Children & Society, 20*, 313-323.

Pugh, G. (1998). Children at risk of becoming socially excluded: An introduction to the 'problem'. *In Comprehensive spending review: Cross-department review of provision for young children.* Supporting Papers, vols 1 and 2. London: HM Treasury.

Robinson, R., Anning, A., Cottrell, D., Frost, N., & Green, J. (2004). *New forms of professional knowledge in multi-agency delivery of services for children (the MATch project).* Report to Economic and Social Research Council.

Sloper, P. (2004). Facilitators and barriers for co-ordinated multi-agency services. *Child Care, Health and Development, 30*, 571-580.

Statham, J., Cameron, C., & Mooney, A. (2006). *The tasks and roles of social workers: A focused overview of research evidence.* London: Thomas Coram Research Unit.

Sylva, K., & Pugh, G. (2005). Transforming the early years in England. *Oxford Review of Education, 31*, 11-27.

Tiotto, J. with Hutchinson, R., & Pugh, G. (2006). *Getting our house in order: Better results for children and young people.* London: Improvement and Development Agency.

Utting, D., Rose, W,. & Pugh, G. (2001). *Better results for children and families: Involving communities in planning services based on outcomes.* London: National Council of Voluntary Child Care Organisations.

Vulliamy, G., & Webb, R. (2003). Supporting disaffected pupils: Perspectives from the pupils, their parents and teachers. *Educational Research, 45*(3), 275-286.

Webb, R., & Vulliamy, G. (2001). Joining up the solutions: The rhetoric and practice of inter-agency cooperation. *Children & Society, 15*, 315-332.

Gillian Pugh
Institute of Education
University of London
UK

DEIRDRE MARTIN

PART THREE
RESEARCH DIRECTIONS IN LEADING AND
MANAGING COLLABORATIVE PRACTICE

The context of integrating children's services into schools, although differing somewhat across the four countries of the UK, carries many similarities in terms of opportunities and challenges to leadership and management. Leadership of schools that integrate children's health and social services with education services, as in Full Service Extended Schools, must engage with challenges and opportunities to position schools for success in the future.

The chapters by Warmington, *et al.* and Hartley both draw on sociocultural (cultural historical) activity theory, a theory of organisational learning which has developed to interpret certain aspects of organisational epistemology. The particular interpretation of activity theory offered here is Vygotsky's and Engeström's perspective of learning, and learning in work organisations, which is used to interpret and understand the integration of services into schools. In this approach:

> Standard theories of learning are focused on processes where a subject (traditionally an individual, more recently possibly also an organization) acquires some identifiable knowledge or skills in such a way that a corresponding, relatively lasting change in behaviour of the subject may be observed. It is a self-evident presupposition that the knowledge or skill to be acquired is itself stable and reasonably well defined. There is a competent 'teacher' who knows what is to be learned. The problem is that much of the most intriguing kinds of learning in work organizations violates this presupposition. (Engeström, 2001, p. 137)

For Engeström integrating services into schools is

> a learning challenge that cannot be met by training individual practitioners and parents to adopt some new skills and knowledge. The issue at stake [is] organizational, not resolvable by a sum total of separate individuals. (Engeström, 2001, p. 140)

Engeström defines learning as being able to interpret our worlds in increasingly complex ways and being able to respond to these interpretations. He defines this as

J. Forbes and C. Watson (eds.), Service Integration in Schools, 93–97.
© *2009 Sense Publishers. All rights reserved.*

'expansive learning' and it is the driver for personal and organisational change. He sees activity systems as collective and orientated towards a problem, a 'focus of learning' (an object) and mediated by tools and signs (Engeström, Engeström & Vahaaho, 1999). The elements of human activity are the subject (learners), the object, and the mediating artifacts, the community, rules and division of labour.

Schools could be called 'well bounded work units' that are identifiable as communities of practice or functional systems, that could be conceived as a centre of co-ordination of learning activity. They contrast with the multi-organisational field of children's services and medical care which are much less bounded work units (Engeström, 2001). Practitioners often consider that learning at work and in organisations involves assuming the collectively-based routines, (that is, the forms, rules, procedures, conventions, strategies) around which organisations are constructed (Levitt & March, 1988). From the perspective of sociocultural activity theory, formation of routines occurs horizontally across and between providers of different provisions and vertically between management and managed within the organisational system. Boundaries are created by practitioners' routines. Boundary zones are learning spaces created across activity systems for boundary-crossing.

The main theme that emerges across the three chapters in Part Three is the notion of leadership, particularly distributed leadership at system and multiagency levels. Brown defines system leadership of service integration as a 'philosophical approach to the delivery of services for an area, community, family or child in a way that aims to transcend organisational and professional boundaries'. System leadership is underpinned by a set of leadership behaviours that includes distributed leadership arising out of system roles, where distributed leadership across heads, deputy heads and others encourages and facilitates other people's leadership and spreads the leadership focus. Using activity theory Warmington *et al.* analyse systemic change as vertical learning which demands a capacity to recognise and access expertise distributed across local systems. While Hartley, on the other hand, interrogates the notion of distributed leadership as a construct emerging from a complex of theories and discourses of marketing, work order and organisations.

The chapter by Paul Warmington and colleagues is entitled *Learning leadership in multiagency work for integrating services into schools*. It draws on evidence from a four year research project, *Learning in and for Interagency Working* (LIW) funded by the Economic and Social Research Council (ESRC), Teaching and Learning Research Programme (TLRP), on which the authors were collaborating. The project is orientated by activity theory as developed by Engeström, and involved the methodology of developmental work research (DWR) to engage multiagency professionals in reflecting and resolving systemic dilemmas arising from their interagency working. One of the LIW project's concerns is with what might be termed 'learning leadership', defined here as the creation of environments that foster the kinds of professional learning necessary to develop on-going, integrated partnerships between service professionals. This learning in and for multiagency working demands a capacity to recognise and access expertise distributed across local systems and to negotiate the boundaries of responsible professional action with other professionals and with service users. The chapter explores the nexus between professional learning, organisational leadership and service integration in the context of current shifts in English local authorities towards 'joined up' working. Its focus is the professional learning of organisations and individuals engaged in emergent forms of multiagency practice, wherein providers operate across traditional service and team boundaries to support children and families 'at risk' of social exclusion.

The second chapter, *Leadership and capacity in the public sector: integrated children's services and schools*, is by David Brown, Executive Director of Children's Services, Walsall, and formerly an Executive Headteacher in Birmingham. Brown discusses some of the implications for leadership, organisation and governance of services and schools stemming from multiagency working as initiated by the government's proposals in the 2003 Green Paper, *Every Child Matters* (HM Treasury, 2003). He argues that the complexities surrounding implementation at different levels within the system need to be understood in the context of other significant recent changes and developments. Current attention has often been focused on the most immediate issues for policy-makers rather than the long-term implications for practitioners of what is potentially a very significant change in the way in which statutory and other bodies may operate and work with each other. A brief review of the background to this, the outcomes and target-driven framework in which we operate is followed by some early examples of areas of multiagency work which many local authorities are focusing on with their partners. Finally, Brown discusses the leadership challenges and opportunities which this context presents for both 'system' leaders and for those more generally whose leadership, to be effective, will need to operate in a multiagency context outside of traditional organisational parameters. The extent to which leadership at different levels is prepared to use the opportunities presented by recent developments will be critical to the level of impact upon children and young people.

In the final chapter in Part Three, *Education policy and the 'inter'-regnum*, David Hartley offers a critical reflection on the discourses and logic of joined-up policy making and policy implementation, in a context of collaboration and inter- and multiagency working. In the UK the vocabulary of public services is becoming infused with the prefixes 'inter'-, 'multi-' and 'co-'. Hartley refers to this tendency as the 'inter'-regnum in education policy, by which he does not mean an interregnum in the sense of being between modes of governance, but rather he uses the term 'regnum' to emphasise that this propensity for the 'inter' is asserting itself as a fashion, a new 'reigning philosophy'. Examples of the 'inter'-regnum include the fact that public-sector agencies are being encouraged to adopt 'multi'- or 'inter-agency' configurations; 'workforce reform' seeks to dissolve once-impermeable professional boundaries; leadership is to be 'distributed'. Taken together these strands comprise a network regime of governance which parallels the existing regimes of hierarchies and markets. Why this 'inter'-regnum has emerged now is of interest. Hartley proposes three reasons. First, 'inter' discourses resonate with the culture of consumerism, and take further the earlier market-based regime of

95

governance which was associated with the new public management. Second, 'inter' practices are functional for the 'new capitalism' as a new work order of affinity and solution spaces. Third, the 'inter'-regnum has important intellectual supports: that is, in addition to its association with recent marketing theory, its philosophy emerges from recent theory and research in organisational learning, especially activity theory. Hartley critically reflects on the difficult task facing the UK government to legitimate its strategy of simultaneously weaving together into a seamless social policy two different discourses orientated by distinct philosophies: marketisation and hierarchies orientated by neo-liberalism; and network theory informed by social democracy.

Together, the three chapters raise a number of questions around the concept of professionalism and issues of professional knowledge, skills and identity which merit further study. Leadership within a multiagency team of practitioners working with children 'at risk' or with recognised needs, raises issues of professional identity, and beliefs (both cognitive and emotional) which may result in resistance to multiagency working. Is there evidence of disciplinary knowledge and practices becoming less 'owned' by particular groups, or of hierarchies of power being contested across and within professional groups, resulting in 'flattened' and more democratic hierarchies? What evidence is there for the apparent advantages of working collaboratively: and are there any discernible disadvantages, for example, in relation to loss of previous professional identity and specialist skills and knowledge? To well position schools and children's services for the future, engagement with the challenges and opportunities of such a research agenda would now seem timely and necessary.

REFERENCES

HM Treasury (2003). *Every child matters*, London: HMSO.

Engeström, Y. (2001). Expansive learning at work: Toward an activity theoretical reconceptualization. *Journal of Education and Work, 14*, 133-156.

Engeström, Y., Engeström, R., & Vahaaho, T. (1999). When the centre does not hold: The importance of knotworking. In S. Chaiklin, M. Hedegaard, & U.J. Jensen (Eds.), *Activity theory and social practice*, Aarhus: Aarhus University Press.

Levitt, B., & March, J.G. (1988). Organizational learning, *Annual Review of Sociology, 14*, 319-340.

Deirdre Martin
School of Education
University of Birmingham
UK

PAUL WARMINGTON, HARRY DANIELS, ANNE EDWARDS,
JANE LEADBETTER, DEIRDRE MARTIN, DAVID MIDDLETON,
STEVE BROWN, ANNA POPOVA AND APOSTOL APOSTOLOV

LEARNING LEADERSHIP IN MULTIAGENCY WORK FOR INTEGRATING SERVICES INTO SCHOOLS

INTRODUCTION

This chapter explores the nexus between professional learning, organisational leadership and service integration in the context of current shifts in English local authorities towards 'joined up' working. Its focus is the professional learning of organisations and individuals engaged in emergent forms of multiagency practice, wherein providers operate across traditional service and team boundaries to support children and families 'at risk' of social exclusion. It draws on evidence from the *Learning in and for Interagency Working Project* (LIW), a four-year Economic and Social Research Council (ESRC) Teaching and Learning Research Programme (TLRP) study of interprofessional learning in multiagency settings. One of the LIW Project's concerns is with what might be termed 'learning leadership': defined here as the creation of environments that foster the kinds of professional learning necessary to develop on-going, integrated partnerships between service professionals. This learning in and for multiagency working demands a capacity to recognise and access expertise distributed across local systems and to negotiate the boundaries of responsible professional action with other professionals and with service users.

Here we give an outline of conceptual and methodological issues that have emerged during the *Learning in and for Interagency Working Project*, which commenced in January 2004 and ended in December 2007. In the most recent phases of the LIW Project we have conducted intervention research in five English local authorities. The focus of the research has been on 'learning in practice' among education, social care and health professionals working within 'multiagency' children's services (Leadbetter, Daniels, Edwards, Martin, Middleton, Popova, Warmington, Apostolov & Brown, 2007). In each local authority our research methodology has been organised around a series of 'developmental work research' workshops. In these workshops researchers worked with children's services professionals to analyse the development of current knowledge and practices and, by identifying existing tensions and contradictions, to point towards new practices that might support the development of new forms of multiagency working. The aim of the LIW Project is to try to explain what and

J. Forbes and C. Watson (eds.), Service Integration in Schools, 97–107.

how professionals learn in multiagency settings across education, health and social services. That is, how does multiagency working change the practices and perceptions of services professionals? What tools, contexts and values support or challenge the development of 'joined up' working?

THE LEARNING IN AND FOR INTERAGENCY WORKING PROJECT

The Learning in and for Interagency Working Project (LIW) is one of 12 research projects that comprise Phase 3 of the ESRC's Teaching and Learning Research Programme. Directed by Professor Harry Daniels (University of Bath) and Professor Anne Edwards (University of Oxford). The LIW Project was conducted in the policy climate that produced *Every Child Matters* (HM Treasury, 2003) and the Children Act (2004). These policy developments addressed the needs of young people and families identified as being at risk of social exclusion. They called for 'joined up' responses from professionals and stressed the need for new, qualitatively different forms of multiagency practice, in which providers operate across traditional service and team boundaries. The LIW Project was concerned with examining and supporting the learning of professionals engaged in the creation of new forms of multiagency practice. Our research was driven by activity theory and informed by three particular concerns:

- the identification of new professional practices emerging within multiagency settings;
- the creation of new knowledge rooted in reflective, systemic analysis, which can be levered into more effective multiagency working;
- the location of emergent multiagency practice within an understanding of the changing character of service provision and user engagement.

Local authority interventions

In Stages 1 and 2 of the project the LIW research team produced an extensive literature review (Warmington, Daniels, Edwards, Leadbetter, Martin, Brown & Middleton, 2005), conducted a series of regional workshops with 17 English local authorities and began to develop conceptual models of professional learning. In Stage 3 LIW moved to a detailed examination of multiagency work practices via small-scale intensive studies in two local authorities. In the first the LIW team worked with a Youth Offending Team that included professionals from social services and probation services, plus police, parenting, education, health and drugs and alcohol officers. In the second the team worked with a newly created multi-agency project, a 'virtual' team comprising professionals from a range of services and agencies: social care, health, educational psychology, family support and CAMHS (Child and Adolescent Mental Health Services).

In its final stage (Stage 4) the LIW Project repeated this intervention research on a larger scale with multiagency groupings in three local authorities. This involved work in three multiagency settings: (a) an extended school; (b) a children in public care team; (c) a multiprofessional team comprising education and social care professionals. All three settings were characterised by shifts towards service integration in and around schools.

ACTIVITY THEORY

The LIW Project's analytical framework derived from current innovations in activity theory, particularly the work of Engeström (1987, 2001, 2004 and Engeström, Engeström & Vahaaho, 1999), who has studied the creation of new professional practices in public services. Like Engeström, we define learning as being able to interpret our worlds in increasingly complex ways and being able to respond to those interpretations. Engeström (1987, 2001) refers to this as 'expansive learning'; it is a driver of individual and organisational change. Expansive learning produces culturally new patterns of activity; it expands understanding and changes practice. Standard theories of learning fail to explain how new forms of practice are created and organisations transformed. How we respond as professionals very much depends on whether the workplace allows the responses that are necessary. We therefore argue that individual learning cannot be separated from organisational learning (Daniels, Leadbetter & Warmington, 2007). The LIW Project built on this view in two ways. Firstly, we looked at learning across traditional organisational and professional boundaries and not simply within one organisation or team. Secondly, we examined professional learning by following the object of professional actions.

Activity theory provides a framework in which to analyse these dimensions of professional learning. It is rooted in the work of the Russian social psychologist L.S.Vygotsky and his successors in the field (Vygotsky, 1978, 1986; Leont'ev, 1978). In essence, Vygotsky was concerned to understand human activity in terms of the dynamics between human actors (*subjects*) and the *tools* that they developed in order to impact upon aspects the world around them (the *object* of their activities). This is an object-orientated analysis of human activity; that is, its starting point is a desire to understand what it is that individuals (or organisations) are seeking to change or to shift. In the course of work in local authorities, therefore, we have asked different groups of professionals to explain what it is that they are 'working on'. When we ask this kind of question we are not just concerned with the broad outcomes that professionals want to achieve, such as, for instance, improving referral systems; we want to encourage professionals to explain the exact practices that they think they will have to transform in order to improve referral processes. It might be, for example, that they are trying to find a way to ensure that a child and family only have to complete one assessment form, rather than a series of forms. In this case the transformation of the assessment form process becomes the *object* of the activity; the various children's services professionals carrying out the activity are the *subjects*; their *tools* are the means by which they work on improving assessment forms (this could be anything from a new electronic entry system to the appointment of a key worker/case co-coordinator to a new diary system or any other 'tool').

In order to develop activity theory Engeström (1987, 2001, 2004, 2007) has focused on examining systems of activity at the level of the collective and the community, in preference to concentrating on the individual actor. This 'second generation' of activity theory aims to represent the collective nature of activity through the addition of elements such as *community*, *rules* and *division of labour* and an emphasis on their interactions with each other. An important aspect of Engeström's version of activity theory is an understanding that object-oriented activity is always characterised by ambiguity, surprise, interpretation, sense making, and potential for change. In short, when we ask participants in our research what they are 'working on' the answers we receive are complex, diverse and often contradictory. Engeström (1987, 2001) also emphasises the importance of contradictions within activity systems as the driving force of change and development. By 'contradictions' we mean structural tensions that emerge over time in organisational practices. These contradictions may constrain professional practice at certain points but they may also provide a source of change and development. For instance, in the LIW study we have identified numerous instances in which the efforts of different professional groups (such as teachers, educational psychologists, health workers, social care staff) to work on a shared object (such as the wellbeing of at-risk young people) have been shaped by the contradictions that emerge from having to work to different professional targets, referral thresholds and assessment procedures (that is, conflicting sets of rules).

DEVELOPMENTAL WORK RESEARCH

The LIW Project worked with children's services practitioners in five local authorities to examine and develop emergent multiagency practices. In each authority we organised our research around a series of workshops mainly involving operational staff. These workshops adapted the format used by Engeström in what he terms *developmental work research* (Engeström, 2001). This is a methodology for applying activity theory in order to develop expansive learning in workplace settings. Its value to the LIW Project is that it does not assume that practitioners are always learning to master stable, defined bodies of knowledge and skills; instead it focuses on the kind of 'process' learning required in many contemporary settings, wherein work practices and organisational configurations are undergoing rapid change and workers are creating new knowledge and new ways of working. Developmental work research-style workshops are apposite to research in current UK children's services settings, wherein policy demands for 'joined up' provision stress the need for new, qualitatively different forms of practice, in which providers must operate across traditional service and team boundaries. Developmental work research workshops begin with the 'germ cell' of individuals questioning embedded workplace practices and progressing through stepwise transformations towards new forms of practice. Building upon the principle of expansive, collective transformation, researchers work with practitioners to interrogate the deep-seated rules underpinning past and current work practices in order to point towards new potential practices. This cycle offers opportunities for reconceptualising existing activities and, ideally, for actively and collectively developing new patterns of professional activity.

In the final phase of the LIW Project we worked with multiagency groupings in three local authorities. In each local authority our research interventions were organised around a sequence of six workshops involving operational staff and operational managers working in areas of children's services. Prior to the workshops the research team collected interview and observational data that were later jointly scrutinised in workshop settings by researchers and professionals. The workshops enabled the LIW research team to examine practitioners' 'everyday' interpretations of the professional learning emerging in the shift towards multiagency working and the organisational conditions that support such learning (Daniels *et al.*, 2007). Using activity theory as a shared analytical framework, the workshops were designed to support reflective systemic analysis by confronting 'everyday' understandings with critical analysis of the ways in which current working practices/activities either enabled or constrained the development of innovative multiagency working.

In each workshop analyses of professional learning in and for multiagency working were developed collaboratively between the LIW research team and children's services professionals. These focused upon:

- Present practice: identifying structural tensions (or 'contradictions') in current working practices;
- Past practice: encouraging professionals to consider the historical development of their working practices;
- Future practice: working with professionals to suggest new forms of practice that might effectively support innovations in multiagency working.

The aim of the workshops was to address the challenges of multiagency professional learning by encouraging the *recognition* of areas in which there was a need for change in working practices and suggesting possibilities for change through *re-conceptualising* the 'objects' that professionals were working on, the 'tools' that professionals used in their multiagency work and the 'rules' in which their professional practices were embedded.

Multiagency working and co-configuration

Our research in Stages 1 and 2 suggested that forms of work currently emerging in multiagency children's services settings share something in common with what Victor and Boynton (1998) term *co-configuration*: the production of intelligent, flexible services with a high degree of client participation. This definition resembles innovations evident in some current children's services provision, wherein a range of agencies and otherwise loosely connected professionals coalesce to work with young people and their families. Co-configuration is, therefore, characterised by shifts away from compact teams or professional networks; children's services professionals working with particular families may not share a common professional background or values, or even a common physical location and they may meet quite fleetingly in a variety of configurations. Increasingly, children's services professionals may be operating on the cusp between new co-configuration type work and longer established professional practices. This is apparent in some of the tensions the LIW Project identified between strategic and operational practice, ambivalent attitudes towards interprofessional collaboration and changes in professional identity.

Distributed expertise

One of the pervasive features of the settings in which the LIW Project has worked is the emergence of distributed expertise. Multiagency service provision means that the case of an 'at risk' child is rarely the province of one 'team' but entails diverse professionals from education, social care, health and other agencies coalescing around the child's case trajectory. Therefore, issues of how expertise and specialist knowledge are claimed, owned and shared are important and often problematic. It is not only how expertise is distributed between professionals and around cases that is important; the emergence of patterns of distributed expertise has also prompted examination of professional values and beliefs and about learning to work with other professionals whose values, priorities, targets and systems might be different (Leadbetter *et al.*, 2007). In order to understand distributed expertise, it is important to explore the dynamic, relational ways in which professional learning and professional practice unfolds. One challenge presented by distributed expertise is the need to develop tools to support joint/holistic readings of young people's cases, wherein education and social care professionals try to address cases through parallel collaboration rather than producing 'discrete', sequential analyses of case needs. Our work with children's services professionals has suggested that the learning which is most critical, post-*Every Child Matters*, involves professionals grasping the deep-seated rules of emergent multiagency practice. Across the course of each workshop series participants have shown a concern to construct readings of current practices and have repeatedly emphasised processes of *coming to know* the potential networks or 'trails' of colleagues and resources; these may pre-figure effective multiagency working. These trails were more fluid and dynamic than formal teams or networks but suggested potential ways for practitioners to navigate their way around the distributed expertise existing in their local authorities and to utilise the resources contained in diverse professional expertise.

MULTIPROFESSIONAL LEARNING: BOUNDARIES AND TRAILS

The concept of *boundary-crossing* offers a potential means of conceptualising the ways in which collaboration between workers from different professional backgrounds might generate new professional practices (Kerosuo & Engeström, 2003). Standard notions of professional expertise imply a vertical model, in which practitioners develop competence over time as they acquire new levels of professional knowledge, graduating 'upwards' level by level in their own specialisms. By contrast, boundary-crossing suggests that expertise is also developed when practitioners collaborate horizontally across sectors.

Among the multiagency groups involved in the LIW Project the development of 'knowing who' trails has been a key element of effective multiagency working. This entails the building of knowledge about the kinds of skills and expertise other professionals can offer and a confident understanding of how to access others' expertise. In workshops practitioners have questioned the extent to which these trails work informally or need to be formalised through tools such as meetings, referral processes and information sharing databases. However, accessing distributed expertise is also dependent on professionals understanding the rules within which other professionals' practices are embedded. Contradictions emerge in multiagency activities because of contrasting professional values and also because different professionals may work to divergent targets, statutory guidelines and thresholds of concern. Therefore, boundary-crossing is predicated not only on knowledge of what other professionals do but *why* they operate as they do. Thus there is a need to focus on the ways in which professional knowledge, relationships and identities incorporate learning 'who', 'how', 'what', 'why' and 'when'. Moreover, it is important to explore the dynamic, relational ways in which professional learning and professional practice unfold. This means asking *with* whom practices are developed, where current practices lead *to,* where practices have emerged *from* and *around* what activities and processes new practices emerge. These are concerns which recognise that professional learning in and for multiagency working is embedded in fluid social and cultural contexts.

Tools, resources and systems

One of the ways in which emergent professional activities are addressed in our research is by examining the *tools* or resources that professionals draw upon and develop in order to work upon the objects of their practice. These may be concrete tools, such as case meetings or assessment forms or they may be conceptual tools. Other professionals may also become resources. In the LIW workshops professionals have been asked to present summaries of cases in which they have been involved. As well as asking questions about who was involved in each case and how the different professionals coalesced around the case, questions about tool/resource creation were also explored. In reflecting upon the practices that emerged around a particular case, workshop participants were asked:

- *What* tools/resources do you already have?
- *How* are you using them?
- Can they be used more *systemically,* i.e. built into the system?

The last question is central to our concern with learning in practice and knowledge creation in emerging multiagency settings. The cases presented by professionals in the LIW workshops surfaced multiple tensions in rapidly changing multiagency systems between the objects of practice, tools used to work on them and the rules within which practitioners operate. A scenario that has emerged in a number of instances suggests that professionals sometimes develop isolated innovations in practice that leave wider systems of activity untouched. For example, in a multiprofessional team with which we worked in Stage 4 of the LIW Project an educational psychologist and an education welfare officer worked beyond the call of duty with a child who had experienced severe bullying in her secondary school. Their informal contacts with each other suggested that they had laid effective trails that had enabled them to access each other's expertise. They also felt able, within reason, to bend referral rules where necessary in order to secure the wellbeing of the child. However, what was absent was any sense that their practice made a systemic impact on the school with which they were working. As such, they remained hero-innovators but isolates. Their practice was driven by expanding the object of their practice in an 'ideological' sense, so that the 'whole child' became their object, rather than just attendance issues (her absence from school). The wellbeing of the child, rather than the process rules of the school, was the key driver. The flexible, innovative practice that they produced addressed the immediate problem but there was no 'systemic' expansion of the object. In short, there was an unproductive contradiction between new multiagency practice and old system rules that remained in place. This suggested that, were a similar case to arise, its solution would again be dependent on the goodwill and heroic practice of individual professionals.

Similar constraints on systemic expansion were apparent in an extended school where our research focused on the boundaries between the 'extended' and 'core' activities of the school. Multiagency practitioners, such as counsellors, educational psychologists and health workers, were regularly called upon to address crises but this was largely a one-way flow across the boundary between extended services and the school; there was minimal opportunity for multiagency staff to inform broader school practices, which remained steadfastly orientated around attendance, behaviour and attainment objects. In short, there was little sense that school and services might function as equal, mutually informing learning partners.

Rule-bending

In the LIW workshops it became apparent that responsive, 'joined up' service provision often called for a degree of 'rule-bending' on the part of staff. Rule-bending occurred in cases where staff had identified the need for non-routine, partially improvised decision-making in order to meet highly personalised client needs and/or rapidly changing situations. In such cases professionals sought to ensure that local authority processes and routines did not unduly constrain their responses to clients' needs. We suggest that constructive forms of rule-bending rely upon the creation of organisational climates that support flexible, responsive action by professionals and promote learning for future practice from the ways in which staff have negotiated structural tensions between rules, tools, objects and professional identity.

Glisson and Hemmelgarn's (1998) study of the effects of organisational climate and interorganisational co-ordination on the quality and outcomes of US children's services systems offers noteworthy findings in respect of rule-breaking. They conclude that efforts to improve children's services provision should focus on developing positive organisational climates that are conducive to practitioner improvisation. They argue that, while high quality services are characterised, in part, by forms of process-orientation that ensure availability, comprehensiveness and continuity, 'process-related requirements for quality service are not necessarily related to outcome criteria'. In short, approaches that are overly process-orientated risk limiting 'employee discretion and responsiveness to unexpected problems and opportunities'. Their analysis indicates that improved outcomes for young people are strongly related to practitioners' 'tenacity in navigating ... bureaucratic hurdles ... to achieve the most needed services for each child' (Glisson & Hemmelgarn, 1998, p. 416).

We argue that organisational climates that allow for rule-bending have much in common with 'co-configuration'. That is, they are predicated upon highly responsive, highly personalised case work and customised relationships between professionals and young people that emphasise the need for client participation in planning and decision-making. Moreover, these climates are driven by results in relation to whole child wellbeing, rather than rigid adherence to process. Discussion in the LIW workshops surfaced the role that rule-bending (negotiating and challenging the structural tensions that exist in professional systems) can play in expanding professional learning in multiagency children's services settings.

Change and resistance

The LIW Project identified the considerable resistance to change that may arise when participants in our workshops have understood that they should make changes in practice and organisation but cannot yet engage with the processes of making changes (Daniels *et al.*, 2007). Our current thinking regarding this issue is being influenced by Vasilyuk (1991), who discussed such examples of inner resistance and subsequent actions whereby 'a person overcomes and conquers a crisis, restores lost spiritual equilibrium and resurrects the lost meaning of existence' (Vasilyuk, 1991, p. 10). This work directs attention to the affective dimensions of change which are too often under-theorised in studies of the development of new forms of professional practice. In Engeström's (2007) latest interventionist research he has noted that whilst individual practitioners were happy to construct new models and tools for changing their work, they appeared reluctant to proceed with implementation. This resistance to the construction of new professional identities presents a challenge to the overly cognitive orientation of much activity theory-based research. In the last year of his life, Vygotsky (1986) turned his attention to a new unit of analysis, namely, *perezhivanie*. This concept may be equated with 'lived or emotional experience'; it is a concept that we hope will help us to unpack the emotional dimensions of professional identity and practice in settings such as those we have encountered in our local authority sites, wherein new forms of multiagency working and new configurations of professional expertise are emerging (Daniels *et al.*, 2007).

CONCLUSION

The LIW Project was concerned with the learning in practice of professionals and organisations engaged in the creation of new 'joined up' solutions aimed at meeting complex and diverse client needs. The professional learning challenges that we identified demand a capacity to access expertise distributed across local systems, to negotiate the boundaries of responsible professional action with other professionals and, in certain instances, to push those boundaries through non-routine, partly improvisational bending of existing rules. These are forms of learning driven by a concern to support whole child wellbeing, rather than rigid adherence to organisational processes. Distributed, multiagency expertise is created when practitioners collaborate *horizontally* across sectors. However, it is likely that spaces in which practitioners are able to learn in and for multiagency working are only effectively created where there is also *vertical learning*, developed within boundary zones between *strategic* and *operational* levels of practice. Intersections between vertical and horizontal learning ideally support flexible, responsive action by professionals and promote learning for future practice by enabling professionals to negotiate structural tensions between rules, tools, objects and professional identity. Our observation of different ways in which professionals are learning to negotiate these contradictions continues to inform our research into learning in and for multiagency working.

ACKNOWLEDGMENTS

This paper draws upon on conceptual and methodological developments emerging from the Economic and Social Research Council (ESRC) funded Teaching and Learning Research Programme III study, *Learning in and for Interagency Working*, directed by Professor Harry Daniels (University of Bath) and Professor Anne Edwards (University of Oxford).

For further information about the LIW Project contact: Professor Harry Daniels, Department of Education, University of Bath, Claverton Down, Bath, BA2 7AY. E-mail: h.r.j.daniels@bath.ac.uk

The Learning in and for Interagency Working Project website can be accessed at: http://www.education.bham.ac.uk/research/projects/liw/index.shtml

REFERENCES

Daniels, H., Leadbetter, J., & Warmington, P. with Edwards, A., Martin, D., Middleton, D., Popova, A., Apostolov, A., & Brown, S. (2007). Learning in and for multi-agency working. *Oxford Review of Education, 33*(4), 503-519.

Engeström, Y. (1987). *Learning by expanding. An activity-theoretical approach to developmental research.* Helsinki: Orient-Konsultit.

Engeström, Y. (2001). Expansive learning at work: Toward an activity theoretical reconceptualisation. *Journal of Education and Work*, *14*(1), 133-156.

Engeström, Y. (2004). *New forms of learning in co-configuration work*. Paper presented to the Department of Information Systems 'ICTs in the contemporary world' seminar, LSE, January 2004.

Engeström, Y. (2007). Putting activity theory to work: The change laboratory as an application of double stimulation. In H. Daniels, M. Cole, & J. Wertsch (Eds.), *The Cambridge companion to Vygotsky*. Cambridge: Cambridge University Press, pp. 363-382.

Engeström, Y., Engeström, R., & Vahaaho, T. (1999). When the center does not hold: The importance of knotworking. In S. Chaiklin, M. Hedegaard, & U. Jensen (Eds.), *Activity theory and social practice*. Aarhus: Aarhus University Press.

Glisson, C., & Hemmelgarn, A. (1998). The effects of organizational climate and interorganizational coordination on the quality and outcomes of children's service system. *Child Abuse and Neglect*, *22*(5), 401-421.

HM Treasury (2003). *Every child matters*. London: HMSO.

Kerosuo, H., & Engeström, Y. (2003). Boundary crossing and learning in creation of new work practice. *Journal of Workplace Learning*, *15*(7/8), 345-351.

Leadbetter, J., Daniels, H., Edwards, A., Martin, D., Middleton, D., Popova, A., Warmington, P., Apostolov, A., & Brown, S. (2007). Professional learning within multi-agency children's services: Researching into practice. *Educational Research, 49*(1), 83-98.

Leont'ev, A. N. (1978). *Activity, consciousness, and personality*. Englewood Cliffs, NJ: Prentice Hall.

Vasilyuk, F. (1991) *The psychology of experiencing: The resolution of life's critical situations*. Hemel Hempstead: Harvester.

Victor, B., & Boynton, A. (1998). *Invented here: Maximising your organization's internal growth and profitability*. Boston, MA: Harvard Business School Press.

Vygotsky, L. (1978). *Mind in society*. Cambridge, MA: Harvard University Press.

Vygotsky, L. (1986). *Thought and language*. Cambridge, MA: Massachusetts Institute of Technology Press.

Warmington, P., Daniels, H., Edwards, A., Leadbetter, J., Martin, D., Brown, S., & Middleton, D. (2005). *Interagency collaboration*. Bath: University of Bath, Learning in and for Interagency Working Project.

Paul Warmington, Jane Leadbetter, Deirdre Martin
University of Birmingham
UK

Harry Daniels, Anna Popova
University of Bath
UK

Anne Edwards, Apostol Apostolov
University of Oxford
UK

David Middleton, Steve Brown
University of Loughborough
UK

107

DAVID BROWN

LEADERSHIP AND CAPACITY IN THE PUBLIC SECTOR: INTEGRATED CHILDREN'S SERVICES AND SCHOOLS

INTRODUCTION

Every Child Matters (HM Treasury, 2003) heralded a number of highly significant changes in the leadership, organisation and delivery of education and children's services in England. The aim of this chapter is to look at the implications of these changes for leaders in education and children's services more widely, with particular discussion around the place of schools. In this chapter I argue that the complexities surrounding leadership and implementation at different levels within the system need to be understood in the context of these wider changes and developments. There is a brief review of the background to this, the outcomes and target driven framework in which we operate and then some examples of initial areas of multi-agency work which are a focus for many local authorities and their partners. Finally, there is a discussion of the leadership challenges and opportunities which this presents, both for 'system' leaders and for those more generally, for whom effective leadership will need to operate in a multi-agency context outside of traditional organisational parameters.

Every Child Matters

The Children Act 2004 was one of the most far reaching and possibly most widely supported of recent Acts of Parliament concerning public sector delivery in England. The policy outlined in *Every Child Matters: Change for Children* (Department for Education & Skills, 2004) alongside the *Outcomes Framework* (Department for Education & Skills, 2005a) contains an explicit desire to achieve a 'radical change in the whole system of children's services' (Department for Education & Skills, 2004, p. 4) with a shift from intervention to prevention and an emphasis on services working together more effectively. These changes are far reaching in scope and especially so for the statutory or voluntary organisations who provide services for children, both for the internal operations and culture of such organisations, and more significantly in how they work in relation to each other. The creation of a Children's Trust in each local authority is one of the most significant aspects of changed organisational relations. Such developments stem from a variety of sources, of which *The Victoria Climbié Report of an Inquiry by Lord Laming* (Department of Health and Home Office, 2003, 'Laming Report') is

J. Forbes and C. Watson (eds.), Service Integration in Schools, 109–125.

probably one of the best known. However, it would be a mistake not to place this change in a much wider context than child protection as there are equally many systemic, strategic and operational issues which follow from the move towards more integrated children's services. There is certainly a leadership dimension which has a critical connection with the wider context of public sector reform and changes in schools.

Public sector reform

The current wave of public sector reform relating to education and children's services more generally, can be placed in the wider Thatcher-Blair[i] period of policy change which has seen some fundamental shifts towards accountability based target-setting and marketisation. Significant policy development provides a powerful context for such shifts. Whether or not one believes that this represents a set of integrated policy objectives or a response to a set of political-economic drivers, this has clearly represented a centre-driven, top-down model of change. Within the educational context, the National Curriculum, Local Management of Schools (LMS), and more recently the National Strategies to support school improvement[ii] and the Education and Inspections Act (2006), indicate this very clearly. What has been generally less developed is a sense of the organisational and leadership implications of this which are either implicit or a necessary part of the realisation of these changes.

In *Reforming our public services* (Office of Public Services Reform, 2002) the government set out four key principles underpinning its strategy for such reform of which the children's services agenda is one part. Two of these principles relate to (1) the role of the government in setting standards and developing a framework of accountability; and (2) the issue of choice and the flexibility of supplier – the implications of which I will consider through the role of schools as semi-autonomous bodies. The two additional principles highlight the integrated leadership and organisational culture aspirations explicit in their approach. These state that:

- These standards can only be delivered effectively by devolution and delegation to the front-line, giving local leaders responsibility and accountability for delivery, and the opportunity to design and develop services around the needs of local people.
- More flexibility is required for public service organisations and their staff to achieve the diversity of service provision needed to respond to the wide range of customer aspirations. This means challenging restrictive practices and reducing red tape; greater and more flexible incentives and rewards for good performance; strong leadership and management; and high quality training and development (p. 7).

In terms of Children's Services the recommendations of the Laming Report (Department of Health and Home Office, 2003) also developed approaches that require a leadership change at local levels. The report made a series of recommendations including the need to:

- Ensure services to children and families are properly co-ordinated and that the inter-agency dimension of this work is managed effectively.
- Develop strong links with community-based organisations that make significant contributions to local services for children and families.
- Appoint a director responsible for ensuring that inter-agency arrangements are appropriate and effective, and the development of services to meet local need.
- Ensure that gaps in information should be passed on to the relevant authority in accordance with local arrangements.
- Establish a 'common language' for use across all agencies to help those agencies to identify who they are concerned about, why they are concerned, who is best placed to respond to those concerns, and what outcome is being sought from any planned response.
- Disseminate a best practice approach.
- Establish an agreed plan to safeguard and promote the welfare of the particular child.

In parallel the Joint Chief Inspectors Report (2002, p. 2) recommended that all agencies:

- Take all appropriate actions, working to agreed local policies and procedures in full partnership with other local agencies.
- Develop integrated planning processes as an inter-agency priority.
- Ensure robust management information processes with a shared understanding across all local agencies.

Thus at the national level the aspiration for a different style of inter-agency relationship with implicit recognition of leadership at local levels to produce this was established. Subsequent structural changes facilitated by the Children Act 2004 occurred alongside additional developments at policy level. In all English local authorities from 2008, for instance, there will be a Director of Children's Services (DCS) with responsibility, accountability and the ability to direct all statutory agencies to co-operate in order to ensure and improve the well being of all children and young people in a local authority area. The Chief Education Officer and Director of Social Services for Children roles have been combined creating a single leadership role for education, social care, health, youth services, young offending and all other areas affecting the lives of children and young people, which is reflected in the roles of a wider group of leaders and managers in local authorities. Schools, although not covered as statutory partners and thus without being subject to a potential 'duty to co-operate', are now inspected under a framework which includes reference to *Every Child Matters* (HM Treasury, 2003).

There is now also a responsibility placed upon the governing bodies of all maintained schools to enhance the 'well being' of children, i.e. a responsibility in law beyond ensuring educational standards. Ofsted (Office for Standards in Education), is itself now the regulatory body for all aspects of children's services, where previously education and social care were split between two inspectorates. Both the existing local education authority, in place since the 1944 Education Act, and the structure of social services, are swept away as a result of this reform process with local authorities acting as the Children's Services Authority.

These developments clearly represent a very fundamental change in the provision of education and the integration of statutory functions relating to children and young people. However, these macro changes actually tell us very little about the realities on the ground and my intention here is to explore this new system architecture to analyse how leaders will face the challenges of 'multi-agency leadership' or system leadership in this newly reconfigured world.

POLICY AND CHANGE

Senior and middle leaders in the statutory agencies, schools and the voluntary sector operate within a complex political and policy context. They find themselves within an environment of considerable public sector reform, a culture of marketisation, target-setting and scrutiny which have a number of different drivers. In attempting to understand the dynamic forces which exist at a local level therefore it is important to set these within the national context of changes in overall government policy and especially to examine how this relates to education, social care and other children's services.

Education and children's services continue to form a very critical part of the policy agenda for central government as evidenced by the creation of the Department for Children, Schools and Families (previously the Department for Education & Skills). The Department for Children, Schools and Families has set out the *The Children's Plan*[iii] (2008, no pagination) with the ambitious aim of making 'England the best place in the world for children and young people to grow up'. The current work on the new Local Area Agreements (LAAs)[iv] for 2008 and beyond, which local authorities are subject to, will bring together all targets for all local authorities and partners, a larger proportion of which will be within education and children's services. Thus we have an area of policy littered with initiatives, very open to public and governmental scrutiny and one where the target setting approach of recent public service reform is very much part of the fabric of the culture.

This regime has, however, generated some contradictory forces at local level. In establishing the LAAs and the *Every Child Matter: Outcomes Framework* (Department for Education & Skills, 2005a), there is a ready set of targets designed to produce a more integrated response to improving the lives of children and young people. In part this has indeed resulted. However, aspects of the system of reporting, and the maintenance of single governmental departmental ownership of specific targets at the national level, has the effect of generating the intention of integrated working whilst at the same time creating powerful pressures to focus upon those key targets which impact upon each organisation and its perceived success or failure rather than the wider system. Schools, Primary Care Trusts and Local Authorities are all in their own way subject to this pressure.

In organisational terms the government's 'Choice and Diversity' approach to schools (see for example, Department for Education & Skills, 2005b) can be seen as an extension of autonomous school management initiated under LMS, and alongside the creation of hospital trusts, as examples of the perceived need to generate innovation and flexibility of provision for local delivery of public services. This approach occurs whilst the local authority, certainly in the case of the DCS, is moving towards a more strategic and commissioning role, rather than, as formerly, the delivery of services.

In the context of this movement in roles we see a shift of power to delivery organisations along with a shift in some responsibilities and accountabilities. Handy's (1994) 'loose-tight' analysis of leadership systems is probably pertinent here. Alongside a tight target setting regime we have elements of policy which aim to release local leadership to create the capacity to generate local solutions to some challenging social problems and issues. It could be argued that this is simply part of a shifting of responsibility and costs, or that it leads to a more effective targeting of resource. It does however, create for leaders the environment in which the challenge and opportunity of service integration around school and communities takes place.

Some current issues relating to service integration in relation to schools/education

Taking these developments as a whole, how can we begin to make sense of their potential impact and the need for change arising from the Integrated Children's Services (ICS) agenda from the perspective of public sector leadership and organisations? There are many different issues which need to be addressed in the development of a more integrated approach which affect schools either deeply or more peripherally. I have chosen not to highlight large and significant areas of work such as educational attainment, school improvement and child protection, all of which are critical and central elements of the role of the Director and the wider partnership but which are covered elsewhere. Instead I will consider some new areas of multi-agency work highlighting potential challenges for leaders. Some examples of current areas of work which have a connection to, or impact upon schools, are set out in Table 1.

Common Assessment Framework (CAF)
This framework is designed to engage a wider group of professionals including schools to understand and plan for the needs of vulnerable children and families without necessarily using social care as the first action. It will increasingly become ICT-based via the 'eCAF' and sits alongside the statutory development of an integrated database of professionals' involvement with children and families.

Table 1. Current areas of work which have a connection to, or impact upon schools

Policy area	Purpose/Detail	Agencies
Common Assessment Framework[v]	Establishment of thresholds for social care involvement and more co-ordinated family support	Education, health and social care
Integrated Youth Support/PAYP (Positive Activities for Young People)[vi]	Focus on reducing youth crime and Anti Social Behaviour	Youth and youth offending services, Leisure, Connexions,[vii] education
Extended Schools/services,[viii] Children's Centres[ix] and Sure Start[x]	From full service provision to family support. Preventative services in the community	Education, with some 3rd sector leads and potentially all other agencies
Looked After Children[xi]	Improved standards of care, decreased numbers in care	Social care, health, leisure and education
Family Nurse Partnerships and work on sexual health	To build on health professionals as frontline workers with families and schools	Health and education
Childhood and Adolescent Mental Health Services (CAMHS)	Support for the most vulnerable children and young people with identified mental health issues	Health led but increasing interest in looking more holistically at mental health
Post-16 Not in Education, Employment or Training (NEET)	Focus on reducing the NEET figure related to crime. Aspirational implications of NEET	Education in its widest sense. Social care interest in Looked After Children in EET, potentially all partners
'Voice' of children and young people	Developing a more coherent and systematised engagement with young people's views	All

This builds on some existing practices such as child protection networks, and existing relationships between police, health and social services, to which education and school colleagues, at least on the pastoral side of the school, are already connected.

Child protection has been a key driver of ICS change, on the basis of the much publicised tragedies which have occurred over recent years and the consequential comment on public sector delivery. There has been a recognition of the need to prioritise early intervention rather than just reactive prevention. However, for locally based leaders there are huge implicit pressures to focus resources and attention on child protection and family support and for this to be a central rationale for structural developments. There is both agreement on the need for a CAF in principle but also a concern by some in education that this is a shift of responsibility and accountability. The CAF both becomes a hugely useful tool for exploring professional spaces and shared knowledge and one that also potentially challenges practice very directly.

Integrated Youth Support, PAYP & NEET
This is an attempt to bring together the many agencies involved with young people. The significant national focus on this via the Youth Task Force, and the NEET agenda means that this is an area of a high expectation. There are, however, some considerable cultural and philosophical differences among professionals which become a central issue whilst attempting to establish co-ordinated action.

Extended services/schools, Children's Centres and Sure Start
This is the area where many schools will recognise *Every Child Matters* as having its greatest impact. How schools tackle the more challenging issues is one of the areas I discuss here, along with a consideration of how the wider system might capture the most innovative work. It is also an area that raises many professional boundary issues.

Improving the life chances of 'Looked after children'
This is one of the weakest areas in children's services nationally. The involvement of more senior level leaders and design of more holistic approaches co-ordinated across several sectors is now key. This approach aims to support practitioners in terms of designated teachers and key social workers who had previously championed individual children but had sometimes lacked the organisational/ agency influence to effect change and ensure effective support on behalf of the child.

Family Nurse Partnerships and Child and Adolescent Mental Health Services
These are both areas where traditional forms of work in health are moving towards a potentially more pro-active less clinically based model, whilst building on some traditional areas of multi-agency working between health and education in schools.

Voice/engagement with young people
A significant element of the Children Act (2004) centres on engagement with the child or young person themselves. The recent discursive shifts between individualisation and personalisation, and social and inclusive, professional and institutional elements, has implications for how new forms of working will be designed and scrutinised for effectiveness by young people themselves.

All this creates areas of challenge for leadership including issues surrounding professional boundaries and changing priorities, ownership beyond the school institution, resources, and facilitating engagement to develop new solutions and ways of working. How schools relate to this strategic environment will depend on the level at which they interact and the motivation they have to be involved. These initiatives produce generic leadership challenges beyond the 'normal' challenges of partnership within additional areas of activity. For example, the Cummings, Dyson, Papps, Pearson, Raffo, Tiplady and Todd, (2006) *Full Service Extended Schools Report* (FSES) explores how this is working on the ground, citing a case where

> [O]ne FSES appointed a schoolbased co-ordinator, held bi-monthly extended school management meetings for cluster head teachers, had regular multi-agency steering group meetings with representation from community members and students, had a working party to focus on a parental engagement strategy, and was in the process of establishing multi-agency operational groups (for childcare, sexual health and for PAYP) to drive forward developments in these areas. (p. 39)

Typology of school involvement in multi-agency work

Schools' involvement and experience of multi-agency working varies tremendously. Some schools already have well-established patterns of work with other agencies, others less so. The following typology considers the nature of such school involvement and the rationale from a leadership perspective.

Activity
– Case based: Individual child, child protection, family support;
– Agency based: Working relationships with health, Connexions;
– Area based: Newer relationships based around Children's Centres, Sure Start or local version of a Children's Area Partnership focus on transactional activity;
– School leader/manager relationship with external children's services managers;
– School led area initiatives;
– School leader involvement in local area/authority planning/strategic discussion.

Rationale
– Legislative, policy and statutory: This operates much more weakly as a driver down the system with the exception of areas such as child protection and more traditional school-social services and school-health services links. However, the Education and Inspections Act (2006) brought in the 'well-being' duty on Governing Bodies.
– Inspection frameworks and activity: work to support positive inspection results.
– Professional role: school leaders, both senior, community focused and pastoral, may see this professional role either traditionally or as part of 'children's services'. For some this might encompass the role of 'social entrepreneur'.
– Moral: given that much of the service integration agenda concerns the most vulnerable children and families, schools and school leaders/managers may be driven by a moral purpose to work with other services.
– Pragmatic response to service integration: for some schools especially in the most deprived areas there may be a belief that this will provide support and additional capacity/knowledge to assist in ameliorating some existing social/family challenges.

- Pragmatic response to resource availability: LMS commands a more efficient use of school resources, e.g. some extended use of the site can bring access to a variety of other funds and thus capacity for the school.
- Community focused schools: for some schools multi-agency work is a continuation of existing work and traditionally part of the ethos of the school.
- Impacts of marketisation: Extended schools as operated via extensions of nursery or childcare provision may, in part, have been driven by issues around competitive school admissions.
- Political: Schools operate within the micro-political context of the local area, there may be advantages for individuals or conversely pressures to be involved.

Service integration and wider children's services transformation, alongside the profound changes in schools, creates leadership development opportunities for a wide range of senior and middle leaders. Some local authorities and schools are consciously using children's services change as a vehicle for management structure changes and for giving a more strategic brief to individuals from a variety of professional backgrounds. In this, as in all change, there are leaders and managers who are seizing the opportunity to re-make their own role in the new context of a more strategic role for children's services and schools. As Cummings *et al* (2006) note, complex activities and partnerships of Full Service Extended Schools are characterised by multi-strand models of leadership and management.

We are beginning to see new relationships between managers in statutory agencies and senior leaders from schools and although only at an emergent stage it does indicate a shift. Such changed relations form the context in which future leaders will operate. The complexity and scope of the change agenda in children's services means that from a leadership perspective system leadership and distributed leadership become, whether by necessity or design, key attributes of the more effective work in this area (Harris, Brown & Abbott, 2006). These key themes are now explored.

THE LEADERSHIP CHALLENGE

Organisational co-operation and mutual dependence

Wilkinson (2003, p. 12) considers the rationale for mutual dependency if groups and individuals are to fully develop their inherent potential:

> Cooperation...allows for the full exploitation of the technical complementarities... and facilitates the sharing of knowledge necessary for effectiveness... (it) fuels the learning process by which new information and knowledge are created, incorporated and diffused, and by which new products, processes and organisational forms are developed. The resulting operational and dynamic efficiencies are crucial determinants of the ability of organizations (to be effective and) ... to respond flexibly to changing circumstances and new opportunities. These efficiencies are also important because they generate value added.

117

Many leaders appear to have an almost instinctive perception of the importance of these change forces, and successful organisations draw on this. However, a critical element in any system, whether related to public sector organisations, family, firm or nation is that alongside mutual dependence, with its advantages of cooperation, come issues of power relations, 'the exploitation of which could result in a retaliatory withdrawal from full cooperation and a consequent lowering of efficiency' (Wilkinson, 2003, p. 11).

Cooperation is very necessary and has evident benefits but clearly this is a critical issue where individuals, communities or organisations are, or perceive themselves to be, politically at risk. Few would publicly question support for 'partnership', which features high in the action plans of most parts of the public sector but the fundamental nature of the changes proposed to organisational practice in children's services are likely to generate 'change concerns'. Although the driving public sector interest of *Every Child Matters* will produce a moral momentum for change it would be naïve not to consider the implications for leaders, in schools at least, charged with turning a legislative and real moral vision into a practical reality, while at the same time operating in a climate where there is considerable scrutiny of academic standards.

All of those involved in any partnership work are aware of the potential for damaging forces triggered by moves towards change which impacts on individuals and organisations. Those concerned with parallel work in the 'adult' sphere have talked about the potential for 'Territorialism, traditionalism, timidity, tribalism, terrorism' (Lorimer, 2005) and McAteer (2005) discusses 'staff resistance' to perceived 'take over by social services'. Thus the challenge for leaders is to produce change for children and young people which adds value to the work of professionals rather than reduces the impact of services already at times struggling with aspects of delivery. Current factors such as those considered above can act to make organisations less likely to co-operate despite appreciating the long term benefits in doing so.

Leadership and service integration

We have seen a number of influences on both statutory and non-statutory agencies to operate together which go beyond partnership for mutual interest to potentially a way of working which will impact upon professional boundaries, career pathways, organisational budget plans and leadership. As Muijs (2007) has observed, the aim to improve outcomes for children, young people and families via partnership work and especially community orientated work is not new. In terms of education the 1970s witnessed the development of the community school concept in which adult learning especially, but also aspects of community orientated provision, were significant. In social care, the 1970s saw the inception of community social work following the Seebohm Report (1968). More recently there have been other aspects of policy development in relation to specialist schools and colleges, where there has been a more systemic look at provision and a wider role to effect change through a more integrated involvement of partners to improve outcomes.[xiii] Such policies collectively concern a strategic level of engagement between statutory agencies and communities. However, what is critically different in the current context is the overall and concerted policy direction underpinning *Every Child Matters* where many government departments in England including Department for Children Schools and Families, Department of Health, Home Office and Department for Business, Enterprise and Regulatory Reform (formerly Department of Trade and Industry) have collaborated, at least in theory and partially in practice, to create an outcomes and policy framework for multi-agency working in its own right.

I have discussed the aspirations to achieve multi-agency working at national level, but underpinning it at the local and regional level is the leadership required to make a reality of these aspirations. The implementation of multi-agency working requires a 'system leadership' or leadership which takes account of a role beyond one agency or institution, which moves beyond traditional boundaries. However, as Muijs (2007) has noted, there has been comparatively little discussion of the leadership implications of this.

System leadership and leadership development

The concept of 'system leadership' has developed, at least in the context of children's services in schools, to describe the need for school leaders to have a wider perspective of their role. Extended schools, federations and other new external relationships take system leadership beyond an expression of an idealised perspective to a set of potential and real structures in which roles might develop to be very different from those originally conceived when the parameters of each agency were originally defined. Some of this arises from the *Every Child Matters* agenda, some from the government's diversity and choice agenda and the new public sector and marketisation trend and there are tensions here which are being worked through. Although many such tensions are unstated at the national level, most leaders who operate across agencies recognise that different forces operate at national and local agency levels and possibly the first aspect of the leadership challenge is for this to be explicitly stated. Policy concerning admissions, inclusion, and the requirements placed on all schools by Ofsted, for instance, are some of the areas in which this potential tension between autonomous schools and integrated working may be played out, but there is no *a priori* reason why the forces which apply in terms of the typology given above will be different for schools enjoying different forms of governance relationship with the local authority. Schools may of course attempt to withdraw from local authority control but this will not necessarily be related to their status. A World Bank study in the USA (Patrinos & Sosale, 2007) for instance, describes those schools serving more deprived communities as more likely to engage in the Charter School movement (these are schools which are not affiliated with local school districts). In practice deprivation may be a key determinant of change to integrated working, alongside an awareness amongst the school leadership of how their relationship to external agencies is related to their vision for the school, and how successful relationships may support their core purpose. This view is endorsed by Cummings *et al.* (2006)

> The theories of change held by FSES [Full Service Extended Schools] leaders tend to focus on the role of schools in engaging with children, families and community members, overcoming the 'barriers to learning' which they experience, developing their commitment to learning and their sense of themselves as learners, and generating outcomes in terms of attainment, accreditation and better prospects in the labour market. Their expectation is that these processes will transform cultural aspirations and expectations across communities ... there is initial evidence that FSES approaches can be associated with benefits for schools in terms of improvements on performance measures (such as student attainment and exclusion rates) and increased intake numbers. (p. iv)

Thus vision, leadership, moral purpose and strong links to the community may prove to be longer term determinants of the extent to which some schools engage with other agencies. Caldwell and Spinks (1998) have observed that working in a major change environment, many leaders will seize a number of different strategic opportunities: 'In the midst of this turbulence and uncertainty...leaders must position their institutions for success in the future, for that is the essence of their work' (p. 197), and Stoll, Bolam and Collarbone (2002, p. 62) note that,

> Improving schools appear to have the capacity to take charge of change... more successful schools appear to be in the driving seat, setting their own direction, adapting mandates to fit their vision, colonising external education reforms. Successful school improvement is based upon an ownership mentality where schools define their own direction... the vision needs to come from within.

Some schools and school leaders will use the opportunities afforded by multi-agency working to establish a pro-active system role. Three examples which give a sense of the extent of multi-agency working in my local area are:

Bentley West School and Children's Centre, Walsall
The Headteacher is both the Executive Headteacher of two primary schools, one of which was subject to an Ofsted Notice to Improve, and runs a highly effective children's centre in one of the most deprived local government wards in England which demonstrates some excellent examples of multi-agency working.

Frank F Harrison School, Walsall
A cross-phase Federation involving secondary and primary schools, which has a significant emphasis upon community provision, again in one of the most deprived local authority wards in England. Family learning constitutes a key aspect of their work and a new build special school for children with physical disability is being constructed on the site.

Hamstead Hall School, Birmingham
The Assistant Headteacher, from a pastoral background, leads extended services integrated work at this secondary school and participates in macro level planning work in wider networks. The Assistant Headteacher for Sport fulfils the same role in the community sports partnership.

System leadership throughout children's services, is defined not by the size of the role but the breadth of perspective. In terms of service integration it indicates a philosophical approach to delivery which focuses upon area, community, family or child in a way that aims to transcend organisational and professional boundaries. Such leadership is underpinned by a set of leadership behaviours which are likely to include distributed leadership arising out of system roles. There are a number of pragmatic reasons for this link between system and distributed leadership:

- Wide ranging scope of role generally;
- Technical scope of integrated work necessitates a more open style, and the sharing of knowledge;
- Interplay of partners requires a level of emotional engagement unlikely to be achieved by single individuals;
- Complex change process – requires a championing of different professional and organisational contexts and system leaders at different levels will attempt to cut across boundaries and find strategic opportunities for professionals to want to cross boundaries;
- The growth of non-teaching staff in schools provides a further link and facilitates working in different forms.

Full Service Extended Schools (FSES) already demonstrate such principles. Cummings *et al. (*2006, p. 38) provide two examples,

> … [T]he model was one of distributed leadership with the head teacher and deputy head teacher having responsibility overall for FSES developments in school and other staff having responsibility for different elements. Here, the head teacher stated, 'To be a leader of an extended school you can't do it alone' and said that FSESs need 'lots of leaders' and a head teacher who, 'facilitates other people's leadership' and 'spreads the leadership focus'. Elsewhere, the entire school leadership team was being restructured around Every Child Matters priorities and outcomes, and termly meetings were held with partners from other agencies to plan delivery of outcomes.

Thus we may see in the context of greater system leadership in education, a larger community of leaders which will connect across agencies at different levels.

THE ROLE OF CHILDREN'S SERVICES LEADERS

The statutory role of the Director of Children's Services (DCS) has line management responsibilities for services around children and young people and a wide role in ensuring that health services, housing, leisure and so forth address the issues contained in *Every Child Matters* and co-operate to create 'joined-up' provision for children and young people which improves outcomes. This marks a change for the role of local authorities and signifies a shift in the power relations amongst different agencies given the statutory duty to co-operate with the local authority, acting as the Children's Services Authority. However, in practice this legislative 'sledge-hammer' is unlikely to be as productive as the leadership of effective partnerships and joint commissioning in order to achieve synergy and impact at the local level.

The DCS and senior staff have to build upon existing partnerships and create new ones as needed to effectively manage current work and create new approaches to integration and preventative strategies of which the Children's Trust model is one. Impact however will be profoundly affected by the extent to which the macro partnership has symbiotic relationships with 'local line leaders' (Senge, Kleiner, Roberts, Roth, Ross & Smith, 1999) and significant 'players', including community and political, at a local level. In the new agenda much emphasis has rightly been placed upon considerations of multi-agency working but it is the link to leadership in a multi-agency world which will create the environment in which such a multi-agency approach operates.

At the senior level there is a need to create strategic environments which give the space to innovate, facilitating sufficient 'buy-in' of key players, senior officers, managers from schools, health professionals, Sure Start, voluntary sector, police service and the wealth of other agencies and groups which support children and young people in some way. The leadership of significant organisational change in an external environment which is at times somewhat hostile and itself changing must, in the context of a wider vision for service integration, achieve a pragmatic acceptance of partners as well as a philosophical basis. Each local authority has created a system wide Children's Plan which should bring coherence to this work and provide a backdrop to action plans and priorities.

Key managers within the statutory agencies will need support to see their role in a wider and more strategic, or commissioning, role as distinct from a service delivery context. In the short to medium term they may have to ensure moves towards service integration whilst improving the delivery of targets, which (as discussed above) is where accountability systems are out of step with the new ethos at central government level.

Leaders will need to create a degree of coherence out of two fundamental areas of tension: school and system needs, and professional identities, which will require very clear and open dialogue about the issues and needs, pressures and specific challenges of different service areas, professional approaches, cultures and values, and where accountability lies. Such changes will necessitate confidence building as professional boundaries become blurred, whether between senior/pastoral colleagues in school, or between different statutory agencies: the role of the lead professional for each vulnerable child being especially challenging to practice and boundaries. However, in this context the ability of a wider range of local leaders to articulate a direction of travel towards more integrated working will be critical, requiring, as Bennis and Nanus (1997, p. 82) point out,

> a mental image of a possible future and desirable future state of the organization ... as vague as a dream or as precise as a goal or mission statement ... a view of a realistic, credible, attractive future for the organization, a condition that is better in some important ways than what now exists.

Finally, the sharing of professional knowledge has already become one of the key elements at local level of multi-agency leadership:

> Successful organizations access tacit knowledge...their success is found in the intricate interaction inside and outside the organization – interaction which converts tacit knowledge to explicit knowledge on an ongoing basis ... there is a link between knowledge building and internal commitment ... to make good things happen. (Fullan, 2001, p. 80)

Fullan identifies complex 'change lessons' in the context of schools, which most crucially concern behaviour and practices, and beliefs and understanding. For Fullan, alterations to behaviour and practices bring about deeper change, while modifications in beliefs and understanding bring deeper changes still. Thus for teachers, and for all professionals, service integration is about the difficulty of re-doing and rethinking. It is important for leaders to involve people in an interactive process to allow people to acquire new beliefs. It is also about leaders facilitating sharing of the knowledge, perspectives and challenges of those with immediate family, child and community experience often based in schools and in social work or health teams, without which multi-agency working is unlikely to be sufficiently grounded.

Overall, and at all levels, it is a leader's awareness of the forces at national level and their ability to use such knowledge to support colleagues' collaboration on target areas for service integration which are most likely to achieve practitioners' ownership and commitment.

CONCLUSION

The scale of the change in children's services necessitates the creation of a wider community of system leaders. At local authority level there is a clear role for senior colleagues from across education, health and social care to articulate and develop leaders throughout the system. This is about place shaping, about futures thinking and setting in context a vision for improved outcomes which start from the perspective of the child. Thus we may see the gradual rise of different forms of leadership, overlapping with existing institutional leadership in the context of creating and supporting both commissioning models to deal with particular social challenges, and frameworks around different models of professional working. Such

DAVID BROWN

new forms of leadership developing 'learning capabilities...skills and proficiencies that, among individuals, teams and larger communities, enable people to consistently enhance their capacity to produce results that are truly important to them' (Senge *et al.*, 1999, p. 45).

System leadership places its own challenges upon individuals and organisations and the development of distributed leadership cultures will be critical to facilitating types of integrated working that are effective in local areas. In the context of tight financial settlements for local authorities, considerable pressures on schools and a challenging external environment, there may be criticism that changing children's services is more concerned with efficiency gains rather than a holistic view of a child's development as an overall philosophy. In the real world of public sector economics it will in the end be for individual leaders to establish their moral compass.

> Tomorrow's successful leaders will value principles more than they value their companies ... and be deeply involved on a continuous basis in personal and professional development. (Covey, 1996)

NOTES

[i] A term which indicates a continuation of Margaret Thatcher's (UK Conservative Prime Minister, 1979-1990) Neoliberal policies in Tony Blair's (UK Labour PM 1997-2007) administration
[ii] http://www.standards.dfes.gov.uk/
[iii] http://www.dcsf.gov.uk/publications/childrensplan/
[iv] Local Area Agreements (LAAs) are currently voluntary, three-year agreements between central government and local authorities and their partners, which deliver national outcomes in a way that reflects local priorities. http://www.everychildmatters.gov.uk/strategy/laas/
[v] The CAF is a standardised approach to conducting an assessment of a child's additional needs and deciding how those needs should be met. It can be used by practitioners across children's services in England. http://www.everychildmatters.gov.uk/deliveringservices/caf/
[vi] The Positive Activities for Young People programme (PAYP) is a targeted programme which has provided diversionary activities since April 2003. Young people across the country aged 8-19, who are at risk of social exclusion and community crime, are able to participate in positive activities during the school holidays and access out of school activities throughout the year. Those young people who are most at risk are encouraged to engage in learning and/or employment with key worker support. http://www.connexions.gov.uk/partnerships/index.cfm?CategoryID=6&ContentID=384
[vii] A service providing 'Information and advice for young people'. http://www.connexions-direct.com/
[viii] Extended schools: Access to opportunities and services for all. A prospectus (2005) DfES.
[ix] A Children's Centre for Every Community (July 2005) DfES, Sure Start Unit.
[x] Sure Start is the Government programme to deliver the best start in life for every child, bringing together early education, childcare, health and family support. http://www.surestart.gov.uk/
[xi] Children looked after by local authorities
[xiii] http://www.standards.dfes.gov.uk/specialistschools/

REFERENCES

Bennis, W., & Nanus, B. (1997). *Leadership: strategies for taking charge.* New York: HarperCollins.
Caldwell, B. J., & Spinks, J. M., (1998). *Beyond the self-managing school.* London: Falmer Press.

Covey, S.R. (1996) *Principle-centred leadership* London: Simon & Schuster.

Cummings, C., Dyson, A., Papps, I., Pearson, D., Raffo, C., Tiplady, L,. & Todd, L. (2006). *Evaluation of the full service extended schools initiative, second year. Thematic papers.* University of Manchester/DfES Research Paper RR795.

Department for Education & Skills (2005a). *Every child matters: Outcomes framework.* London: Her Majesty's Stationery Office. Available: http://www.everychildmatters.gov.uk/aims/outcomes/

Department for Education & Skills (2005b). *Higher standards, better schools for all, more choice for parents and pupils.* London: Her Majesty's Stationery Office.

Department for Education & Skills (2004). *Every child matters: Change for children.* London: HMSO.

Department of Health & Home Office (2003). *The Victoria Climbié Report of an inquiry by Lord Laming.* London: HMSO.

Fullan, M. (2001). *Leading in a culture of change.* San Francisco: Jossey-Bass.

Handy, C. (1994). *The Empty Raincoat: Making Sense of the Future.* London: Hutchinson.

Harris, A., Brown, D., & Abbott, I. (2006). Executive leadership: another lever in the system? *School Leadership and Management, 26*(4), 397-409.

HM Treasury (2003). *Every child matters.* Green paper. London: HMSO.

Joint Chief Inspectors. (2002). *Safeguarding children. A joint chief inspectors' report on arrangements to safeguard children.* London: Department of Health.

Lorimer, P. (2005). Models of partnership – The 'nuts & bolts' of integration. Presentation at Integrated Care Network Midlands Conference, Feb. 2005.

McAteer, K. (2005). Walsall integrated learning disability service. Presentation at Integrated Care Network Midlands Conference, Feb. 2005.

Muijs, D. (2007). Leadership in full-service extended schools: communicating across cultures. *School Leadership and Management, 27*(4), 347-362.

Office of Public Sector Reform (2002). *Reforming our Public Services.* Available: www.pm.gov.uk/output/page257.asp (Accessed: 05/08/2008)

Patrinos, H.A., & Sosale, S. (2007). *Mobilizing the private sector for public education.* World Bank Publications.

Seebohm, F. (1968). Report of the Committee on Local Authority and Allied Personal. Social Services (the Seebohm Report). London: HMSO.

Senge, P., Kleiner, A., Roberts, C., Roth, G., Ross, R., & Smith, B. (1999). *The dance of change: The challenges to sustaining momentum in learning organizations.* New York: Doubleday.

Stoll, L., Bolam, R., & Collarbone, P. (2002.) Leading for change: Building capacity for learning. In: K. Leithwood, & P. Hallinger (Eds.), *Second international handbook of educational leadership and administration* (pp 41-73). Dordrecht: Kluwer Academic Publishers.

Wilkinson, F. (2003). Productive systems and the structuring role of economic and social theories. In Burchell, B.J., Deakin, S., Michie, J., & Rubery, J. (Eds.), *Systems of production: Markets, organizations and performance* (pp. 10-39). London: Routledge.

David Brown
Executive Director of Children's Services
Walsall
UK

DAVID HARTLEY

EDUCATION POLICY AND THE 'INTER'-REGNUM

INTRODUCTION

There is an increasing trend for collaboration and partnership in education. Joined-up policy-making is prompting joined-up policy implementation. In the UK, the vocabulary of public services is becoming infused with the prefixes 'inter'-, 'multi'- and 'co'-. Public-sector agencies are being encouraged to adopt 'multi'- or 'inter-agency' configurations; 'workforce reform' seeks to dissolve once-impermeable professional boundaries; leadership is to be 'distributed'. More generally, networks of affiliation abound. I refer to this tendency as the 'inter'-regnum in education policy. (This does not mean an *interregnum* in the sense of being *between* modes of governance.) I use the term 'regnum' to emphasise that this propensity for the 'inter' is asserting itself as a fashion, a new 'reigning philosophy' (Tyack & Hansot, 1982, p. 158). The purpose here is twofold. First, I present examples of the 'inter'-regnum from the Prime Minister's Strategy Unit (2006), and I locate this conceptually within Thompson's (2003) analysis of hierarchies, markets and networks. Second, I shall consider the cultural, intellectual and economic contexts which allow for the 'inter'-regnum to emerge as policy.

In 1990, Chubb and Moe published their influential work *Politics, markets and America's schools*. Their broad conclusion, based on a secondary analysis of the *High school and beyond* data-set,[i] was that the public (that is, the state) schools of America were overly constrained by external bureaucratic controls from school boards and state legislatures, unlike their private school counterparts, whose endeavours were driven more by the consumers who paid for them. The higher levels of academic achievement within private schools could be attributed to the relatively low levels of external bureaucratic interference therein. Notwithstanding strong criticism (Goldstein, 1993), Chubb and Moe's work arguably strengthened the ideological current taking schools towards the market. In sum, the 'market' became an emerging regime of governance in education, purporting to replace an allegedly more self-serving bureaucratic model. That said, the expansion of an audit culture did nothing to 'free' the market or to lessen central administrative control: highly bureaucratic procedures, such as national testing, were adopted in order to provide would-be 'customers' with the objective information which would allow them to compare different providers. Of late, a new 'network' mode of governance and regulation is beginning to emerge. It comprises one of three governance regimes typified by Thompson (2003). Figure 1 presents Thompson's typology.

J. Forbes and C. Watson (eds.), Service Integration in Schools, 127–140.

	Hierarchical order	Market order	Network order
Type of order envisaged:	Designed and consciously organised outcomes	Spontaneously generated outcomes	Designed outcomes; or spontaneously generated outcomes
Behavioural agents:	Rule-driven and active authoritative inputs	Private competitive decisions	Cooperation and consensus seeking
Mechanism of operation:	Hierarchically organised bureaucratic administration/ monitoring/scrutiny/ interventions	Price mechanism, competition self-interest, self-regulation	Loyalty, reciprocity and trust
Type of overall coordination or governance offered:	Overt, purposeful guidance and 'active governance' *ex ante* coordination	Unseen 'guiding hand', 'non-governance' but *ex post* coordination	Formally organised coordination and governance; or 'self-organised' informal 'non-governance'

Figure 1. Types of governance regimes (after Thompson, 2003, table 2.1, p. 490)

Thompson's typology maps very neatly onto the UK government's recent working document on the reform of the public services (Prime Minister's Strategy Unit, 2006, p. 6), depicted in Figure 2. The government's new 'model of public service reform' comprises a mutually-supportive amalgamation of bureaucracy, markets and (now) inter-agency working. To elaborate: rather than set bureaucracy and markets against each other, the government has continued to combine them, elaborating upon the complementarity of the 'citizen' and the 'consumer', the 'public' and the 'private'. In the government's model, 'top down performance and management' reveals itself in 'targets, regulation, inspection and intervention'. This accords with Thompson's *hierarchy* regime of governance. The government's 'market incentives to increase efficiency and quality of services' and its 'users shaping the services from below' both correspond to Thompson's *market* regime of governance. And thirdly, the government's 'capability and capacity' approximates Thompson's *network* regime of governance. The government's model implies a consensus: bureaucracy, markets and networks are in mutual adjustment, each segment being functional for the others, all in self-improving harmony, acting in concert to provide better public services for all. That is the direction of policy.

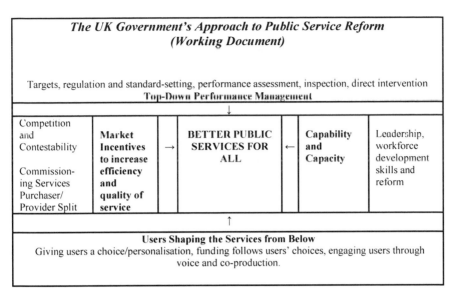

Figure 2. Adapted from Prime Minister's Strategy Unit (2006, p. 6) The UK Government's Approach to Public Service Reform (Working Document): Chart A: The UK government's model of public service reform: a self-improving system

Thompson's market-based model, which is conceptually close to the 'new public management' model depicted in Figure 3, privileges the consumer as an individual who chooses (after being informed) from what is on offer. In this, the stress is on *individual* choice, and on a *separation* between consumer and provider. It associates the customer with the term 'service user'. But the government has now elaborated upon this: it has introduced *personalisation*. This is a stronger version of 'customer', for it is a customer who is an active proponent of what she or he wants: that is to say, the customer is not simply a chooser of what is on offer. Personalisation, in turn, may require some form of networked multi-agency working so that personalised needs can be met. In other words, personalisation – notwithstanding the implication of individual choosing – requires for its implementation not a separation between customer and provider, but two kinds of *co*-production: first, that between customer and provider so as to identify the need; and second, if it be deemed necessary to the success of a solution, a co-production among the providers themselves in some kind of networked configuration of inter-agency working.

In order to achieve effectively the personalised needs or wants of the individual, new solution spaces which cut across existing organisational structures might need to be configured – hence the emphasis on inter- and multi-agency arrangements. Policy documents such as *Every child matters* (HM Treasury, 2003) or (in Scotland) *Report of the Joint Future Group* (Scottish Executive, 2000), exemplify this 'inter'-regnum as a way of accomplishing personalised needs. Structural arrangements have been formed which give a new institutional status to this trend, as in 'integrated children's services', and the 'children's index'." 'Extended schools' (Department for Education and Skills, 2005) and 'workforce remodelling' (Tabberer, 2005) are other enabling processes. Having introduced the concept of 'inter'-regnum, I turn now to consider why, now, it has currency. That is to say, what are the cultural, economic and intellectual contexts which are allowing for its expression as policy? Each is discussed below, in turn.

	New Public Management	Personalisation
Ethos	Market-based	Democratic, personalised, user-centric
Users	Consumers, some self-service	Co-producers, creating solutions with professionals
Delivery model	Contracted services	Mixed market of providers. Solutions assembled from a variety of sources around user needs.
Performance objective	Inputs and outputs managed for efficiency	Multiply-agreed with stakeholders, users, including user-experience and social value.
Professional role	Commission and monitor	Adviser, broker, advocate, solutions assembler
Accountability	To politician and users through market comparisons and contracts	To users directly as well as taxpayers, stakeholders and politicians

Figure 3. Models of public service provision (adapted from Leadbeater, 2004, pp. 62-65)

CULTURE AND THE 'INTER'-REGNUM

Late modernity has borne witness to the dissolution of once-rigid classifications. Bauman, for example, assigns the adjective 'liquid' to this tendency, as in 'liquid modernity' (Bauman, 2000). This is in contrast to the once-'solid' modernity which preceded it, what Foucault referred to as a 'disciplinary society', a society of 'enclosures' wherein the individual moved from one discrete space to another: from the family to the school, thence to the military barracks, or to the factory; perhaps, occasionally, to the hospital or to the prison (Deleuze, 1992). These well-demarcated spaces – these enclosures – had their own rhythms, rationales and rituals. But now the points of reference used by individuals and groups to plot their life-courses during the 'solid' modern period – that is, in the period of disciplinary power – are disappearing. The pessimism is considerable: the quest for certainty and stability, and the adherence to fixed boundaries and classifications – both now seem to be slipping out of reach (Bauman, 2000, p. 22). Life is to be lived provisionally (Melucci, 1996, p. 22). The 'environments of enclosure' – prisons, hospitals, factories and schools – are all under constant revision and reform. This is especially the case for the school which is said to be in 'an advanced state of decay' (Touraine, 2000, p. 37; see also, Kiziltan, 1990, p. 358). So public institutions which in the modern age had given us a sense of belonging and certainty, are in decline, even 'finished' (Deleuze, 1992, no pagination).

Alternative sources of what Durkheim (1995 [1912]) called 'collective effervescence' are now being sought. There is a pre-modern atavistic tendency towards communities whose basis is an appeal to the non-rational, to the emotional; as in a fondness for drugs, gambling, astrology, nationalism and nature. Now even management theory refers to missions, enchantments, visions, passion and transformations – all of them arguably rational appropriations of the nonrational (Hartley, 2004). Some of these trends are referred to in a recent analysis of *Currents in British Society* by the MORI polling organisation. They include: a 'growing gap between institutions and people'; a 'move from self-centredness to autonomy'; a 'flow from ideology to more meaning in life'; a trend 'from organized social structure to network culture'; and a 'drifting from [the] rational to polysensuality' (Page, 2006, unpaginated). All this raises a question: '[....] how can we live together in a society that is increasingly divided up into networks that instrumentalize us, and into communities that imprison and prevent us from communicating with others?' (Touraine, 2000, p. 14). Put another way, at one and the same time we are witnessing economic globalisation and harmonisations, on the one hand, and a quest to *belong* to communities rather than *use* networks for a performative or instrumental purpose, on the other. Whilst a globalised economy may be typified by networks, these networks tend neither to be permanent nor deep. They are calculative. They are associations, not communities.

But this pessimism may be over-stated. It can be argued that what is occurring is not so much a *de*-institutionalisation, but a *re*-institutionalisation. Here enters the 'inter'-regnum, which was discussed earlier. That is to say, institutional structures can be rendered more open, less enclosed; and this is both within and among organisations. There are now looser, ephemeral and more widespread 'connections'. These looser connections – Gee (2004, pp. 98-99) refers to them as 'affinity systems' – are typified by weak communal ties, largely devoid of 'bonding'. Within liquid modernity, power is conferred on those whose identities and interactions are fluid and ephemeral, fast and loose. In sum, the weakening of all forms of classification; the rise of the network society; the trends towards de-socialisation and towards de- or re-institutionalisation – all of them are signs of contemporary culture. Public policy is beginning to go with the grain of that culture (Hood, 2000, p. 178). Multi-agency and inter-agency working – arrangements which are often short-lived 'projects' and which have no clear geographical 'location' – strike a chord with the flexible 'liquid modern' view of time and space. So much for the cultural 'context' of the 'inter'-regnum. I consider below the economic context.

The 'new' capitalism and the 'inter'-regnum

Production during the past 100 years has been largely along Fordist lines: mass production typified by routine and the repetition of tasks. That is now changing. In what Gee *et al.* (1996) call the 'new work order', or the 'new capitalism' (Gee, 2000), workers are required to be 'self-programmable', able to re-train themselves, able to adapt to new projects and processes (Castells, 2000, p. 12). What is central to the production process of the new capitalism are not commodities, but design: how to design and market new 'identities', 'affinity spaces' and 'networks' (Gee, 2004, p. 97). An affinity space is:

> a place (physical, virtual, or a mixture of the two) wherein people interact with each other, often at a distance...primarily through shared practices or common endeavour ... and only secondarily through culture, gender, ethnicity, or face-to-face relationships. (Gee, 2004, p. 98)

Logically, the new work order requires that schools will prepare young people for it. But there remains a continuing mismatch between the new work order and classroom pedagogy. There are few examples of a 'productive pedagogy' which anticipates the 'new work order' (Hartley, 2003; Lingard, Hayes & Mills, 2003); rather there is strong evidence of a continuing 'transmission' pedagogy (Hardman, Smith & Wall, 2003) as schools remain mindful of their performance and place within national league-tables. The classroom rewards individual, not distributed, knowledge; pupils usually work alone, not in groups, not in a common endeavour. Knowledge is gained from a limited repository, often the book, or the teacher. Tacit knowledge – which, by definition, is not expressed formally – is given little recognition (Gee, 2004, p. 89). The contemporary classroom is no affinity space: the pedagogical mismatch between the work regime of the new capitalism and the school classroom is considerable. Similarly, the school itself – notwithstanding calls for 'distributed leadership' – is not, paradoxically, a learning organisation, although there have been calls for it to become so (Hargreaves, 1999). Classrooms remain locked into Bauman's 'solid modernity', their 'grammar' resolutely rooted in the 'old capitalism' of mass production and bureaucracy (Tyack & Tobin, 1994).

To return to the 'new capitalism': just as patterns of production are changing, so too are those of consumption. In the age of mass-production, mass-consumption had prevailed. Later came mass-customisation: that is, as a result of market-surveys, or surveys of customer satisfaction, producers attempted to give consumers what, in the aggregate, they had said they wanted. No longer does that suffice. Those who have met their subsistence needs now wish to express themselves, to reveal their preferred identity, to gain a stylistic edge over others, symbolically, through the goods and services which they buy. To focus only on the supply-side will not do: instead, a co-creation – a 'direct involvement in the production process by what we still call the consumer' – is now required (Miller, 2003, p. 117). An *inter*-relationship between the customer and the producer is called for: that is, a *co-production* [see Figure 3] between the customer and the provider, a relationship which brings satisfaction to the former and profit for the latter. It has resonance with that concept which is acquiring some currency within

UK public policy: *personalisation*, which was referred to earlier, and which will be considered again later. Suffice it to state here that, in order both to define and to meet the personalised needs of consumers, it may be necessary to construct inter-agency configurations to serve as networked productive 'spaces'. These spaces may intersect both private and public agencies, a structural isomorphism emerging within both. In the production process within the 'new capitalism' in its new work order – the prefix 'inter' assumes a crucial significance, for it privileges the network and the team over the fixed role and the individual who fills it. Fluid affinity spaces become the new solution spaces. They can be real or virtual; or both. And now, too, the old demarcation between producer and customer is becoming weakened, for there is to be an inter-relationship between the two, as they are said to come together in a new continuing collaboration of co-production, a process referred to as personalisation (Leadbeater, 2004).

Intellectual movements and the 'inter'-regnum

It has been argued so far that contemporary culture reveals a number of trends: *socially*, towards de-socialisation and towards looser connections, or to calculative affinities and networks; and *temporally*, towards ephemerality. In general terms, the social, spatial and temporal demarcations within the 'solid' modern period have weakened. After Gee, and secondly, I have suggested that the 'new' capitalism (or, if preferred, Bauman's 'liquid modernity') has strong elective affinities to these cultural trends.

The 'inter'-regnum has an intellectual and epistemological dimension. One aspect of it is what Gee (2000) refers to as the 'social turn'. The social turn was in part a reaction against the emphasis on the individual mind which was central both to behaviourism and (later) to cognitive science. In particular, he argues that meaning and context are mutually constitutive of each other – a social interaction. He includes within the social turn the following disciplinary configurations: sociohistorical psychology (Wertsch, 1991); situated cognition (Lave, 1996); recent evolutionary work on the relationship between mind and environment (Clark, 1997); and new studies of science, technology and society (Latour, 1991). Gee states that work on sociocultural approaches to literacy and to related aspects of education often include references to many of the strands within the 'social turn' movement. Contained within the social turn are theoretical insights into *how* the 'inter'-regnum in public policy can be implemented. Specifically, I consider here – very briefly – one theory which is incorporated within the social turn, namely sociocultural activity theory, a theory which has relevance for the *implementation* of the 'inter'-regnum.

In order to implement personalisation, the government has belatedly drawn upon theories of organisational epistemology, or organisational learning. Noteworthy is Engeström's theory of 'expansive learning', or 'knotworking' (Engeström, 2000, 2004).[iii] The theory cannot be explored fully here, but what is being pointed up is its potential use in the furtherance of multi-agency, networked services provision. Engeström's expansive learning is based upon a seven-stage ideal-typical

DAVID HARTLEY

'expansive cycle'. Engeström's first stage consists of the *questioning* of current practice within a collective activity system. Before discussing the subsequent six stages, I shall refer briefly to the meaning of *activity system*, and to the concepts which comprise it . There are a number of dimensions to an activity system. The *subject* of the activity system comprises the individual or sub-group, which brings its gaze and intention to the *object*; or, crudely, that which the 'subject' is working on. So the 'object' itself is not a goal, fixed and formal. It is 'a heterogeneous and internally contradictory, yet enduring, constantly reproduced purpose of a collective activity system that motivates and defines the horizons of possible goals and actions ... The object is projective and transitory, truly a moving horizon' (Engeström, 2004, p. 6). The object, therefore, is that to which the activity is directed and which will be changed, with the aid of *tools*, thereby generating *outcomes*. ('Tools' may be physical or symbolic, external or internal.) By way of illustration, and again put simply, the 'subject' could comprise a group of professionals who are providing services for children; and the 'object' in this case could be to learn how to accomplish inter-agency and inter-professional working. The *community* consists of other individuals and groups who share that same general object. Within this community there exists a *division of labour*, differentiated by task, power and status. The activity system also has *rules*, both formal and implicit, which support or constrain actions and interactions within the system (Engeström, 1987). Furthermore – and this has relevance to the implementation of the 'inter'-regnum – two activity systems themselves may interact horizontally with each other, their respective 'objects' combining to form a third object (Engeström, 2001, p. 135). Engeström's theory of expansive learning, therefore, comprises a theoretical strand within Gee's 'social turn'. It forms part of an emerging process of theory development within organisational epistemology which has the purpose of informing and of enabling inter-agency working. For example, studies such as the *National Evaluation of the Children's Fund* in England (Edwards, Barnes, Plewis & Morris, 2006); and the Economic and Social Research Council (ESRC)-funded *Learning in and for interagency working* project (Daniels, Edwards, Creese, Leadbetter, Martin, Brown & Middleton, 2004) have both drawn on Engeström's theory of expansive learning (see also Edwards, 2004).

There is a second aspect to the intellectual basis informing personalisation and the 'inter'-regnum. Perhaps not surprisingly within a consumerist society, it refers to contemporary marketing theory. Whereas theory in organisational epistemology has informed the *tactical* implementation of multi-agency working, it is marketing theory which has informed the *strategic* decision to push for personalisation. For example (Horne, 2005), the Department for Education and Skills Strategy Unit refers to influential works such as *The support economy* (Zuboff & Maxmin, 2002); *The customer-centric enterprise: advances in mass customization and personalisation* (Tseng & Piller, 2003), and *Markets of one: creating customer-unique value through mass customization* (Gilmore & Pine, 2000). In contemporary marketing theory there are two central concepts: co-configuration and co-customisation. These concepts replace that of 'mass customisation'. Mass customisation, it will be recalled, required a flexible and rapid response to give

134

customers 'exactly what they want', the result being 'low-cost, high-quality goods and services' (Pine, Victor & Boynton, 1993, p. 117). But these were averaged wants, not individual wants. Co-customisation, however, purports to focus on the individual customer, and is a theme central to Victor and Boynton's (1998) *Invented here*. In this work they elaborate upon the process of co-configuration in an age of co-customisation:

> Co-configuration work occurs at the interface of the firm, the customer, and the products or services. It requires constant interaction among the firm the customer and the product. The result is that the product continuously adjusts to what the customer wants. Co-configuration creates *customer-intelligent* value in products or services where the line between product and customer knowledge becomes blurred and interwoven. (Victor & Boynton, 1998, p. 14; emphasis in the original)

In this process of co-configuration it is not the product which is of central importance: it is the identity, the experience and the relationship which are created and maintained in association with the product. By retaining and sustaining this personalised relationship with the consumer, the business seeks thereafter to offer new imaginings and new identities (Gee, 2004, p. 97), or even new 'sensations' and 'transformations' (Pine and Gilmore, 1999, p. 177). These insights are now being applied to the public services. In this way – that of personalised co-production – it is expected that both the definition of the problem and the co-production of the solution can avoid the asymmetries of power whereby problems and solutions are defined by professionals alone (Milbourn, Macrae & Maguire, 2003, pp. 32-33).

CONCLUSION

The concern here has been twofold: first, with an emerging 'inter' dimension within the model of public services provision; and second, with a consideration of the cultural, economic and intellectual contexts which have allowed for its expression, either as policy and/or as practice. This emerging dimension of governance was termed the 'inter'-regnum. It can be regarded as an 'inter'-regnum in two senses: first, in the sense that the government's model of public services provision implies that there can be a seamless affinity – a functioning interaction – among Thompson's three governance regimes: hierarchy, market and network; and second, in the sense that there can be inter-agency provision which can meet the personalised needs of individuals. This latter no longer purports to position the customer as a mere service-user, but as an active co-producer of personalised needs and solutions.

In summary, the 'inter'-regnum can appeal to cultural, economic and intellectual considerations. First, it resonates with the culture of consumerism. This is so because recent marketing theory sets great store by personalising products and services. It takes further that earlier market-based regime of governance which was associated with the new public management, as defined by Leadbeater (Figure 3 above). Second, it is functional for the 'new capitalism' as a new work order of affinity and solution spaces. Third, it has important intellectual supports: that is, in addition to its association with recent marketing theory, it can appeal to theory and research in organisational learning, itself part of what Gee (2000) calls the 'social turn'.

The emergence of the 'inter'-regnum warrants some comparison to the emergence of post-Fordist work regimes in the aftermath of the 1968 demonstrations in France. Boltanski and Chiapello (1999) argue that the workers' critique of Fordist capitalist work regimes in the 1960s – that they were too managerial, too destructive of workers' creativity – were themselves incorporated into the new post-Fordist mode of working which set great store by autonomous, empowered and self-managing workers. In other words, a progressive political agenda was appropriated by private and public institutions in their new managerial regime, that of post-Fordism. Similarly, today, the intellectual 'social turn' movement is becoming appropriated as a means of maximising profit, albeit within a new work regime which has the 'appeal' of empowered workers who collaborate and network in 'teams' (Gee, 2000, pp. 187-188). But it can be argued that Gee's analysis is focused mainly on the private for-profit sector (and therefore has little relevance to public-sector agencies such as education). Even so, it is becoming clear that the continuing blurring of the public-private divide at the level of policy – and the push for 'personalisation' – allows for, but does not necessarily ensure, a growing convergence of work regimes within both private and public work settings.

At present, the policy is ahead of the evidence. There appear to be three concerns. The first arises in the co-production (between 'customer' and provider) of the 'need'. The process assumes that the provider shall in the first place agree to regard the 'customer' not simply as a passive 'service user', but as an actively engaged co-producer of a personalised need (Clarke, 2004, p. 39). But this is problematic. Even among policy-makers at local and central government levels there are differences in the definition of what shall count as 'customer', with central government more likely to distance itself from a passive notion of the customer (as 'service user') in favour of an active customer who co-produces a need which can be met; and this by inter-agency configurations if required (Needham, 2006, p. 852). Furthermore, although the government stresses 'personalisation' as the way in which providers can co-produce the personalised need of the customer, the matter of who shall comprise this 'co' (in the co-production among the providers) is left unexamined, it being assumed that all shall have equal facility and desire to engage in this co-production, a matter which earlier 'partnership' (of provider) studies has found to be problematic, if not conflictual (Jones & Bird, 2000, p. 504; Seddon, Billet & Clemans, 2004, p. 138). There is a second difficulty. The policy of personalisation assumes that the 'customer' shall indeed identify herself or himself as a 'customer' or as a 'consumer', rather than, as hitherto, a 'service user' or 'patient' or 'parent'. But the evidence for this identity-shift is to the contrary (Clarke & Newman, 2005). And even if the necessary identity-shift is made, the customer's capacity to give voice to a need is uneven, because different 'active customers' will bring to the personalisation process quite different forms of cultural capital. Finally, there is a third concern. It is financial. Personalisation – and the organisational re-configurations which it might require – may be expensive (Johnson, 2004).

The UK government has sought to give the impression that hierarchy, markets and networks can converge easily, within an elegantly-drawn structure of curved spaces and mutually supportive arrows joining them all up. But Crouch (2003) points up the difficult task which the government has in legitimating its strategy: 'Contradictory though they are, the Labour government seeks to honour simultaneously the citizenship model and the new marketisation strategy' (p. 34). In Hall's (2003, no pagination) view there is a 'double' or 'hybrid' regime comprising an always-dominant neo-liberal strand and a subordinate social democratic one. But these strands are not separate: the discourse of the 'inter'-regnum purports to weave them together as a preferred policy 'package'. It remains an empirical question whether or not the lived experiences of those whose lives are touched by the co-configuration of hierarchy, markets and networks will be socially harmonious and productive, as intended.

ACKNOWLEDGEMENT

This chapter originally appeared as: David Hartley (2007), Education policy and the 'inter'-regnum. *Journal of Education Policy*, *22*(6), 695-708. Reprinted by permission of the publisher, Taylor & Francis Ltd. http://www.tandf.co.uk/journals.

NOTES

i   'The National Education Longitudinal Studies (NELS) program of the National Center for Education Statistics (NCES) was established to study the educational, vocational, and personal development of young people beginning with their elementary or high school years, and following them over time as they begin to take on adult roles and responsibilities'. http://nces.ed.gov/surveys/hsb/

ii   The 'children's index' is the popular name given to the Information Sharing Index for England and Wales (with Welsh powers being devolved to the Welsh Assemby). The provision for this is contained in Section 12 of the Children Act 2004 [available online at http://www.opsi.gov.uk/ acts/acts2004/40031-c.htm.] The draft regulation is subject to a consultation which ended in December 2006.

iii A related approach, but not discussed here, is the process of 'knowledge creation' (Nonaka *et al.*, 2000; Takeuchi and Nonaka, 2004).

REFERENCES

Bauman, Z. (2000). *Liquid modernity*. Cambridge: Polity Press.
Boltanski, L., & Chiapello, E. (1999) *Le nouvel ésprit du capitalism*. Paris. Gallimard.
Castells, M. (2000). Materials for an exploratory theory of the network society. *British Journal of Sociology, 51*(1), 5-24.

Chubb, J.E., & Moe, T.M. (1990). *Politics, markets and America's schools*. Washington, D.C.: The Brookings Institution.

Clark, A. (1997). *Being there: Putting brain, body, and world together again*. Cambridge, MA: MIT Press.

Clarke, J. (2004). Dissolving the public realm? The logics and limits of neo-liberalism. *Journal of Social Policy, 33*(1), 27-48.

Clarke, J., & Newman, J. (2005). *What's in a name? New Labour's citizen-consumers and the remaking of public services*. Paper presented to the CRESC conference: Culture and social change: disciplinary exchanges, Manchester, 11-13 July.

Crouch, C. (2003). *Commercialisation or citizenship: Education policy and the future of public services*. London: Fabian Society.

Daniels, H., Edwards, A., Creese, A., Leadbetter, J., Martin, D., Brown, S., & Middleton, D. (2004). *Learning in and for interagency working*. Available online: http://www.tlrp.org/proj/phase111/daniels.htm) (Accessed 1.12.2005).

Department for Education and Skills (2005). *Extended schools: Access to opportunities and services for all: A prospectus*. London: DfES

Deleuze, D. (1992). Postscript on the Societies of Control. *October, 59*, Winter, 3-7. Available online: http://www.n5m.org/n5m2/media/texts/deleuze.htm (Accessed 17.11.2006).

Durkheim, E. (1995 [1912]). *The elementary forms of religious life*, translated by Karen E. Fields. New York: The Free Press.

Edwards, A. (2004). *Multi-agency working for the prevention of social exclusion: Using activity theory to understand learning across organizations*. Available online: http://ne-cf.org.uk/briefing.asp?section=000100040009&profile=000100080005&id=1035 (Accessed 17.11.2006).

Edwards, A., Barnes, M., Plewis, I., & Morris, K. (2006). *Working to prevent the social exclusion of children and young people: Final lessons from the National Evaluation of the Children's Fund*. Birmingham: University of Birmingham.

Engeström, Y. (1987). *Learning by expanding: An activity-theoretical approach to developmental research*. Helsinki:Orienta-Konsultit.Available online: http://lchc.ucsd.edu/MCA/Paper/Engestrom/expanding/toc.htm (Accessed 17 .11.2006).

Engeström, Y. (2000). Activity theory as a framework for analysing and redesigning work. *Ergonomics, 43*(7), 960-974.

Engeström, Y. (2001). Expansive learning at work: Toward an activity theoretical reconceptualisation. *Journal of Education and Work, 41*(1), 133-156.

Engeström, Y. (2004). New forms of learning in co-configuration work. Seminar presentation, London School of Economics, 22nd January, 2004. Available online: http://www.is.lse.ac.uk/events/ESRCseminars/Engeström.pdf (Accessed 1.12.2005).

Gee, J.P. (2000). The New Literacy Studies: from 'socially situated' to the work of the social, in D. Barton, M. Hamilton, & R. Ivanic (Eds.), *Situated literacies: Reading and writing in context*. London: Routledge.

Gee J. P. (2004). *Situated language and learning: A critique of traditional schooling*. London: Routledge.

Gee, J.P., Hull, G., & Lankshear, C. (1996). *The new work order: Behind the language of the new capitalism*. St Leonards, New South Wales: Allen and Unwin.

Gilmore, J.H., & Pine, B.J. (Eds.) (2000). *Markets of one: Creating customer-unique value through mass customization*. Boston, MA: Harvard Business School Press.

Goldstein, H. (1993). *Review of* Chubb, J.E. & Moe, T.M. (1990) *Politics, Markets and America's Schools* Washington, D.C.: The Brookings Institution. *British Educational Research Journal, 19*(1), 116-118.

HM Treasury (2003). *Every Child Matters*. London: HM Treasury. Available online: http://www.everychildmatters.gov.uk/_files/EBE7EEAC90382663E0D5BBF24C99A7AC.pdf (Accessed 22 .11.2006).

Hall, S. (2003). New Labour's double-shuffle. *Soundings*, Summer. Available online: http://www.lwbooks.co.uk/journals/articles/nov03.html (Accessed 1 .02.2007).

Hardman, F., Smith, F., & Wall, K. (2003). 'Interactive whole class teaching' in the National Literacy Strategy. *Cambridge Journal of Education, 33*(2), 197-215.

Hargreaves D.H. (1999). The knowledge-creating school. *British Journal of Educational Studies, 47*(2), 122-144.

Hartley, D. (2003). New economy, new pedagogy? *Oxford Review of Education, 29*(1), 81-94.

Hartley, D. (2004). Management, leadership and the emotional order of the school. *Journal of Education Policy, 19*(5), 583-594.

Hood, C. (2000). *The arts of the state: Culture, rhetoric and public management.* Oxford: Oxford University Press.

Horne, M. (2005). *Personalised learning.* London: DfES Strategy Unit. Available online: http://www.becta.org.uk/page_documents/research/conf2005/matthew_horne.pdf (Accessed 19.1.2006)

Johnson, M. (2004). *Personalised learning – An emperor's outfit?* London: Institute for Public Policy Research. Available online: http://www.ippr.org.uk/uploadedFiles/projects/PL%20paper%20for%20publication.PDF (Accessed 19.1.2006).

Jones, K., & Bird, K. (2000). 'Partnership' as strategy: Public–private relations in education action zones, *British Educational Research Journal, 26*(4), 491-506.

Kiziltan, M.U., Bain, W.J., & Canizares, M.A. (1990). Postmodern condition: Rethinking public education. *Educational Theory, 40*(3), 351-369.

Latour, B. (1991). *We have never been modern.* Cambridge, MA: Harvard University Press.

Lave, J. (1996). Teaching, as learning, in practice. *Mind, Culture, and Activity, 3*(3), 149-164.

Leadbeater, C. (2004). *Personalisation through participation: A new script for public service.* London: Demos.

Lingard, B., Hayes, D., & Mills, M. (2003). Teachers and productive pedagogies: Contextualizing, conceptualizing and utilizing. *Pedagogy, Culture and Society, 11*(3), 399-424.

Melucci, A. (1996). *The playing self: Person and meaning in the planetary society.* Cambridge: Cambridge University Press.

Milbourne, L., Macrae, S., & Maguire, M. (2003). Collaborative solutions or new policy problems: Exploring multi-agency partnerships in education and health work. *Journal of Education Policy, 18*(1), 19-35.

Miller, R. (2003). Towards the learning society. In T. Bentley & J. Wilsdon (Eds.), *The adaptive state: strategies for personalising the public realm.* London: Demos.

Needham, C. (2006). Customer care and the public service ethos. *Public Administration, 84*(4), 845-860.

Nonaka, I., Toyama, R., & Konno, N. (2000). SECI, *Ba* and leadership: A unified model of dynamic knowledge creation. *Long Range Planning, 33*(1), 5-34.

Page, B. (2006). *Issues to consider: social demographic and organizational trends.* London: Ipsos MORI Social Research Institute. Available at: http://www.strategy.gov.uk/downloads/seminars/social/social.pdf (Accessed 17.11.2006).

Pine, B.J., Victor, B., & Boynton, A.C. (1993). Making mass customisation work. *Harvard Business Review*, September-October, 108-119.

Pine, J.P., & Gilmore, J.H. (1999). *The experience economy: Work is theatre and every business a stage.* Boston: Harvard Business School.

Prime Minister's Strategy Unit (2006). *The UK government's approach to public service reform* (Working Document): Chart A: The UK government's model of public service reform: A self-improving system. London: Cabinet Office. Available online: http://www.strategy.gov.uk/downloads/work_areas/public_service_reform/sj_pamphlet.pdf (Accessed 17.11.2006).

Scottish Executive (2000). *Report of the Joint Future Group.* Available online: http://www.scotland.gov.uk/library3/social/rjfg-00.asp (Accessed 17.11.2006).

Seddon, T., Billett, S., & Clemans, A. (2004). Politics of social partnerships: A framework for theorizing. *Journal of Education Policy, 19*(2), 123-142.

Tabberer, R. (2005). People development. Presentation to the TDA Stakeholder 2005 Day. October, 17th London: TDA.

Takeuchi, H., & Nonaka, I. (Eds.) (2004). *Hitotsubashi on knowledge creation.* Singapore: John Wiley (Asia).

Thompson, G.F. (2003). *Between hierarchies and markets: The logic and limits of network forms of organization.* Oxford: Oxford University Press.

Touraine, A. (2000). *Can we live together: Equality and difference.* Cambridge: Polity Press.

Tseng, M.M., & Piller, F.T. (2003). *The customer-centric enterprise: Advances in mass customization and personalization.* New York: Springer.

Tyack, D., & Hansot, E. (1982). *Managers of virtue.* New York: Basic Books.

Tyack, D., & Tobin, W. (1994). The 'grammar' of schooling: Why has it been so hard to change? *American Educational Research Journal, 31*(3), 453-479.

Victor, B., & Boynton, A.C. (1998). *Invented here.* Boston, MA: Harvard Business School Press.

Wertsch, J.V. (1991). *Voices of the mind: A sociocultural approach to mediated action.* Cambridge, MA: Harvard University Press.

Zuboff, S., & Maxmin, J. (2002). *The support economy.* New York: Viking.

David Hartley
School of Education
University of Birmingham
UK

AUDREY HENDRY

PART FOUR
FUTURE SCHOOL SERVICES, 'GLOBAL SOLUTIONS'

Many studies of service integration in schools are concerned with activities at the personal, organizational and local service delivery levels. Perhaps this is unsurprising when service delivery is normally centred round individuals and the organization in which they work. Yet, as borne out in the previous chapters in this book, it would seem that service integration, both in the challenges it faces and the aims it hopes to achieve, could usefully be more broadly conceived. If integrated service delivery in our schools is to improve, current approaches may be insufficient. Looking differently at problems or in different places for solutions may be necessary. A number of the issues raised in the chapters which follow may seem a long way from the work of some professionals who are involved in our schools at present, but wider conceptualisation and contextualisation of the issues is likely to provide a clearer perspective on the kind of challenges faced by schools. It may also offer insights into how interprofessional and interagency policy and practice might be adapted to meet the future needs of those on whom service reform impacts.

New Labour's attempts to modernise and remodel the workforce employed in schools are explored in the chapter by Graham Butt and Helen Gunter. Their chapter outlines some of the ways in which schools have been reconstructed in response to the National Agreement (Department for Education & Skills, 2003) in England which redefined the roles of teachers, non-teaching staff and other professionals in schools. The study presented here looks in detail at how these changes have been experienced by teachers and others and comments on how teachers' work-life balance has been altered as a result of the Agreement. The impact of the National Agreement is contingent on local circumstances, Butt and Gunter observe, but nationally it would seem that there is some evidence of positive change resulting from this remodelling.

Butt and Gunter compare and contrast the situation in England with modernisation and remodelling in other developed countries, finding distinct parallels between systems. They draw on the work of Berkhout in South Africa where successive administrations have sought to restructure and reculture schools and schooling. In contrast to England where, according to Butt and Gunter, remodelling has taken place largely in response to teacher shortages, workforce

J. Forbes and C. Watson (eds.), Service Integration in Schools, 141–143.

changes in South Africa are set against the backdrop of democratisation and structural transformation. Despite these differences, similarities are found between the two settings in the ways in which change has been experienced by teachers.

Drawing on the work of Fitzgerald in New Zealand and Vidovich in Australia the chapter goes on to outline the marked similarities in how reform has proceeded in England and in these other contexts. While the reforms have taken place at different times and are underpinned to some extent by differing political ideology, the writers suggest that there are lessons to be learned from each context about successful reform and the role of the teacher within it. Their findings lead the writers to conclude that the relationship between teachers, reform and teacher morale is complex, contingent and problematic.

The chapter by Cate Watson invites us to consider the complexities inherent in global discourses of service integration through an exploration of the local. Watson outlines research conducted in Scotland which explored initial teacher education students' narrative construction of their identities as beginning teachers. The study draws on Laclau and Mouffe's theory of discourse. While the work of Laclau and Mouffe is more usually applied at the macro level, Watson opens her chapter with a discussion of the usefulness of this approach to discourse as a way of understanding subject positions within current discourses of interprofessional practice. These discourses are, she reminds us, often unstable, contested and competing. Watson proposes that a 'miniaturisation' of Laclau and Mouffe's approach in a critical microanalysis of discourse may reveal possibilities for change. Having argued for this particular methodology, Watson uses it to examine beginner teachers' narratives of 'need' as generated within the current political discourse of social inclusion. She takes a narrative fragment, and moving back and forth between the global and the local, uses the fragment to illuminate issues central to current educational policy. Like Butt and Gunter, Watson's work uncovers tensions and dilemmas in the ways in which teachers are positioned by discourses. At the local level instability is experienced, while at the global level closure and uniformity appears to be imposed. In closing Watson urges that interprofessional practice may require us to move away from notions of consensus and perfect communication and instead consider alternative ways of dealing with the problematic.

In the final chapter Jon Nixon picks up some of the themes introduced by Watson. Nixon argues that interprofessional practice is not simply a matter of structures or systems but is concerned with the culture of organizations and with relationships within and across these organizations. Central to the argument is a concern for people and their well-being and the quality of the associations they form. Thus, Nixon suggests, mutuality and reciprocity between people improve integrated service delivery.

Nixon offers the Aristotelian concept of 'virtuous friendship' as one way of conceptualizing how interprofessional relationships might be reconfigured. Nixon advocates that, as a step towards reconfiguring interprofessional relationships, a new vocabulary is needed, one which is able to use terms such as hope, friendship and trust. Interprofessional activity based on virtuous practice might then allow practitioners the space and opportunity to think together about the ends and purposes of interprofessional practice and the actions needed to bring it to life.

The chapter – and book – ends with a series of questions; questions which challenge and extend the themes and issues developed over the four seminars in the series from which this book has emerged. Nixon asks that as professionals involved in services for children and young people, for families and the community, we examine current practices critically and with humility, placing ourselves in the position of others, valuing others equally and accepting that our understanding of what constitutes knowledge is subject to change. Nixon invites us to consider building locally the conditions needed for change while remaining sensitive to what might be termed global.

Audrey Hendry
Quality Improvement Officer
Education, Learning and Leisure
Aberdeenshire Council
UK

GRAHAM BUTT AND HELEN GUNTER

MODERNISING AND REMODELLING SCHOOLS: ARE THERE 'GLOBAL SOLUTIONS' TO TRANSFORMING THE SCHOOL WORKFORCE?

INTRODUCTION

The current agenda of modernisation and remodelling of the school workforce, as promoted by New Labour, reflects an attempt to re-structure and re-culture all England's public sector workforces. Here we consider the process of modernisation within education, whilst drawing on the work of colleagues from other countries who have sought to understand the transformation of school workforces within their national contexts. We seek to address whether workforce modernisation, in whatever form, offers a meaningful way forward for the teaching profession in England and in other countries. Connections will be made to the enhanced roles of support staff and teaching assistants within the modernised school, with reference being made to both interagency and interprofessional policy and practice.

Since coming to power ten years ago New Labour has been keen to both re-structure and re-culture public sector workforces, including the workforce employed in state schools. Two terms that have come to the fore when describing this process of changing public services are 'modernisation' and 'remodelling' – we will deal with each of these concepts in turn. In this chapter we attempt to illustrate how the English experience of modernising schools has distinct parallels elsewhere and explore the extent to which adopting 'global solutions' to transforming the school workforce is sensible. Where pertinent, direct reference is made to interagency and interprofessional policy and practice in different national contexts. There is currently evidence of considerable 'policy borrowing' in education amongst developed countries. We draw upon accounts from South Africa (Sarie Berkhout), New Zealand (Tanya Fitzgerald) and Australia (Lesley Vidovich) to explore the extent to which other countries have pursued similar approaches to modernisation and remodelling in their schools, whilst also seeking to assess whether these developments have resonance with the English experience.

Remodelling of the school workforce was introduced into English schools from September 2003 through the National Agreement (Department for Education & Skills, 2003). In essence this attempted three things: to reduce the current and projected shortage of teachers in schools, to transform the culture of the education workforce, and to change the workload of teachers. With large numbers of teachers choosing not to teach (around 300,000 according to Horne, 2001), and with around one in three teachers expecting to leave the profession in the next five years

J. Forbes and C. Watson (eds.), Service Integration in Schools, 145–156.
© *2009 Sense Publishers. All rights reserved.*

(Woodward, 2003), the staffing situation in schools could not be ignored. The National Agreement has been forged between the government, employers and unions (except the National Union of Teachers) and aims to reform the education workforce through:

- defining the work teachers should and should not do;
- removing routine administrative tasks from teachers (the '25 tasks');
- reducing teachers' hours of work;
- providing support staff for teachers (both inside and outside the classroom);
- providing 'new managers' with experience from outside education;
- training headteachers in change management.

The National Agreement has been implemented in English schools in a series of phases (Phase 1 from September 2003, Phase 2 from September 2004, Phase 3 from September 2005) and is supported by a variety of agencies: the Workforce Agreement Monitoring Group (WAMG), the Implementation Review Unit (IRU) and the National Remodelling Team (NRT).

Modernisation

Modernisation, in the context of English schools, is a word which has been used to cover a variety of new 'things to be done'. The necessity for change has been stressed, within a concept that also encompasses a perceived need for new jobs, new roles, new responsibilities and a new set of values for the workplace. New Labour seems to be closely wedded to the concept of modernisation – often adopting the language of 'new' and 'modern', combining it with an imperative to discover novel ways of doing things through centrally funded 'pathfinder' and 'testbed' projects. Specifically, New Labour has sought to develop a 'third way' with respect to public sector reform, attempting to bring together two prominent 'drivers' of educational change which have been apparent since the Second World War: firstly, the requirement for generous public funding of education, underpinned by principles of social equality and inclusion; and secondly, the drive to increase private provision of education, with an emphasis on competition and choice. The New Labour 'third way' therefore strives to bring together both the state and market through the involvement of the private sector in state education.

The implications of this are evident in the recent educational policies created by New Labour. Take, for example, the *Every Child Matters* (Department for Education & Skills, 2004a) legislation. There is much here to be commended by the education profession, particularly the focusing of services on the needs of the child. However, the integration of education with other public services (health, police, social services) has not been straightforward – particularly when there are recent suggestions that schools may no longer be led by an educationist (a headteacher, in the traditional sense), but by a Chief Executive (who previously may have had little, or nothing, to do with education).

The reform agenda of modernisation in schools has advanced rapidly over the past decade. The focus for intervention has swung from the curriculum (with a loosening of the National Curriculum and a concentration on numeracy and literacy strategies), to structural change of schools (specialist schools, beacon schools and academies), to workforce remodelling (performance management, leadership training, removal of bureaucracy) and to the support for social inclusion (the 'Excellence in Cities' programme). More is on the horizon: increased choice for parents and children, interagency and interprofessional 'providers' being drawn into the delivery of education, greater independence for headteachers/chief executives and governors, further staff development, and wider partnerships (Department for Education & Skills, 2004b).

Remodelling

Remodelling questions 'who does what' in schools, whether these arrangements are still successful, and how they might be changed for the better.

New Labour faced an immediate dilemma when it entered power in 1997, for the national supply of teachers was not meeting either predicted or existing demand. The imperative to train more teachers through a variety of different routes, was supplemented by a shift in policy that looked towards the employment of greater numbers of 'para-professionals' in educational provision. The traditional teaching workforce was therefore enhanced by a variety of teaching and learning assistants (as well as support staff) who were to take some of the commonly accepted roles of the teacher, thus easing labour supply problems. This has extended, in recent years, to greater links with other agencies and professional groups. This model envisages the future teaching workforce consisting of fewer, higher status, teachers supported by a variety of other staff within a culture of 'new professionalism' (Department for Education & Employment, 1998; Department for Education & Skills, 2002). The expectation is that teachers will be 'freed to teach', whilst others will be assisting them by taking away non-teaching (largely bureaucratic and administrative) tasks that have traditionally diverted the teachers' efforts away from the classroom. The allocation of time for planning, preparation and assessment (PPA) has also, in theory at least, enabled teachers to reduce their workload and strike a better work-life balance. However, there are those who would argue that by removing 'non-teaching' roles from teachers one takes away a significant element of their professionalism, commitment and dedication to caring for the whole child. In addition, many teachers are concerned about their *raison d'être* being undermined by a new workforce that is trained on the job, receives lower wages and is of lower status. As such there are a number of important questions that have not yet been appropriately answered about the remodelling of the education workforce. For example, with the increasing employment of para-professionals what effect will this have on the status of teaching as a graduate entry profession?

One major shift has been to 'upgrade' the role of teaching assistants (TAs) to support teachers in the classroom – either through the 'traditional' TA roles of

147

working with specific children who have particular needs, or by supporting specific teaching, learning and assessment tasks for a whole cohort of children. This has often widened the job of the TA to providing support not only for pupils and teachers, but also for the curriculum and the whole school. The low status, training and pay of TAs has, in part, been addressed through the creation of Higher Level Teaching Assistants (HLTAs), who are now trained to take on greater responsibility for teaching and learning in the classroom. The overall aim of introducing greater numbers of support staff, both inside and outside the classroom, has been to provide teachers with a more reasonable work-life balance, to increase their job satisfaction and ultimately to retain them in their jobs. There are parallels within other developed countries where TAs have recently accepted similarly enhanced roles in schools.

Job satisfaction and work-life balance

The government has become increasingly interested in the connections between teacher workload, job satisfaction and work-life balance over the past few years. This interest is perhaps not so much driven by altruism, but rather by the need to recruit and retain teachers in greater numbers than is currently the case. Poor teacher recruitment, loss of high percentages of new teachers in their first years of teaching, and an ageing national teacher population are all major concerns – which will not be solved simply by recruiting more teachers in the short term. The deep-seated issues of teachers' work-life balance clearly need addressing. Commissioned reports from PriceWaterhouseCoopers (2001) and the School Teachers' Review Body (STRB) (2004) have each highlighted the need to tackle teachers' hours of work, but have hinted that the problem is not simply statistical. As the STRB commented, workload reduction and the maintenance of high job satisfaction are 'of at least equal importance to pay in helping to address problems of recruitment, retention and morale' (p. 25).

Recent research into levels of teachers' job satisfaction within the modernised and remodelled school environment has produced some interesting findings (Thomas, Butt, Fielding, Foster, Gunter, Lance, Pilkington, Potts, Powers, Rayner, Rutherford, Selwood & Szwed, 2004). When teachers have been asked about how they might reduce workload and increase job satisfaction they highlight the negative impact of the non-teaching tasks they regularly undertake (photocopying, filing, money collection, form filling, duplicating information, etc). The second most common reason given for high workload is MARRA (monitoring, assessment, recording, reporting and accountability), whilst third is the time spent in covering for absent colleagues and the subsequent loss of non-contact time. The last two causes of excessive workload are the number of government school initiatives that require implementation and the excessive demands for planning in schools (including target setting, duplication of plans, and planning that is not fit for purpose) (Butt & Lance, 2005). Here the case for increasing the number and roles of administrative staff is viewed positively, as is the greater deployment of teaching assistants. Possibilities of employing staff – or their experience, via consultancies – from a variety of other professional groups have also presented themselves. Many teachers also commented on their own use of ICT. They felt that gaining access to better training in ICT use – as well as updated hardware, software and networks – would decrease their workload and increase their job satisfaction.

With regard to modernisation and remodelling current research can reveal 'no systematic relationship between job satisfaction and hours worked – findings which emphasise that job satisfaction is dependent on a more complex set of factors than hours worked' (Butt & Lance, 2005, p. 420). The assertion that people who work long hours do not have high levels of personal job satisfaction is therefore not supported, nor is the opposite the case. Highly motivated people often gain huge satisfaction from their work and choose to work long hours. Therefore many teachers' sense of job satisfaction is located in a complex set of factors, beliefs and attitudes which are tied up with their commitment to their job, their working relationships with colleagues and children, and the ethos of their school. In part, this may explain why some teachers apparently like working long hours, even when there are possible ways to avoid this; why the increase in classroom-based support has not been welcomed more fully by some teachers; and why there is little realisation that intensive work during term times may not equate to a similar, less intensive, workload spread over an entire year. There is some evidence that teachers may not object to working long hours, as long as they have some control and choice about when they carry out non-teaching duties.

THE WAY FORWARD?

Initial evaluations of the remodelling and modernisation of the education workforce in English schools are revealing (Thomas *et al.,* 2004). Many schools that had 'bought into' the remodelling and modernisation agenda *before* the launching of the National Agreement in 2003 have found the transitions relatively straightforward. Some were already moving in the direction of change that is now being suggested by the government. Others have not found transition so easy, getting bogged down in issues of staffing, definition and deployment of tasks, and disputes over 'who does what'. All schools have had to face up to the problems created by the backdrop of an often contradictory policy and practice regime from the 1980s and 1990s.

Nationally there is some evidence of positive change resulting from modernisation and remodelling. Year-on-year statistics of the number of teachers employed have shown gains – an increase of 3,700 teachers in England in January 2006 (to a total of 435,600) and a decrease of vacancies by 250 (to 2,230). The number of support staff is also rising (up by 22,700 to 287,000), which includes an increase of 6,100 new teaching assistants (Department for Education & Skills, 2006). Locally the picture is more piecemeal – some schools have witnessed revolutions in the composition of their staffing (beyond the traditional employment of teaching and support staff) and the roles they undertake, increased use of ICT in labour saving and educationally supportive ways, and the extension of a more pleasing work-life balance resulting in greater job satisfaction. Others are just beginning to make progress, or are finding the challenge of changing working cultures in their schools very difficult to achieve. It is perhaps ironic that the laudable drive to reduce teachers' workload has been achieved through the dedicated 'out of hours' work of selfless individuals, often from senior management teams, at the expense of their own free time. There is also evidence of headteachers making changes that they do not necessarily believe in, and we need to ask serious questions about what this means for morale and professional judgement.

The experience of modernisation and remodelling in education in other developed countries

Here we draw on the accounts of three international authors who have explored the ways in which modernisation and remodelling are playing out within their own national contexts. Each comments on the effects of 'policy borrowing', largely from the English context, and notes the extent to which transformation of their school workforces has been successful. Some reference is made, where appropriate, to interagency and interprofessional policy and practice.

Sarie Berkhout (2007) engages with the transformation agenda in South Africa and considers the extent to which policy development in other countries has influenced change in the national context; Tanya Fitzgerald (2007) explores the remodelling of schools and schooling from the perspective of New Zealand, illustrating similarities with the situation currently being experienced in English schools; whilst Lesley Vidovich (2007) uses an analytical lens to look at globalisation and how the forces associated with this have impacted on education in Australia and elsewhere – affecting teachers' professional identity, teaching and learning, and the need for modernisation.

South Africa

Berkhout (2007) describes the 're-making' of teachers in the South African context, played out against the backdrop of democratisation and transformation in the post-apartheid era. The past 12 years have seen a major restructuring of the education system where 'expectations built on notions of an all-powerful apartheid state that constructed an unjust education system were transferred to the new state and its promise to transform society into a more just and equitable system' (p. 152). She reports how the transformation agenda has increasingly been influenced by policy development in other countries, as well as by a managerialist discourse. There appears to be a growing disjunction between policy texts and education practice in South Africa, such that the anticipated participatory democratisation of education has found teachers trapped within traditional contexts and power relationships, whilst being viewed by the state as increasingly in need of 're-making'. Berkhout sees this as taking real power away from teachers, who now find themselves at the bottom of a hierarchical system of decision making and reduced to 'acting out their respective roles' (p. 149).

South Africa is currently attempting to modernise all its public sector workforces. Within state education teachers are seen as part of a fairly general problem with regard to reform, modernisation and the achievement of policy delivery. The transformation of the education system is viewed by Berkhout as 'very much related to the English restructuring of the 1960s which was underpinned by values of equity and democratic development and aspired to deliver the comprehensive ideal' (p. 150). She describes how South African teachers are 'expected to abandon cultures and practices of the past and reform their identities in the image of the modern global citizen' (p. 151). A new curriculum, Curriculum 2005, was launched in 1996 and was accompanied by the redeployment and rationalisation of teachers – partly in an attempt to standardise the pupil:teacher ratios in schools. The effect of this was that 'large numbers of teachers, mostly experienced, were retrenched and left the system. Schools located in privileged areas were able to charge school fees that enabled them to employ additional staff, whereas the traditional disadvantaged schools did not gain sufficient numbers of teachers to realise the expected relief' (p. 153). The geographic distribution of schools, linked to the history of racial segregation of residential areas, remains the same, perpetuating traditional inequalities. As such, the divide between privileged schools and the rest has become more visible and entrenched.

Similar to the English education system 'wave upon wave of policy change and reform (has) sorely challenged leadership in schools and 2004 saw large-scale investigations into the morale and workload of teachers' (p. 154) in South Africa. Teachers are seen as in need of 're-making', or of being equipped with new skills, to enable a modern standardisation of provision. They are considered to be the lynch-pin of transformation, but are generally believed by the government 'to lack capacity and to require "remodelling" ' (p. 155). Indeed they may be forced to 'develop a strategic mimicry of the policy expectations which are counter-forces to the traditional conceptions of teaching and learning that teachers themselves believe in' (Mattson & Harley, 2002, p. 284). Berkhout (2007, p. 156) concludes that

contrary to the modernisation project in England, which is very much focussed on the provision of additional support to alleviate the burden of teachers, inequalities in resource provision fundamentally drive the discourse of education transformation. Although the national and provincial structures provide for a major overhaul of the system, they have left the education institutions largely untouched – much as they did during the apartheid era.

She notes serious dissatisfaction and despondency amongst teachers – issues which she relates to the waves of transformations that do not seem to 'settle', to teacher workload and job satisfaction, to low morale, and to the impact of HIV/Aids on young people. In essence 'South African educational policy is strongly inclined to follow the English example…policy development is also strongly influenced by English consultants and civil servants. In this regard "modernisation" is no exception' (p. 162).

New Zealand

Fitzgerald (2007) also notes that 'the educational reform agenda and the resultant restructuring of schools in New Zealand has proceeded with marked similarity to England' (p. 163). Whilst the language of 'modernisation' and 'remodelling' are largely omitted from policy rhetoric in New Zealand, their processes have functioned to effect structural changes in schools and contractual changes for teachers that 'have implicitly produced an unambiguous level of workforce reform that has re-formed schools and schooling, teachers and teaching' (p. 163). The links with English educational policy making are clear for Fitzgerald when she states 'New Zealand, at the geographical periphery, continues to transport and re-work policies from its ideological centre' (p. 163).

Fitzgerald describes workforce reform in New Zealand schools as occurring in two modernisation phases. The first (1989-1995), has aligned schools with the demands of the market through structural changes, whilst remodelling has radically transformed the ways in which schools were led, managed and governed; the second (1996 to date), emphasised the public accountability of teachers within a managed profession. More recently problems of recruitment and retention of teachers have resulted in 'contractual remodelling of teachers' professional work and activities that has the worrying potential to invoke irrevocable changes to the school workforce' (p. 164). Teachers have again been constructed as 'the problem' and therefore are subjected to a culture of performance management which increasingly controls and regulates their work.

As Codd (2005) explains, schools have been transformed to compete in an educational marketplace, from local to global, where the community served is re-visioned as 'clients' or 'consumers'. Here education is largely seen as a private product. As with any product, education has a life cycle as a marketable commodity, such that reduced spending on education prompts schools to act in entrepreneurial ways as a means of making themselves more financially viable – hence schools increasing their demand for 'voluntary' parental contributions, looking for corporate sponsorship, accepting curriculum materials made by commercial companies in exchange for advertising rights, conducting international marketing to attract overseas (fee-paying) students, and re-branding themselves (for example Baird's Intermediate School in South Auckland becoming Baird's Mainfreight Intermediate School after accepting sponsorship from a haulage company). Fitzgerald explains how modernisation has also eroded the professional autonomy of teachers, as they have become central to the financial, strategic and entrepreneurial objectives of the school. Teachers have therefore become producers of the 'commodity' of student skills, knowledge and abilities which in turn contribute to the global economy. Thus 'the modern school and the modern market place share a symbiotic relationship. A modernised school however, requires amongst other things, a modernised workforce' (p. 169).

These changes in New Zealand's schools have resulted in a new climate in which teachers work. As a modernised workforce they now experience increased hours of work, larger class sizes, more administrative tasks and greater accountability, whilst sensing a loss of their professional autonomy. Given that these are the problems which modernisation in English schools has tried to *eradicate*, some believe that the New Zealand government will again seek to borrow policy initiatives from England, to solve their problems (Thrupp, 2001; Robertson & Dale, 2002). Political concerns about workload issues, the age of the school workforce and teacher retention are similar to those in English schools, as highlighted by a small scale quantitative study commissioned by the Ministry of Education (2002).

Fitzgerald concludes that remodelling and modernisation of schools and schooling has been continuing in New Zealand since 1989, with further reform based on changing the purposes, structure and function of schools along English lines being on the horizon. However, in the New Zealand context, the 'shift in responsibility for schools and schooling from the State to schools was accompanied by demands for fiscal and organizational efficiency and the re-production of education as a commodity that was subject to the demand of local and global consumers' (p. 175). Teachers have also become the objects of reform in terms of their contracts, performance management and introduction of standards.

Australia
Vidovich (2007) looks to the forces of globalisation to help explain the growth of modernisation policies in education in Australia. She has witnessed the ways in which the 'global knowledge economy' has moved to centre stage in public policy making, with international economic competitiveness becoming a key driving force behind policy development. This has resulted in the reconstruction of the professional identities of teachers, with implications for the future quality of teaching and learning.

Taking a definition of globalisation which essentially locates it within the greater economic interconnectedness of the world, Vidovich focuses on technical and ideological aspects of the globalisation process. Here she notes the growth of neo-liberalism, market ideology and principles of competition and the effects these have had on education and policy formation. Indeed, the very acts of policy borrowing and policy convergence across international boundaries have been facilitated by the forces of globalisation. Education policy making in Australia, according to Vidovich, has been strongly influenced by that in England, USA, Canada and New Zealand – although the term 'modernisation' is new within Australian educational circles. Nonetheless, teachers have already been highlighted as a key 'policy problem', as they have in other countries.

Australia has witnessed corporatisation and privatisation of education since the late 1980s. Since the election of the Howard Coalition Government in 1996 unions have not been routinely invited to the policy 'table', whilst the passing of highly controversial Industrial Relations legislation in 2006 has severely limited union power – with individual Australian Workplace Arrangements prevailing over collective agreements. Hence teachers are generally portrayed as having lost their previous powers of negotiation. The problems faced by education are similar to those in England: teacher shortages, poor retention of teachers, low status of the profession and poor teacher supply (particularly in maths, sciences and ICT).

Combined with a central drive for greater teacher accountability and a demand for a 'new professionalism' within the teaching workforce, the parallels with English state education are therefore strong.

Many in Australia hoped for significant education policy borrowing from England when New Labour was elected to power in 1997 on a platform of 'education, education, education', but this enthusiasm changed as the English policies played out. Nonetheless, similar education policies have been adopted by parties of significantly different ideological traditions (Labour in England and a Conservative Coalition in Australia). Both governments have favoured centralised control of markets and competition, within a neo-liberal framework, although the Australian government has not attempted the 'third way' coupling of left and right as a driver of policy development. Australian educational policy is generally less unified and less coherent across the whole country, due to Australia's federal political structure, but the central state still uses financial levers to steer policy despite the size and diversity of the education sector fragmenting its centralised control.

Vidovich concludes by noting the marginalisation of teacher voice in policy making in Australia, whilst Sachs (2003) contrasts the idealised position of the teacher with that of the prevailing managerial (economic) discourses which have promoted an individualistic, competitive, controlling, regulative, externally-defined and standards-led identity for teachers. The 'new professionalism' of teachers should reveal a critical and active engagement with policy, which is currently far from the case. With globalisation as a common antecedent to modernisation policies across many countries there has been an ideological consistency amongst different policies at different sites. However, Vidovich calls for a clear differentiation between a 'global knowledge society' and a 'global knowledge economy'. There is, in the English and Australian cases, a convergence of education policy goals and discourse, but not in the structures and processes adopted in state schools in each country. Organisations and individuals have negotiated central policies differently, changing the resultant practice within the different school contexts.

CONCLUSIONS

Modernisation and remodelling are concerned with the creation of flexible workforces through the challenging of previous conventions of 'who does what' in the workplace. As such they are as much about changing cultures as they are about changing structures (Butt & Gunter, 2007).

New Labour governments in England have argued that globalised economies now require national workforces to be capable of acquiring transferable skills, to be accepting of the need to retrain, and to be flexible in the ways in which they work. They have also introduced the prospect of greater interagency and interprofessional work in schools, within a modernised and remodelled education workforce. Flexibility is increasingly demanded of those who make up the education workforce – where traditional role boundaries are no longer static, but open to question. Within this new reality is a tension concerning who should now be providing the nation's schooling. This can be approached from the macro level – should education be seen as a public good, or a private service? Or from the micro level – should classroom teaching always be carried out by trained teachers? At the heart of this debate lies the professional identity of teachers, alongside the desire of both parents and students that teaching should still be carried out by fully trained professionals.

Internationally, based on case study evidence from South Africa, New Zealand and Australia, the drive towards modernisation and remodelling of the education workforce continues apace. The influence of the market, neo-liberal economic policy and globalisation are seen to have had noticeable impacts on schools and the working lives of teachers. The prospect of greater diversification within the education workforce, through interagency and interprofessional working, are realities within the English state education system and appear in other national contexts. What is perhaps most significant in the pursuit of 'global solutions' to workforce modernisation is the strong and continuing tradition of policy borrowing amongst certain developed countries – from predominantly English sources. At present, there is perhaps only rather limited evidence of interagency work in schools in the case study countries selected here, although in the future one suspects that a lead may be taken from the English example.

In the international context some observers have commented that attempts at modernising and remodelling education workforces have concentrated more on creating lists of what teachers should *not* be doing, rather than clearly articulating a model of what teachers should expect in their professional practice. The latter approach orientates arguments around whether pedagogy is kept at the forefront of teachers' work (or the work of other para-professionals) and whether the care of students, both academically and pastorally, is still seen as important. There is a danger in approaching remodelling and modernisation from the perspective of the school as an organisation – focusing on its structures and management – rather than from the perspective of teaching, learning and caring. In short, there is an issue about what should now be at the centre of 'modernised education' – structures, or students?

REFERENCES

Berkhout, S. (2007). Democratisation and the re-making of teachers in South African Schools. In G. Butt, & H.M. Gunter (Eds.), *Modernising schools: People, learning and organizations* (pp. 149-162). London: Continuum.

Butt, G., & Gunter, H.M. (Eds.) (2007). *Modernising schools: People, learning and organizations.* London: Continuum.

Butt, G., & Lance, A. (2005). Secondary teacher workload and job satisfaction: Do successful strategies for change exist? *Educational Management Administration and Leadership, 33*(4), 401-422.

Codd, J. (2005). Teachers as 'managed professionals' in the global education industry: The New Zealand experience. *Educational Review, 57*(2), 193-206.

Department for Education & Employment (1998). *Teachers: Meeting the challenge of change.* London: DfEE.

Department for Education & Skills (2002). *Time for standards: Reforming the school workforce.* London: DfES.
Department for Education & Skills (2003). *Raising standards and tackling workload: A national agreement.* London: DfES.
Department for Education & Skills (2004a). *Every child matters: Change for children.* London: DfES.
Department for Education & Skills (2004b). *Raising standards and tackling workload: Implementing the national agreement.* London: DfES.
Department for Education & Skills (2006). *School workforce in England, January 2006* (revised). London: DfES.
Fitzgerald, T. (2007). Remodelling the agenda, schools and schooling: A New Zealand perspective. In G. Butt, & H.M. Gunter, (Eds.), *Modernising schools: People, learning and organizations* (pp. 163-175). London: Continuum.
Horne, M. (2001). 'Teacher knows best'. *The Guardian*, 4th September, 2001.
Mattson, E., & Harley, K. (2002). Teacher identities and strategic mimicry in the policy/practice gap. In K. Lewin, M. Samuel, & Y. Sayeed (Eds.), *Changing patterns of teacher education in South Africa* (pp. 279-288). Sandown/Cape Town: Heinemann.
Ministry of Education (2002). *Recruitment and retention in New Zealand secondary schools.* Wellington: Ministry of Education.
PriceWaterhouseCoopers (2001). *Teacher workload study.* London: DfES
Robertson, S., & Dale, R. (2002). Local states of emergency: The contradictions of neo-liberal governance in education in New Zealand. *British Journal of Sociology, 23*(3), 463-482.
Sachs, J. (2003). *The activist teaching profession.* Buckingham: Open University Press.
School Teachers' Review Body (2004). *Teachers workload survey.* London: STRB.
Thomas, H., Butt, G., Fielding, A., Foster, J., Gunter, H., Lance, A., Pilkington, R., Potts, E., Powers, S., Rayner, S., Rutherford, D., Selwood, I., & Szwed, C. (2004). *The evaluation of the Transforming the School Workforce Pathfinder Project.* Research Report 54. London: DfES.
Thrupp, M. (2001). School-level education policy under New Labour and New Zealand Labour: A comparative update. *British Journal of Educational Studies, 49*(2), 187-212.
Vidovich, L. (2007). Navigating 'global' modernisation policies in education: Responses from Australia. In G. Butt, & H.M. Gunter (Eds.), *Modernising schools: People, learning and organizations* (pp. 189-202). London: Continuum.
Woodward, W. (2003). 'A third of teachers plan to quit'. *The Guardian*, 7th January, 2003.

Graham Butt
School of Education
University of Birmingham
UK

Helen Gunter
School of Education
University of Manchester
UK

CATE WATSON

MYTHICAL SPACES AND SOCIAL IMAGINARIES: LOOKING FOR THE GLOBAL IN THE LOCAL IN NARRATIVES OF (INTER)PROFESSIONAL IDENTIFICATION

INTRODUCTION

According to Marchart (1997), 'Social myths and traditions are nothing else than the outcome of repetitive practices of articulation...which lost their contingent origin in the course of this repetition so that now we perceive them as necessary, incontestable, eternal etc.'. In the course of such repetition, myths lose their temporal quality, becoming social imaginaries – limits or horizons structuring fields of intelligibility (Laclau, 1990) through which social practices are conceived and become naturalized. As such, myths and imaginaries can be understood as shaping spaces at all levels of social and institutional organization. John Law (2003) invites us to consider the complexities inherent in these global and local discourses. Is, he asks, the global large and complexly interrelated? Or could it be (also) small and non-coherent? What happens when different myths and imaginaries, and the global and local worlds they give rise to, collide? In this chapter I explore possible worlds in and among narratives, identifications and discourses, searching for the global as constituted in, and enacted through, the local. Taking as my starting point the idea that narratives are performative, constituting the thread that links us to subject positions within discourse, I explore some methodological possibilities for examining the relationships between personal narratives, institutional discourses and the professional identifications they give rise to.

As has been outlined elsewhere in this collection, current policy surrounding provision of Children's Services is concerned with seamless transitions and joined-up working. The barriers surrounding such aspirations have been discussed at length (see, for example, McConkey, 2006; Shucksmith, Philip, Spratt & Watson, 2006; Tett & McCulloch, 2006) and centre on differences in professional roles, values and language and in the organizational structures within which different professionals work. So, while at the macroscopic level, as Allan (2006a, p. 55) says 'the language used in policy privileges consensus and creates closure' (an aspect of the normalising effect of power), focusing in may disclose a rather different picture in which practice is 'revealed as the source of all kinds of frustrated desires,

J. Forbes and C. Watson (eds.), Service Integration in Schools, 157–166.

unstated criticisms, and endlessly deferred confrontations' (Torfing, 1999, p. 123). For example, in a study of interprofessional working to support pupil mental well-being Spratt, Shucksmith, Philip and Watson (2006, p. 397) describe a situation in which 'teachers questioned the validity of receiving training or advice from individuals without direct experience of classroom management'. In some instances, teachers resorted to bullying tactics such as subjecting other workers to 'rites of passage' rituals, 'undertaking unsupported whole class teaching, or group work with unsuitably large numbers of disruptive pupils, before they were accepted as colleagues by teachers'. Myths and imaginaries may therefore lead professionals to construct the world in diverse ways and once there to occupy it differently. However, it should be remembered that the mantra of joined-up working in current policy discourse is itself assuming something of a mythic status, recognisable as part of the Western social imaginary of progress, one effect of which is to cast professionals in deficit terms.

In this chapter I tease out a 'small story' (Watson, 2007) obtained from narrative research conducted with beginning teachers and use this to investigate the ways in which institutional identifications are manifested in and through narratives of practice, drawing on Laclau and Mouffe's (1985) theory of discourse. I then discuss the implications of this approach to discourse analysis for research into interprofessional/multiagency working and conclude by looking at the possibilities for the development of a critical methodology with the potential for bringing about institutional change.

DISCOURSE AND THE FIELD OF IDENTITIES

Torfing (1999, p. 85) defines a discourse as 'a differential ensemble of signifying sequences in which meaning is constantly renegotiated'. We are always already interpellated or hailed into discourses, as Althusser (1971) would say, as part of more or less stable, socio-culturally and historically situated flows of power in the Foucauldian sense (Foucault, 1980, p. 119) in which,

> What makes power hold good, what makes it accepted, is simply the fact that it doesn't only weigh on us as a force that says no, but that it traverses and produces things, it induces pleasure, forms knowledge, produces discourses. It needs to be considered as a productive network which runs through the whole social body, much more than as a negative instance whose function is repression.

Laclau and Mouffe visualise the social as a discursive field within which are disposed elements of both linguistic and material practice (Howarth, 2000). The identity of these elements is linked by difference in the same sense that language is structured by difference and hence it is the arrangement, or in Laclau and Mouffe's terms, the articulation of these elements in relation to the discursive field that gives them meaning. Thus Howarth gives as an example a forest, the meaning of which depends on the arrangements of elements within the discursive field: 'In discourses of economic modernization, trees may be understood as the disposable means for continued economic growth...In environmentalist discourses, by contrast, a forest might represent a viable ecosystem or an object of intrinsic value and beauty' (Howarth, 2000, p. 102); or indeed, in current discourse as a means to offset carbon emissions. Power inheres in the articulation of the elements of the discursive field and provides subject positions for identification.

Since the elements of the discursive field are related by difference, meaning is always unstable and discourses resist closure. A surplus of meaning therefore exists within the discursive field giving rise to 'a field of identities which never manage to be fully fixed' (Laclau & Mouffe, 1985, p. 111). As Mouffe (1992, p. 2) says,

> The social agent is constructed by a diversity of discourses among which there is no necessary relation but a constant movement of overdetermination and displacement. The 'identity' of such a multiple and contradictory subject is therefore always contingent and precarious, temporarily fixed at the intersection of those subject positions and dependent on specific forms of identification.

Laclau and Mouffe's theory provides an understanding of identity as the product of available subject positions within the discursive field. However, they also show how flows of power in the discursive arrangement create exclusionary spaces. If the discursive field contains surplus meanings which are not articulated into discourses, then these elements are excluded from hegemonic discourses and become unsayable.

In Laclau and Mouffe's theoretical framework, political forces attempt to impose closure and so achieve control, limiting subject positions for identification within discourse. In this way, the effect of power is to establish control in order to articulate the elements of the field in a particular way and hence to fix meaning around a 'nodal point', though this can only ever be partial. In Lacanian terms this nodal point is a *point-de-capiton*, a quilting point, 'a signifier which stops the otherwise endless movement of signification' (Lacan, quoted in Stavrakakis, 1999, p. 59). The impossibility of complete closure renders the discursive field open to multiple meanings among competing discourses but hegemony is achieved when forces are able to articulate and stabilise the discursive field through 'articulating as many available elements – floating signifiers – as possible' (Howarth & Stavrakakis, 2000, p. 15). One way this can be achieved is through the formation of a 'chain of equivalence', which dissolves the differences existing between signifying moments of the discursive field in order to create a united front which 'seeks to divide social space by condensing meanings around two antagonistic poles' (ibid, p. 11). In education, an example of this is given by Qvarsebo's (2004) analysis of the abolition of corporal punishment in Swedish schools in the 1950s. Here he shows how a hegemonic formation aggregated around a nodal point centred on the language of psychology. This articulated two distinct discourses within the discursive field. One, promulgated by the Schools Commission, focused on discipline problems as psychological constructs which were viewed as being incompatible with the practice of physical punishment. The other arising from the

1947 *Commission of Inquiry on School Discipline* centred on 'practical and instrumental language' and argued for the ineffectiveness of corporal punishment as a sanction, except as a last resort, and for more psychological guidance and support in school to provide effective means of discipline. The hegemonic articulation of these two positions within the discursive field occurred in such a way that subject positions for teaching professionals available for identification precluded adherence to corporal punishment. In this way, the nature of teacher professionalism was re-articulated.

In some instances, a relatively stable articulation of elements of the discursive field leads to a naturalisation or sedimentation of meaning, such that 'what is politically constructed is presented as normal or natural, and resistance is constructed as deviant, or unnatural' (Torfing, 1999, p. 123). Certain discourses apparent in education are illustrative of this. Thus I have described (Watson, 2007) how ability has come to be viewed as a moral issue in schools: 'bright pupils' are morally acceptable while 'bottom sets' are seen as deviant. This idea is so pervasive that it is not questioned and new entrants to the profession rapidly construct and perform their identities around such practices. As Torfing (1999, p. 123) notes, sedimentation of practices in this way conceals their political nature.

Laclau and Mouffe also discuss the concepts of social antagonism and dislocation as the means by which discursive articulations are disrupted and reformed in new ways to give new meanings. This draws on a notion of the positioning of the subject within the discursive field and hence to notions of agency. Laclau and Mouffe (1985, p. 121) argue that subjects both position themselves and are positioned by discourses, they refer to these twin aspects as political subjectivity and subject positioning respectively. Their analysis shows how this arises from the inherent inability of the discursive field to achieve fixity of meaning:

> The category of subject is penetrated by the same ambiguous, incomplete and polysemical character which overdetermination assigns to every discursive identity. For this reason, the moment of closure of a discursive totality, which is not given at the 'objective' level of that totality, cannot be established at the level of a "meaning-giving subject", since the subjectivity of the agent is penetrated by the same precariousness and absence of suture apparent at any other point of the discursive totality of which it is part.

In *Hegemony and Socialist Strategy* (Laclau & Mouffe, 1985) this lack of closure is posited as what leads to social antagonisms, seen as arising at the frontiers of discourses and which contest those discourses. However, in later analyses (Laclau, 1990, cited in Glynos & Stavrakakis, 2000) these antagonisms are themselves seen as discursive articulations which rupture hegemonic formations, leading to dislocation, a traumatic event in which the subject position identified with is put in crisis. It is this crisis however which makes new identifications possible,

> If dislocations disrupt identities and discourses, they also create a lack at the level of meaning that stimulates new discursive constructions, which attempt to suture the dislocated structure. In short, it is the 'failure' of the

structure...that 'compels' the subject to act, to assert anew its subjectivity. (Howarth & Stavrakakis, 2000, p. 13)

Thus, Laclau and Mouffe provide a means for understanding how agency (referring to 'an intentionally acting subject' Torfing, 1999, p. 137) can arise within discourse, so countering anxieties aroused by the implications of 'discourse determinism'. The solution to the problem of the relationship between on the one hand a fully determining structure (as posited by Marx) and on the other a fully rational and self-cognizant agent, is provided by the concept of dislocation:

The subject is internal to the structure, but the structure is dislocated by an event which cannot be domesticated by the structure. The dislocation of the discursive structure prevents the full structuration of the structure and also prevents the subject from being determined by the structure. (Torfing, 1999, p. 149)

In this way, as Laclau says, dislocation enables temporality, possibility and freedom (Laclau, 1990, p. 41).

'Honey, I shrunk the grand theory'

Laclau and Mouffe's theories of discourse are generally applied at the level of political movements – how can they be put to use in analysis at the local level? Since the discursive field is conceived as a topological disposition of elements, highlighting the spatial nature of discourse as its visual metaphor, this creates the potential for examination at a microscopic level. Can we miniaturise Laclau and Mouffe, embarking on a Fantastic Voyage (Fleischer, 1966), putting them to work in the service of the local, in effect, looking for the global at the molecular level?

One way of doing this is through an examination of narratives of practice, looking at the meanings attached to concepts and their 'use-value' in terms of genre (Beebee, 1994). Looking for logics of equivalence and difference to see the patterns they make within the discursive field, the antagonistic poles, the points of dislocation. Looking, as Law (2003, p. 6) suggests drawing on Leibniz' *Monadology*, for a complexly Baroque world of 'gardens within gardens and ponds within ponds' which 'resist[s] clarity, mastery and the single point of view' (MacLure, 2006, p. 731).

In the next part I draw on these ideas to explore the methodological possibilities for an approach which offers a microanalysis of discourse. Using a narrative fragment taken from a series of interviews with beginning teachers, I build an improbable edifice for researching professional discourses, an edifice which may partially illuminate (i.e. partially obscure) tensions and proximities in interprofessional/interagency working – or rather, through a focusing back and forth from global to local arriving at a sense of what is illuminated and what is obscured at different levels.

The discourse of 'need'

In this narrative fragment, two student teachers talk about their recent school experience placement. (This is part of a longer extract which is analysed in terms of the narrative construction of teacher identities in Watson, 2007).

> *Andrea: I'd have had, the first time they did something y'know, called you something I'd have had them out the room down to the support unit because that's just not – far as I'm concerned that's not on'. Um, so I sat through this class watching this lot and just thinking tchh yeah right (laughs) but y'know you can imagine how – y'know I think there's three classes like that that he has – and you can imagine that um that kind of experience could be very wearing um so...*

> *Jim: [Is it] inclusion?*

> *Andrea: Well I don't think it was particularly ...that kind of problem I think these boys were doing it because they were being allowed to do it...*

The narrative is generated within the current political discourse of social inclusion, itself part of the lingering Western global social imaginary of utopianism. The political discourse of 'social inclusion' has formed a hegemonic articulation, occupying the position of an unquestionable good in which education is seen as playing a central role. Thus, as Edwards, Armstrong and Miller (2001, p. 420) argue, policy on social inclusion suggests that inequality and exclusion can be overcome by 'better governance and service delivery...Such a view contradicts the idea that exclusion and inequality are generated by the economic mode of production'.

In school, a central element in the discourse of inclusion is that of 'need' or 'lack' and the notion that 'support' provides the necessary scaffold to make good this deficit. In Scotland, the language of 'support' as in 'additional support needs' (Scottish Executive Education Department, 2004a) has supplanted that of 'special educational needs' as a move towards a more inclusive educational policy. The policy discourse ostensibly constructs children behaving problematically in school as in need of support rather than punishment, and this idea has been widely promulgated through the policy conduit by means of documents such as *Better Behaviour, Better Learning* (Scottish Executive Education Department, 2001). The discourse of 'need' and 'support' is therefore a prevalent one in schools forming, under the umbrella of inclusion, a hegemonic articulation such that to be a professional within the current context requires an identification with this subject position within discourse. To adopt a different position would be to have one's identity as professional (partially) negated. But the way in which it is used in this narrative, ambiguously suggestive of a disciplinary measure, is indicative of a point of potential antagonism, which serves to undermine the discursive structure of inclusion in which 'support' is a signifying element. Andrea's narrative is antagonistic, reflecting a subject position for teachers which is at odds with, and potentially threatens rupture of, the hegemonic articulation surrounding inclusion and its attempts to impose closure. In order to extend the hegemonic articulation, the signifier 'support' has to be emptied of meaning, to become a signifier without a signified, in effect signifying a 'totality which is literally impossible' (Laclau, 2006, p. 107). This uneasy alliance enables the teacher to enter into the would-be hegemonic discourse and take up a subject position within it, while at the same time introducing an element of instability into the structure, as a point of resistance. There is thus a tension or undecidability between the logic of difference and the logic of equivalence in the two positions, 'which of the two logics gains the upper hand in this hierarchy, and thus manages to assert itself as the predominant logic, depends on the political struggles over hegemony in this area' (Torfing, 1999, p. 126).

To examine where this tension is coming from it is necessary to look at the competing discourses that teachers are positioned in and by. Whatever meaning Andrea attaches to the term 'support', it is clear that in the setting she is working in at least, it results in exclusion from class – i.e. support, whether this is constructed as punitive or therapeutic, takes place somewhere else. To this extent, it can be argued that there is a discursive articulation providing a subject position for teachers in which pupils presenting as behaviour problems are regarded as forming a constitutive outside to the discourse of schooling, from which they are thus to be literally excluded. The identity as teacher is negated by the presence of the undesirable other, and so through the relational nature of identity that is constituted in sameness and difference, 'every identity is dislocated in so far as it depends on an outside which both denies that identity and provides the condition of possibility at the same time' (Laclau, 1990, cited in Torfing, 1999, p. 131). Pupils with challenging behaviour constitute an antagonistic force which is held responsible for the blockage of the teacher's full identity: 'As a result our political actions will tend to be guided by the illusion that the annihilation of the antagonistic force will permit us to become the fully constituted "we" that we have always sought to be' (Torfing, 1999, p. 129). As Stavrakakis (1999, p. 101) says, 'it is to the existence of this evil agent, which can easily be localised, that all persisting disorder is attributed'. There is an aporetic relationship between this simultaneous creation and denial of identity. For the teacher, the literal exclusion of the untameable other will result in the removal of the blockage which prevents full identification, yet it is the very presence of the other that determines our identity. This contest creates a mythic space for the development of teacher identity predicated on the ability to 'control' the other.

Within this mythic space support becomes an exclusionary practice, part of an apparatus in which 'pedagogical practices are inventions to make who the child is and is to become' (Popkewitz & Lindblad, 2004, p. 232). In the new policy discourse of 'additional support needs' and under the aegis of 'social inclusion' the notion of 'support' has been extended to embrace more and more children, giving rise to more and more difference which must be managed leading to 'a constant reiteration of exclusion' (Allan, 2006b, p. 126).

The problematic construction of 'inclusion', at least for pupils with 'bad behaviour', is referenced by Jim's interjection as to whether the evident difficulties in this class stem from the policy of inclusion. Andrea replies that it is 'not that kind of problem'. At the local or molecular level the policy discourse of inclusion is not about consensus and closure but about available positions – who is or is not worthy of inclusion. Paradoxically, the policy of inclusion with its mantra of 'all children' (no child left behind, getting it right for every child, etc.) functions to further exclude those who cannot, in the words of *A Curriculum for Excellence* (Scottish Executive Education Department, 2004b) develop the capacity to become successful learners, confident individuals, responsible citizens and effective contributors, as discursively constructed and defined by the state apparatus. A dark side of utopianism is inscribed in Curriculum for Excellence, with its obverse focusing on the exclusion of children and young people who cannot be included in the mantra 'all children'.

The aporetic nature of the global discourse is reproduced in the ambivalent and ambiguous narrative. In other words, the instability in the discourse is revealed at the local level while at the global level an attempt is made to impose closure and consensus.

IMPLICATIONS AND POSSIBILITIES

This narrative fragment serves to open up the possibilities for an examination of the discursive practices of teachers and the others they work with. The political moment is revealed in the microanalysis of discourse. By examining the ways and the contexts within which elements of the discursive field are used, the extent to which they are moments within the fluid mosaic structure of discourse, it may be possible to elaborate a topological structure in which tensions, overlaps, alliances, resistances can be articulated – in effect, creating a map of mythical spaces. Moreover, such a map may indicate the points at which dislocation of the structure can occur. Hegemonies are hegemonic precisely because they manage to persuade us that they are 'natural', but they cannot hegemonise completely, so this sedimentation is a fantasmatic illusion. There can be a 'de-fixation of meaning', 'the fixed topography vanishes into a fluctuating wave; land becomes liquid' (Marchart, 1997, p. 5). We need therefore to examine and redefine the 'mythical spaces of the imaginary geographies of schools' (Hargreaves, 2002, p. 196) as a prelude to bringing about change – to create new understandings of what interprofessional working could look like. What if it wasn't the clash of cultures which gives rise to a deficit model of interprofessional collaborative practice in a discourse which privileges consensus – what if discourse itself was recognised as being so inherently unstable as to prevent closure and consensus? Then we would need to construct new imaginaries – not based on a utopian illusion of consensus and perfect communication but on 'contested dissensus' (Gunder, 2005, p. 86) as a more appropriate – grown-up rather than joined-up – model for interprofessional practice. In Futures research, scenarios have been seen as a way to analyse 'probable, possible and preferable' worlds (Börjeson, Hojer, Dreborg, Ekvall, & Finnveden, 2006, p. 725); Inayatullah (1998, p. 815) suggests 'causal layered analysis' can be used as an approach which combines analysis at horizontal and vertical levels of discourse, in effect moving between the global and the local, in order to 'open up space for the articulation of constitutive discourses, which can then be shaped as scenarios' in order to create alternative futures. Microanalysis of narrative fragments potentially provides a useful means of examining discourse as part of this approach.

REFERENCES

Allan, J. (2006a). After the break? Interrupting the discourses of interprofessional practice. In J. Forbes (Ed.), *The research and policy discourses of service integration, interprofessional and interagency working: ESRC Seminar 1 proceedings.* School of Education, University of Aberdeen, *Research Papers* 14, 52-69.

Allan, J. (2006b). The repetition of exclusion. *International Journal of Inclusive Education, 10*(2-3), 121-133.

Althusser, L. (1971). *Lenin and philosophy and other essays.* London: NLB.

Beebee, T.O. (1994). *The ideology of genre: A comparative study of generic instability.* University Park: Pennsylvania State University Press.

Börjeson, L., Hojer, M., Dreborg, K., Ekvall, T., & Finnveden, G. (2006). Scenario types and techniques: Towards a user's guide. *Futures, 38*, 723-739.

Edwards, R., Armstrong, P., & Miller, N. (2001). Include me out: Critical readings of social exclusion, social inclusion and lifelong learning. *International Journal of Lifelong Education, 20*(5), 417-428.

Fleischer, R. (1966). *Fantastic voyage.* USA: Twentieth Century Fox.

Foucault, M. (1980). Truth and power. In C. Gordon (Ed.), *Power/knowledge. Selected interviews and other writings 1972-1977.* Sussex: Harvester Press, pp. 109-133.

Glynos, J., & Stavrakakis, Y. (2000). Encounters of the real kind: Sussing out the limits of Laclau's embrace of Lacan. In S. Critchley, & O. Marchart (Eds.), *Laclau. A critical reader* (pp. 201-216). London: Routledge.

Gunder, M. (2005). Obscuring difference through shaping debate: A Lacanian view of planning for diversity. *International Planning Studies, 10*(2), 83-103.

Hargreaves, A. (2002). Sustainability of educational change: The role of social geographies. *Journal of Educational Change, 3*(3), 189-214.

Howarth, D. (2000). *Discourse.* Buckingham: Open University Press.

Howarth, D., & Stavrakakis, Y. (2000). Introducing discourse theory and political analysis. In D. Howarth, A. Norval, & Y. Stavrakakis (Eds.). *Discourse theory and political analysis* (pp. 1-23). Manchester: Manchester University Press.

Inayatullah, S. (1998). Causal layered analysis: Post-structuralism as method. *Futures, 30*(8), 815-829.

Laclau, E. (2006). Ideology and post-Marxism. *Journal of Political Ideologies, 11*(2), 103-114.

Laclau, E. (1990). *New reflections on the revolution of our time.* London: Verso.

Laclau, E., & Mouffe, C. (1985). *Hegemony and socialist strategy.* London: Verso.

Law, J. (2003). *And if the global were small and non-coherent? Method, complexity and the baroque.* Available from www.comp.lancs.ac.uk/sociology/papers/Law-And-if-the-Global-Were-Small.pdf (Accessed 20/03/2007.)

MacLure, M. (2006). The bone in the throat: Some uncertain thoughts on baroque method. *International Journal of Qualitative Studies in Education, 19*(6), 729-745.

Marchart, O. (1997). *The flaneur and his duck.* Available at: www.nettime.org/Lists-Archives/nettime-1-9711/msg00022.html (Accessed 20/03/2007.)

McConkey, R. (2006). Multi-agency working: An excuse for inaction? In J. Forbes (Ed.), *Service integration in Scottish schools: Values, vision and vital voices* (pp. 12-31). School of Education, University of Aberdeen, Research Papers 12.

Mouffe, C. (1992). Citizenship and political identity. *October, 61*, 28-32.

Popkewitz, T.S., & Lindblad, S. (2004). Historicizing the future: Educational reform, systems of reason, and the making of children who are the future citizens. *Journal of Educational Change, 5*(3), 229-247.

Qvarsebo, J. (2004). *Compulsory school, corporal punishment and changed notions of childhood. The Swedish political process 1946-1958*. Fifth European Social Science History Conference. Humboldt University, Berlin, Germany, 24-27 March.

Scottish Executive Education Department (2004a). *The report of the consultation on the draft Code of Practice, draft Regulations and policy papers for the Education (Additional Support for Learning) (Scotland) Act 2004*. Edinburgh: SEED.

Scottish Executive Education Department (2004b). *A curriculum for excellence*. Edinburgh: SEED.

Scottish Executive Education Department (2001). *Better behaviour better learning. Report of the Discipline Task Group*. Edinburgh: SEED.

Shucksmith, J., Philip, K., Spratt, J., & Watson, C. (2006). Learning how to collaborate? Promoting young people's mental health through professional partnership in schools. In J. Forbes (Ed.), *The research and policy discourses of service integration, interprofessional and interagency working: ESRC Seminar 1 proceedings* (pp. 9-32). School of Education, University of Aberdeen, Research Papers 14.

Spratt, J., Shucksmith, J., Philip, K., & Watson, C. (2006). Interprofessional support of mental well-being in schools: A Bourdieuan perspective. *Journal of Interprofessional Care, 20*(4), 391-402.

Stavrakakis, Y. (1999). *Lacan and the political*. London: Routledge.

Tett, L., & McCulloch, K. (2006). Inter-agency partnerships and school-family-community links to prevent social exclusion. In J. Forbes (Ed.), *Service integration in Scottish schools: Values, vision and vital voices* (pp. 32-46). School of Education, University of Aberdeen, Research Papers 12.

Torfing, J. (1999). *New theories of discourse: Laclau, Mouffe and Zizek*. Oxford: Blackwell.

Watson, C. (2007). 'Small stories', positioning analysis, and the doing of professional identities in learning to teach. *Narrative Inquiry, 17*(2), 371-389.

Watson, C. (2006). Unreliable narrators? 'Inconsistency' (and some inconstancy) in interviews. *Qualitative Research, 6*(3), 367-384.

Cate Watson
School of Education
University of Aberdeen
UK

JON NIXON

THE CONDITIONS FOR INTER-PROFESSIONAL LEARNING: THE CENTRALITY OF RELATIONSHIP

INTRODUCTION

The argument of this chapter is based on two assumptions: (1) service integration is not just a matter of structure and system, but of institutional culture and inter-professional relationship (and therefore of professional agency); (2) global solutions must take into full account the cultural, social and relational factors pertaining within specific national, regional and institutional contexts (and therefore be locally grounded). The argument is concerned primarily, not with the existing conditions of inter-professional relationships, but on hoped-for conditions that would have to be met for inter-professional relationships to aspire to what Aristotle referred to as 'virtuous friendship'. Such relationships, it is argued, constitute the social content of hope in that they look to new perspectives on institutional renewal and professional regeneration. They provide inter-professional spaces of learning within which professionals can begin to realise their functional capabilities. The question then arises as to the conditions necessary for generating and sustaining such relationships within and for a renewed civil society. It is that question which this chapter seeks to address.

THE CONSTITUTION OF CIVIL SOCIETY

Civil society is fragile, and it needs to be extended. (Hall, 1995, p. 27)

Hall was right to assert, in 1995, that civil society needed to be *extended*. It did, and it still does. Ten years later, however, the need to *deepen*, as well as extend, civil society seems equally urgent. Engagement, membership and participation comprise the depth dimension of civil society. This chapter, with its emphasis on human relationship as a constitutive element of civil society, is centrally concerned with this dimension: what would institutions look like if they were managed upon the assumption that they are only ever as good as the relationships they sustain? How would we recognise such an institution if we saw it? How would we recognise the kind of inter-personal and professional relationships that make such an institution possible? Wherein does their goodness lie? This chapter addresses these kinds of questions with specific reference to the quality of professional relationships within and across institutions and organisational structures.

J. Forbes and C. Watson (eds.), Service Integration in Schools, 167–179.

The assumption underlying such questions is that institutional well being is dependent not only on organisational structure, but also on the well being of the individuals involved and the quality and sustainability of the associations they form with one another. *Good* institutions are, from this perspective, constructed around *good* relationships that in turn are based upon the mutual recognition of equal worth and the reciprocity of trust that such recognition generates. Moreover, *good* institutions become *better* institutions through the growth of mutuality and reciprocity at the level of the inter-personal. The quality of civil association in any institution is, therefore, a significant indicator of the well being of the institution as a whole.

This is not an assumption with which many would disagree. Nor, however, is it an assumption that carries much weight among those responsible for the management of corporate institutions. In what Bauman (2001) characterises as these 'times of disengagement' (pp. 39-49), one counter assumption at least carries a much heavier punch: namely, that 'power consists in decision-making and resides with those who make the decisions' (p. 40). Power, in other words, belongs to the managers. It is they who determine the organisational structures, which in turn frame the systems of institutional communication and deliberation, which then circumscribe the culture or ethos of the institution. 'Persons in relation', to draw on MacMurray's (1961) terminology, somehow have to find a niche for themselves and one another in the spaces in between.

The question of terminology, of vocabulary, is crucial. The spaces in between can be imagined only through recourse to a way of talking about professional practice that somehow evades the dominant language of market-management. As McKibbin (2006, p. 6), in his invective against what he sees as the 'destruction of the public sphere', points out:

> we are familiar with the way this language has carried all before it. We must sit on the cusp, hope to be in the centre of excellence, dislike producer-dominated industries, wish for a multiplicity of providers, grovel to our line managers, even more to the senior management team, deliver outcomes downstream, provide choice. Our students are now clients, our patients and passengers customers.

This is a theme to which I return explicitly in the concluding paragraphs. However, it is implicit throughout the ensuing argument. The choice of 'hope', 'friendship' and 'virtue' as key terms in the development of that argument is both deliberate and *oppositional*. This chapter is in part an attempt to highlight the need for developing an alternative language with which to rethink the quality of professional relationships (see Nixon, 2004a; 2004b) and to reconfigure those relationships within the context of inter-professional ways of working (see Nixon, Walker & Baron, 2002a; 2002b; Nixon, Allan & Mannion, 2001).

The social content of hope

This is the *opus contra naturem.* (Mantel, 1990, p. 79)

Because of the nature of goodness – its dependence upon dispositions that can only be acquired in and through practice – we can only grow into goodness through our relationships with others. When those relationships fall apart, or become fraught, our goodness diminishes. We live in a world within which the experience of disintegration – the experience of falling apart, of being fraught – is integral to living. Coping with 'not being good' is, in other words, part and parcel of whatever 'becoming better' might mean. This, as Mantel (1990, p. 79) puts it, is the *opus contra naturem*:

> everything that is going to be purified must first be corrupted; that is a principle of science and art. Everything that is to be put together must first be taken apart, everything that is to be made whole must first be broken into its constituent parts, its heat, its coldness, its dryness, its moisture.

So, argues Mantel, the necessary artificiality of the natural order takes its inevitable course: 'after separation, drying out, moistening, dissolving, coagulating, fermenting, comes purification, re-combination – the creation of substances that the world has until now never beheld' (p. 79).

In order to set about that 'opus', we have to learn not only how to hope, but how to imbue our individual hopes with a sense of social purposefulness. Halpin (2003, p. 60) argues that the notion of 'utopia' is a useful conceptual tool in setting about this task, because, as he puts it, utopianism 'has the potential to enable the personal experience of hopefulness to be interpreted in an explicitly social rather than just an individual way'. Utopianism provides us with the inter-personal, institutional, and social *content* of hope. Utopian thought enables us to imagine interpersonal and institutional structures as they might be. It helps us realise what is as yet emergent or even pre-emergent. In doing so it enables us to think against dominant and residual structures which constitute the blockage: to engage with the *opus contra naturem.*

'Utopia', as Bauman (2002) reminds us, 'refers to *topos* – a *place*'. Utopias were traditionally, as he puts it, 'associated with, and confined to, a clearly defined territory' (p. 223). The utopias with which we are here concerned have no such fixity. They are imagined spaces which we have to reclaim and make together. Bauman is deeply pessimistic regarding the possibility of achieving utopia in this 'no-place, no-land, no-territory' of what he calls 'liquid modernity', within which newly emergent global elites pursue private and highly exclusive pathways to happiness (p. 234). Counter to that pessimistic strain, this chapter argues not only that community is still imaginable, but that imagining new forms of working together for the achievement of a better society is a moral imperative. It renders our claim to professionalism trustworthy and credible.

Conceived in this way, utopianism is not a flight from reality, but a means of radical engagement with reality. 'Hope alone', as Moltmann (1967, p. 25) puts it, 'is to be called "realistic", because it alone takes seriously the possibilities with which reality is fraught. It does not take things as they happen to stand or lie, but as progressing, moving things with possibilities of change'. It is precisely because our experience of the world continually brings home to us the sheer contingency and unpredictability of human affairs that hope is essential: 'only as long as the world and the people in it are in a fragmented and experimental state which is not yet resolved, is there any sense in earthly hopes' (p. 25).

Moltmann's notion of hope was developed within the context of a broader discussion of Christian eschatology, which informed the then still emergent tradition of liberation theology (see, for example, Gutierrez, 1974). However, that notion has profound implications for how within a post-metaphysical age we seek to sustain a sense of moral agency. There is, as MacMurray (1957) points out, a complex and crucial relation between our capacity to act in the world and our capacity to know that world; a sense in which, he argues, agency can only be exercised in a world that is unknowable:

> in action we presuppose that we determine the world by our actions. The correlative of this freedom is that the world which we determine in action must be indeterminate, capable of being given a structure that it does not already possess. We can only know a determinate world; we can only act in an indeterminate world. Therefore, if we really do act, if our freedom of will is not an illusion, the world in which we act must be unknowable. (p. 55)

In his elaboration of this seeming paradox, in terms of 'the self as agent' and of 'persons in relation', MacMurray (1957, 1961) does not explicitly employ the concept of 'hope'. Nevertheless, his argument implies that agency, the capacity to act in an indeterminate and therefore unknowable world, is always reliant upon some human capacity that is not dissimilar to what Moltmann (1967) understands by hope.

Action, involving as it always does some element of incalculable risk, is an expression of our hope that the risk factors are not entirely insurmountable. To lose that hope is to lose our agency: either we give up on action, and thereby lose our agency through our inaction, or action gives up on us, in which case our agency dissolves into a generalised sense of fateful alienation.

The notion of 'virtuous friendship'

A certain reciprocity is essential in friendship. (Weil, 2005, p. 286)

In the *Nicomachean Ethics* Aristotle was clear that 'virtuous friendship' is founded on equality of attitude and belief insofar as these constitute the basis of virtue. He also acknowledged, however, that friendships differ in kind and quality. Indeed, Hutter (1978, p. 115) goes so far as to suggest that 'what Aristotle seems to be saying is that if we understand the psychodynamics of friendship in the narrow sense, we thereby also understand the nature of other human associations. All human associations are forms of friendship, even if only imperfectly'. Friendship may, for example, be tactical and therefore provisional and conditional: a kind of strategic alliance based upon the mutuality of either self-interest or pleasure. Friendship, in either of these two senses, is a matter of being part of the club, part of the enclave. Pahl (2000, p. 21) neatly summarises this set of distinctions in terms of 'friends of utility, friends of pleasure and friends of virtue'.

Much hinges on this set of distinctions, not least the notion of equality. 'Friends of utility' and 'friends of pleasure' are likely to be useful and pleasurable to one another precisely because of their economic and social commonality: who has access to which influential networks; who can afford to dine out at which fashionable restaurants. However, 'friends of virtue', who may be diversely positioned in terms of their economic and social conditions, may still be useful and pleasurable to one another since the 'virtuous friendship' to which they aspire morally re-orientates 'the useful' and 'the pleasurable' towards 'the good': friendship, 'which has virtue as its base and aim is also pleasant and useful. It combines all three aims, since the good in character, when friends, also find each other's company pleasant and useful' (Hutter, 1978, p. 108).

'Virtuous friendship', Aristotle maintained, is between equals who have their own and each others' best moral interests at heart. Such friendship is neither provisional nor instrumental, but unconditional in terms of what is good for oneself and the other: it is both inward-looking and outward-reaching. It is premised on the assumption that we become better people through the reciprocity afforded by our shared aspiration to help one another in doing so. That is why, as Pahl (2000, p. 79) puts it, 'friends of virtue' are also 'friends of hope' and 'ultimately friends of communication': 'our friends who stimulate hope and invite change are concerned with deep understanding and knowing'(see also Vernon, 2005).

The notion of 'virtuous friendship', as referring to a kind of relationship that privileges the recognition of equal worth, is central to our understanding of the conditions of learning. Such relationships are a precondition not only of the deliberative process whereby we ascertain what constitutes right action for ourselves and others; they are also the means by which such processes endure and enjoy some albeit fragile security. They inform our agency, while at the same time providing us with relational structures within which to recognise the agency of others. Thus, as Stern-Gillet (1995, p. 50) puts it, 'friendship plays a unique and crucial role in the noetic actualisation of moral agents'. What Aristotle understood by 'virtuous friendship' becomes a means of rethinking, from the bottom up, what we aspire to in terms of the institutional conditions of learning.

'Virtuous friendship' may, however, require closely guarded formalities to ensure that the principle of 'what is good for the other' is held in supreme regard. There are necessarily asymmetries in the relation between teacher and taught, and indeed between colleagues (with regard to knowledge of the field, breadth of experience, etc.). It is only by acknowledging those asymmetries that the relationship between teacher and taught, and on occasion colleagues, can begin to move towards the common ground that constitutes learning. In the context of any such relationship, 'virtuous friendship' is almost always an aspiration and very rarely an achieved state: what Hutter (1978, pp. 104-105) calls 'a theoretical searchlight' or 'a guiding norm' by which actual relationships can be evaluated. It is a teleological concept which enables us to grasp, ontologically, the underlying purposefulness of the kind of relationship which Giddens (1993, p. 194) characterises as 'pure' in its adherence to 'the imperative of free and open communication'.

Such a perspective suggests that history and narrative are significant components of 'virtuous friendship'; that time, in other words, is a crucial factor in the formation of such relationships. Over time some relationships involve the acquisition of what Hatt (2005, p. 672) calls *'pathic* knowledge' (original emphasis) knowledge, that is, of life as it presents itself to the other person in terms, not only of 'what is' and 'what has been', but of 'what might be'. 'Pathic understanding', as van Manen & Li (2002, p. 219) put it, is 'not primarily gnostic, cognitive, intellectual, technical – but ... relational, situational, corporeal, temporal, actional'. 'Virtuous friendship' sustains, and is itself sustained by, that kind of understanding: an understanding of those imagined futures of which the present is always partially composed.

Mediating between capacity and realization

> ... the capability approach is concerned with showing the cogency of a particular *space* for the evaluation of individual opportunities and successes. (Sen, 1993, p. 50, original emphasis)

Ricoeur (1992) argues that friendship, as conceived by Aristotle, helps put in place the conditions necessary for individuals to realise their capacities through the mediation of 'the other': 'the question is then whether the mediation of the other is not required along the route from capacity to realization' (p. 181). It is, he suggests, 'just this mediating role that is celebrated by Aristotle in his treatise on friendship' (p. 181). Friendship, 'considered in its *intrinsic goodness and its basic pleasure*' (Ricoeur's emphasis), 'works toward establishing the conditions for the realization of life' (p. 186). Another way of putting this, as suggested by 'the capability approach' to human development, is that the quality of our relationships is a major determining factor in enabling us to translate our innate capacities into functioning capabilities (see Stewart, 2005, on 'groups and capabilities').

Sen (1999) links the notion of 'capability' to that of 'freedom': the freedom to exercise agency. Freedom, as he puts it, provides 'the expansion of the "capabilities" of persons to lead the kind of lives they value – and have reason to value' (p. 18). Thus, he argues, while 'income inequality and economic inequality are important' (p. 108), a broader perspective is required 'on inequality and poverty in terms of capability deprivation' (p. 109). Sen has unravelled from this premise a Nobel award-winning corpus focusing upon economic development within relatively disadvantaged localities. His argument, however, also has implications for the ways in which we might conceive of 'capability' at the level of individual and inter-personal development. Indeed, the potential inter-connectivity between the inter-personal and the systemic is one of Sen's major themes.

This line of argument is carried forward by Nussbaum (2000) in her elaboration of what she terms 'functional capabilities' (pp. 78-80). Among these 'capabilities', which she sees as essential to human well being, Nussbaum privileges 'practical reason' and 'affiliation'. These two capabilities, she argues, are fundamental to our functioning as human beings: 'to plan in one's own life without being able to do so in complex forms of discourse, concerns, and reciprocity with other human beings is ... to behave in an incompletely human way.' Taking the example of work, she argues that

> to be a truly human mode of functioning, [work] must involve the availability of both practical reason and affiliation. It must involve being able to behave as a thinking being, not just a cog in a machine; and it must be capable of being done with and toward others in a way that involves mutual recognition of humanity. (p. 82)

To make of work something other than alienated labour requires, then, the capabilities of 'practical reason' and 'affiliation'. What does this entail? Nussbaum defines 'practical reason' as 'being able to form a conception of the good and to engage in critical reflection about the planning of one's own life' (p. 79). Work requires of the worker both a conception of the good and the capacity to apply that conception, through practical reasoning, to particular ends and purposes. So, for example, if I am a medical practitioner, I seek through practical reason to align my practice to the ends and purposes of healing; if I am a lawyer, I seek to align it to those of justice; if I am a teacher, to those of learning. Professional practice, insists Nussbaum, requires a sense of moral purposefulness on behalf of the practitioner. Through practical reason the practitioner meets this moral requirement; the moral requirement, that is, for practice to become morally purposeful and for purposes to be imbued with practical import.

To engage in practical reasoning, then, is to be concerned with both the design of means and the setting of final ends. Moreover, as Carr (2004, p. 61) argues, the setting of the latter is inseparable from the design of the former: 'in practical reasoning, "ends" and "means" stand in reciprocal relationship such that reasoning about the "good" which constitutes the "end" of a practice is inseparable from reasoning about the action that constitutes the "means" for its achievement'. He goes on to argue that 'reasoning about "means" and reasoning about "ends" does not therefore involve reasoning "technically" about the former and "theoretically" about the latter'. They are, he concludes, 'two mutually constitutive elements within the single dialectical process of practical reasoning'. The value of each is dependent upon the value of the other.

In defining 'affiliation' Nussbaum (2000) draws a distinction between, on the one hand, being 'able to imagine the situation of another and to have compassion for that situation; to have the capability for justice and friendship', and, on the other hand, of 'being able to be treated as a dignified being whose worth is equal to that of others; ... being able to work as a human being, exercising practical reason and entering into meaningful relationships of mutual recognition with other workers' (pp. 79-80). What emerges from this distinction is the importance of

173

reciprocity: the way in which 'the capability for justice and friendship' is crucially dependent upon 'being able to be treated as a dignified human being whose worth is equal to that of others' (p. 79). My capability for justice and friendship towards others is, in other words, dependent upon the capability of others for justice and friendship towards myself. The capability of 'affiliation', like that of 'practical reason', is fundamental because without it there is no way of ensuring that our other capabilities can become functional.

The distinction between capability and function is central to both Nussbaum's and Sen's argument. Functioning is an achievement, whereas a capability is the ability to achieve: functionings are more directly related to living conditions, since they are different aspects of living conditions; capabilities, in contrast, denote the opportunities we have regarding the life we may lead. Nussbaum (2000) claims that 'functionings, not simply capabilities, are what render life fully human, in the sense that if there were no functionings of any kind in a life, we could hardly applaud it, no matter what opportunities it contained' (p. 87). Nevertheless, she goes on to argue, citizens must be left to determine what they make of the capabilities that are granted them: 'the person with plenty of food may always choose to fast, but there is a great difference between fasting and starving' (p. 87). Capabilities are 'opportunities for functioning' (p. 88), but do not predetermine that functioning. Indeed, the predetermination of function runs the risk of denying the capability of which it purports to be an expression: 'play is not play if it is enforced, love is not love if it is commanded' (p. 88). Playing, loving and, we might add, learning rely unconditionally upon the agency of those who choose to play, love and learn.

Relationships of virtue depend upon, and at the same time help sustain, the capabilities of 'practical reason' and 'affiliation'. They provide the social space within which we can think together about ends and purposes and about the practices and organisational structures that carry forward those ends and purposes. If relationships are to have these beneficial effects, however, they must not only foster capability but also ensure that capability leads to functioning; leads, that is, to actions that are benign in respect of the individual and of the institution. In such relationships neither party would assume that he or she knows what's best for the other. The purpose of such relationships would be to help the other make the hard choices as to how best to maximise 'opportunities for functioning' and how best to translate those opportunities, or capabilities, into fully functioning, flourishing lives.

The conditions for 'virtuous friendship'

But the world will never be 'just' as long as people do not have the conviction that they all contribute to discovering and moulding a shared human destiny. (Cohen, 2006, p. 169)

The development of ourselves as moral agents – as people who (as Cohen puts it) 'contribute to discovering and moulding a shared human destiny' – is premised on specific human capabilities, the denial of which relegates utopia to the 'no-place, no-land, no-territory' of Bauman's (2002) bleak vision of 'liquid modernity'. The 'capabilities approach', as advanced by Nussbaum (2000) and Sen (1999), enables us to be more specific as to what constitutes the necessary core of relevant capabilities and as to how capability relates to function. It brings us a little closer, that is, to understanding how we might give back to utopia a place, a land, a territory, within the deeply stratified institutional contexts within which we work. 'Virtuous friendship' may be an unrealised ideal, but it is an ideal implicit in those working relationships wherein we aspire to virtue through shared professional practice.

Questions then arise as to what professional relationships would look like if they were modelled on the notion of 'virtuous friendship': what, as professionals working within inter-professional contexts, would we *do* if we were serious about attaining the conditions necessary for 'virtuous friendship'? How would we begin to fulfil the conditions necessary for mutuality and reciprocity, for trust and the recognition of equal worth, for a shared sense of purposefulness? How would we redefine our professional identities in the light of these moral imperatives?

We might start by acknowledging the deeply corrosive effects of current patterns of work and the unequal distribution of those effects across the workplace. Sennett (1999) shows how the steadily increasing insecurity experienced by workers is making it impossible for many to achieve a sense of moral agency. Moreover, he argues, it is those very elements of the post-Fordist working environment that are deemed to be worker friendly – flexibility, team work, specialisation – that are in fact creating the insecurities. They are doing so, he claims, through their re-engineering of time whereby there is an increasing reliance on, for example, worker mobility, part-time and casual contracts, and entrepreneurialism (see, also, Sennett, 2008, pp. 246-252).

We might find ways of becoming more responsive to the differing circumstances of colleagues – within and across professional groups – that render the personal management of time difficult and sometimes chronically crisis-ridden. Pahl (1995) has shown how anxiety is invariably attendant upon success; but the successful very often have the option, or privilege, of living their lives in such a way that the contingent factors that engender anxiety are carefully managed through life style and life choices. The less successful may make other principled choices or simply not have the options open to them: other commitments impinge on the resources of time that the more successful choose – or feel themselves driven – to allocate to work.

We would require of ourselves and others that we take responsibility for the positional power invested in us. The flatter organisational structures associated with post-Fordist work regimes render power more diffuse and therefore more difficult to locate. One's own power is thereby that much easier to deny. To deny one's own positional power, however, is to dis-empower those over whom one ought rightly to be exercising authority. This task becomes that much more

175

difficult when it involves relationships across professional groups whose perceived status may differ significantly. 'Virtuous friendships', in other words, would be equal relationships precisely because they would involve a shared understanding regarding power differentials and a shared dialogue regarding how those differentials might be put to good use.

We would acknowledge that even, or perhaps especially, relationships that aspire to 'virtuous friendship' must respect the competing priorities and pressures acting upon those involved in that relationship. Within the context of 'virtuous friendship' we would acknowledge the agency of the other. We would resist the urge to possess or take over the other, to impose our views on the other, or to make unreasonable claims on the other. With the best of intentions we can sometimes create a culture of dependency, or even oppression, through our failure to recognise and respect boundaries: 'there is not friendship where distance is not kept and respected' (Weil, 2005, p. 288). Without that recognition and respect – that 'distance' – relationships cannot aspire to 'virtuous friendship'. They remain locked in paternalistic modes of thinking and feeling.

Finally, we would acknowledge the diverse professional trajectories to which we are committed and find ways of sustaining one another in pursuing those diverse trajectories. The complex nature of inter-professional practice means that as practitioners we are constantly negotiating a professional identity for ourselves in relation to our specific responsibilities. Becoming a professional involves combining these activities in ways that play to our own strengths and that recognise the priorities of the particular institutions within which we work. Professional identity does not come ready made. It involves the struggle for authenticity and, as such, has to be constructed: 'the incessant (and non-linear) activity of self-constitution that makes the identity of the agent' (Bauman, 1992, p. 193).

Nussbaum (1997) reminds us that education is centrally concerned with 'cultivating humanity' and that such cultivation necessarily involves human flourishing: 'citizens who cultivate their humanity need ... an ability to see themselves not simply as citizens of some local region or group but also, and above all, as human beings bound to all other human beings by ties of recognition and concern. The world around us is inescapably international' (p. 10). If, as I have argued throughout this chapter, relationship is central to professional identity and to inter-professional learning, then the relationships that sustain that identity and learning must be cosmopolitan in their treatment of difference. They must, that is, be seen as part of a purposeful search for what Beck (2006, p. 3) terms 'the truth of others' and its realisation through 'the logic of inclusive differentiation'. The conditions outlined above are all premised, not only on the possibility of, but also the urgent need for 'shaping one's life and social relations under conditions of cultural mixture'.

CONCLUSION

The social imaginary is that common understanding which makes possible common practices, and a widely shared sense of legitimacy. (Taylor, 2007, p. 172)

The argument developed in this chapter is only one part of a necessary and long overdue response to a broad set of concerns regarding the systematic diminution of the public sphere. This diminution is not an inevitable result of the way things are, but is the outcome of a dominant ideology of market-managerialism (see Nixon, 2004a, 2008). The most powerful weapon of that ideology has been its reductionist language. 'It is a language', to return to McKibbin (2006, p. 6), 'which was first devised in business schools, then broke into government and now infests all institutions'. He continues:

> it purports to be neutral: thus all procedures must be "transparent" and "robust", everyone "accountable". It is hard-nosed but successful because the private sector on which it is based is hard-nosed and successful. It is efficient; it abhors waste; it provides all the answers…The language might be laughable, but it is now the language shared by all those who command, Labour or Conservative, and is one way they wield power.

Implicit in this invective is the need to mine an alternative, and indeed oppositional, language from the cultural and historical resources available: what Taylor (2007, pp. 159-211; 2004) terms 'social imaginaries'. 'Hope', 'friendship', and 'virtue' are some of the linguistic resources that I have drawn on in this chapter to set about that task. The idea is neither to deny the current ideological impasse, nor necessarily to confront it head on, but to begin to build locally, at precise points and within specific sectors, the institutional conditions necessary for sustaining alternative ways of being together in the world and of working together for better global futures: what, in the passage quoted above, Taylor refers to as 'that common understanding which makes possible common practices, and a widely shared sense of legitimacy'. The contested legitimacy of the institutions that comprise civil society resides entirely in 'that common understanding'. Without it, institutions become mere organisations and professionals are reduced to technical functionaries.

REFERENCES

Aristotle (1955). *The ethics of Aristotle: The Nicomachean ethics.* London: Penguin Books.

Bauman, Z. (2002). *Society under siege.* Cambridge: Polity Press.

Bauman, Z. (2001). *Community: Seeking safety in an insecure world.* Cambridge: Polity Press.

Bauman, Z. (1992). *Intimations of postmodernity.* London and New York: Routledge.

Beck, U. (2006). *The cosmopolitan vision.* Cambridge: Polity.

Carr, W. (2004). Philosophy and education. *Journal of Philosophy of Education,* 38(1), 55-73.

Cohen, D. (2006). *Globalization and its enemies.* Cambridge, MA and London, England: The MIT Press.

Giddens, A. (1993). *The transformation of intimacy: Sexuality, love and eroticism in modern societies.* Cambridge: Polity Press.

Gutierrez, G. (1974). *A theology of liberation: History, politics and salvation.* London: SCM Press.

Hall, J.A. (1995). In search of civil society. In J.A. Hall (Ed.), *Civil society: Theory, history, comparison* (pp. 1-31). Cambridge: Polity Press.

Halpin, D. (2003). *Hope and education: The role of the utopian imagination.* London & New York: RoutledgeFalmer.

Hatt, B.E. (2005). Pedagogical love in the transactional curriculum. *Journal of Curriculum Studies, 37*(6), 671-688.

Hutter, H. (1978). *Politics as friendship: The origins of classical notions of politics in the theory and practice of friendship.* Waterloo, Ontario: Wilfred Laurier University Press.

MacMurray, J. (1961). *Persons in relation* (2nd volume of the Gifford Lectures delivered in the University of Glasgow, 1953-54). London: Faber & Faber.

MacMurray, J. (1957). *The self as agent* (1st volume of the Gifford Lectures delivered in the University of Glasgow, 1953-54). London: Faber & Faber.

Mantel, H. (1990). *Fludd.* London & New York: Penguin Books.

McKibbin, R. (2006, 5 January). The destruction of the public sphere. *London Review of Books, 28*(1), 3-6.

Moltmann, J. (1967). *Theology of hope: On the ground and the implications of Christian eschatology.* London: SCM Press.

Nixon, J. (2004a). Learning the language of deliberative democracy. In M. Walker, & J. Nixon (Eds.), *Reclaiming universities from a runaway world.* Maidenhead and Philadelphia: Open University Press/McGraw-Hill Education, pp. 114-127.

Nixon, J. (2004b). Education for the good society: The integrity of academic practice. *London Review of Education* [Special Issue: D. Halpin, J. Nixon, S. Ranson, & T. Seddon (Eds.), 'Renewing Education for Civic Society'] *2*(3), 145-252.

Nixon, J. (2008). *Towards the virtuous university: the moral bases of academic practice.* London and New York: Routledge.

Nixon, J., Walker, M., & Baron, S. (2002a). The cultural mediation of state policy: The democratic potential of 'new community schooling' in Scotland. *Journal of Education Policy, 17*(4), 407-421.

Nixon, J., Walker, M., & Baron, S. (2002b). From Washington Heights to the Raploch: Evidence, mediation and the genealogy of policy. *Social Policy and Society, 1*(3), 237-246.

Nixon, J., Allan, J. & Mannion, G. (2001). Educational renewal as democratic practice: 'New' community schooling in Scotland. *International Journal of Inclusive Education, 5*(4), 329-352.

Nussbaum, M.C. (2000). *Women and human development: The capabilities approach.* Cambridge: Cambridge University Press.

Nussbaum, M.C. (1997). *Cultivating humanity: A classical defence of reform in liberal education.* Cambridge, MA and London, England: Harvard University Press.

Pahl, R. (2000). *On friendship.* Cambridge: Polity Press.

Pahl, R. (1995). *After success: 'Fin-de-siecle' anxiety and identity.* Cambridge: Polity Press.

Ricoeur, P. (1992). *Oneself as another.* Chicago & London: University of Chicago Press.

Sen, A. (1999). *Development as freedom.* Oxford: Oxford University Press.

Sen, A. (1993). Capability and well-being. In M.C.Nussbaum, & A. Sen (Eds.), *The quality of life. (A study prepared for the World Institute for Development Economics Research of the United Nations University)* (pp. 30-61). Oxford: Clarendon Press.

Sennett, R. (2008). *The craftsman.* London: Allen Lane.

Sennett, R. (1999). *The corrosion of character: The personal consequences of work in the new capitalism.* New York & London: Norton.

Stern-Gillet, S. (1995). *Aristotle's philosophy of friendship.* Albany: State University of New York Press.

Stewart, F. (2005). Groups and capabilities. *Journal of Human Development, 6*(2), 185-204.

Taylor, C. (2007). *A secular age*. Cambridge, MA and London, England: The Belknap Press of Harvard University Press.

Taylor, C. (2004). *Modern social imaginaries*. Durham, NC: Duke University Press.

van Manen, M., & Li, S. (2002). The pathic principle of pedagogical language. *Teaching and Teacher Education, 18*(2), 215-224.

Vernon, M. (2005) *The philosophy of friendship*. Basingstoke & New York: Palgrave Macmillan.

Weil, S. (2005). Friendship. In S. Miles (Ed.), *Simone Weil: An anthology*. London: Penguin Books.

Jon Nixon
Faculty of Education
Liverpool Hope University
UK

INDEX

Printed in the United Kingdom by
Lightning Source UK Ltd., Milton Keynes
138983UK00001B/151/P

9 789087 905866